CAN MOTHERHOOD
SURVIVE?

CAN MOTHERHOOD SURVIVE?

A Christian Looks at Social Parenting

CONNIE MARSHNER

Wolgemuth & Hyatt, Publishers, Inc.
Brentwood, Tennessee

The mission of Wolgemuth & Hyatt, Publishers, Inc. is to publish and distribute books that lead individuals toward:

- A personal faith in the one true God: Father, Son, and Holy Spirit;

- A lifestyle of practical discipleship; and

- A worldview that is consistent with the historic, Christian faith.

Moreover, the Company endeavors to accomplish this mission at a reasonable profit and in a manner which glorifies God and serves His Kingdom.

© 1990 by Connie Marshner. All rights reserved
Published August 1990. First Edition.
Printed in the United States of America.
97 96 95 94 93 92 91 90   8 7 6 5 4 3 2 1

Unless otherwise noted, all Scripture quotations are from the King James Version of the Bible.

Wolgemuth & Hyatt, Publishers, Inc.
1749 Mallory Lane, Suite 110
Brentwood, Tennessee 37027

Library of Congress Cataloging-in-Publication Data

Marshner, Connaught Coyne, 1951 —
    Can motherhood survive? : a Christian looks at social parenting /
Connie Marshner. — 1st ed.
        p. cm.
    Includes bibliographical references.
    ISBN 1-56121-007-2
    1. Mothers — United States — Religious life. 2. Family — United
States — Religious life. 3. Motherhood — Religious aspects —
Christianity. 4. Motherhood — United States. 5. Parenting — United
States. I. Title. II. Title: Social parenting.
BV4529.M36 1990
261.8'358743 — dc20   90-37034
                                                                        CIP

To my mothers.

CONTENTS

ACKNOWLEDGMENTS

In ancient shadows and twilights
Where childhood had strayed,
The world's great sorrows were born
And its heroes were made.
In the lost boyhood of Judas
Christ was betrayed.

"Germinal" by Æ

I t was probably eight years ago now that Jack Clayton, Washington representative of the American Association of Christian Schools, made the comment at a meeting that "social parenting is the real issue we have to contend with in the future." Unbeknownst to Jack, he planted a seed in my mind, which has come to fruition with this book. Thank you, Jack, for that "good of the order" item.

Many have helped me on the spiritual and intellectual journey which has brought me to this point. Let me mention especially the friendship and instruction and example of Elfriede Richter Ponting, Francis Martin, Marybeth Kielty, Tom and Martie DiIenno, Maria Byrne, Melinda Delahoyde, Sue Arico, Cindy Paslawski, and Mary Holtz.

My husband Bill made this book possible—he sacrificed his entire vacation to doing morning duties so I could write until the wee hours the night before. And he had sacrificed many Saturday mornings before that so I could retreat to silence at the public library to organize my papers and thoughts. Thank you, Bill.

INTRODUCTION

Are you afraid to read a book on motherhood? Are you afraid it will make you feel inadequate somehow?

Please don't be. This is not a book about how to keep kids happy when it's raining or how to help them get better grades. It is a book about our society.

I wrote this book to help you understand how your own motherhood is affected by the cultural, political, and intellectual trends swirling around us all.

Originally, I thought I would write a book on day care. Since it had become a big item on the national agenda, I thought Christians needed to be informed about such a major public policy topic. So I wrote the first five chapters. Mike Hyatt stopped me after five chapters because he didn't think you would buy a book on day care.

But I still felt there was something that thinking Christians needed to be aware of as our nation plunged toward its first major federal child care legislation. And then it came to me: most Christians do not understand quite how widespread and systematic and organized is the drive for social parenting. *We don't understand how we ourselves are victimized by it.*

I am still struggling with my own transition from full-time career woman to full-time mother. As I come, aided by the Holy Spirit, to understand my own thought processes, I can see how much my own life has been influenced by forces that I know are ungodly. I know I'm not unique in my experiences.

I've tried to keep it positive: the first three chapters emphasize why motherhood is important. Then I explore the enemies of motherhood: the ideas, the lobbies, the opinionmakers who are preaching that motherhood is not important. Finally, in Part III, I offer a positive alternative: a new vision of Christian motherhood as a creative, challenging vocation.

How does this book benefit you? If you're already a full-time mother, it will help you understand why motherhood is not honored and respected as it once was. If you are a mother, you feel exasperated and isolated and frustrated more often than you would like to. And maybe you think it's all your fault because you're not a good enough mom. But don't be discouraged: understand that the culture in which we live — all of Western civilization — is being enveloped by a miasma of anti-motherhood, and few of us can escape its effects .

If you're a working mom, this book can be a catalyst to your thinking about your own life and the choices you're making. I made some very serious mistakes when I was a career-centered mother, and I know that plenty of other mothers, even well-intentioned Christian mothers, are repeating the very same mistakes today. I hope this book will help some mothers to avoid making the mistakes I made.

Not that being a working mother is automatically, by definition, a mistake. It isn't. And more and more women don't have any choice in the matter.

But that is all the more reason a mother's sense of balance has to be very informed, and her discernment of the will of God has to be meticulous. With so many cultural trends promoting careers simply for the sake of careers, many women do not know what to look for in providing for their children while they work. *Can Motherhood Survive?* may help fill in a few gaps here. If you're a mom who is thinking about returning to your job or career, you might find that reading this book will help you make your decision.

If you're like I was, though, this book is especially for you: if you have small children and you're working because you like it . . . you're doing some good in your job . . . you depend on the money . . . your husband encourages you . . . your parents feel proud of you . . . you feel as if you're making something of your life . . . it just sort of happened — then you need this book. You need to be challenged, in a gentle, loving way, to take a look at your life and your children's lives from a distance. The perspective of twenty years from now is a good perspective to take. That's what *Can Motherhood Survive?* offers you.

P A R T   1

THE VALUE OF MOTHERHOOD

WHATEVER HAPPENED TO MOTHERHOOD?

(Is This What Childhood Is Meant to Be?)

Rejoice, O young man, in thy youth; and let thy heart cheer thee in the days of thy youth. . . .

Ecclesiastes 11:9

What is modern childhood like? How does an industrial nation in the Western World raise its children? Do we give our children things to rejoice about? Is childhood something that cheers the heart of a child? Or is it a time of confusion and loneliness? Are modern children acquiring memories that will bring them joy throughout their lives? You be the judge; here are a few vignettes, from a variety of sources, describing childhood in America today.

A Day in a Day Care Center

The little ones are clean and well-dressed. We look at them smilingly, but they do not smile in return. They regard us gravely, unblink-

5

ingly. . . . As the day goes on, some children will smile at us. Some will be bold enough to rummage through our purses. Some will come and talk to us. But generally, they will be wary of us. . . . I quickly decide on my own personal favorite child — Elizabeth, a beautiful blue-eyed brunette whose blue-and-white striped designer outfit and multicolored sneakers add up to at least a $100 investment.

Elizabeth immediately sticks her Q-tip into the paint and applies it to her face and most of her pricey outfit. She next proceeds to tear the cotton off the wooden swab. The attendant gives her more paint, and Elizabeth dips her fingers into the plastic cup. "You can't paint with your fingers," she's told. "You've got to take your stick." . . . For the next activity, Elizabeth's group is told to sit in a circle. A mattress is leaning against the crates, and Elizabeth goes over to the mattress and hugs it. She's led firmly back to the circle, and she begins to cry. She doesn't want to do the next activity, fitting little plastic objects into one another.

I conjure up a picture of Elizabeth's mother scaling a career ladder. I wonder how many rungs she has left. Why does she dress this toddler so smashingly and then institutionalize her? How does she think her child spends the day? . . .

The parents begin to come. The reunions are largely unemotional. The parents seem almost embarrassed as they sidle up to the appropriate area and search out their own. Usually, it's just a word or a motion to the little one who emerges quickly, showing very little joy. More fathers than mothers come to pick up the children. They lift them up and kiss them. Most of them say nothing to the women who have tended their children all day.[1]

Day Care: A Major National Industry

An estimated $14 billion was spent on care for children under age 15 in 1986 by families where the child's mother was employed, according to a survey by the Commerce Department's Census Bureau. Provisional data from the Survey of Income and Program Participation conducted from September to November 1986 indicate that 20 million of the children were age 5 to 14, and 70 percent of them were in kindergarten or grade school while their mothers were working.

Most of the 9 million preschool children were cared for outside their home during the hours their mothers worked, 4 out of 10 of them usually in someone else's home. Another 21 percent attended a formal child care facility (day or group care center, nursery, or pre-school).

The proportion of preschoolers cared for in someone else's home increased from 37 percent to 41 percent between this survey and the last child care survey in December 1984-March 1985.[2]

Day Care: A Fashionable Trend

On November 22, Arnold and Porter, a leading Washington, D.C., law firm, celebrated the completion of a new backup child care facility at its 1200 New Hampshire Avenue NW headquarters with a ribbon-cutting ceremony and open house for attorneys, staff, and their children. The facility is located on the ground floor of the firm's main offices and is designed to accommodate up to fifteen children between the ages of three months and ten years. Licensed by the District of Columbia, the facility is under the direction of Maria Elwood and will be staffed by a teacher and assistant teachers. According to Fern O'Brian, co-chairman of Arnold and Porter's Day Care Committee, the purpose of the center is to provide backup child care for attorneys and staff members from 8:30 A.M. to 6:30 P.M. on weekdays, as well as on weekends and firm holidays. Parents will be encouraged to join their children for lunch whenever possible.[3]

What About the Kids?

Every afternoon, around 3:45, the sidewalk across the street from my home starts to fill with the neighborhood children, ages four to fourteen. To a casual observer, these kids would seem to be wandering aimlessly, but I know this routine well. They are waiting for me and my three youngsters to come out for our afternoon play, which we do almost habitually at 4:00 P.M. Then the ritual of surrogate parenthood begins: they talk, I listen, and if it's something they are really concerned about, they make sure I hear and then expect a comment.

I've learned of shoplifting expeditions, heard that drugs have been offered at the middle school, and once saw a distressed 12-year-old wonder why her "steady" dumped her after she refused to have sex with him. I've seen them laugh and cry, fight and make up, dodge policemen and peers.

The conversations I've been privy to disturb me. These words are not meant for my ears; they are searching for their parents' ears. The main problem is that the children landing near my yard each day have no parents home before 6:00 P.M.[4]

Peer Pressure and Social Pressure

When I had my baby, I surprised myself. I quit my high-powered job as a commercial litigator and became a full-time housewife. . . .

Recently, however, . . . all the people I know — from my father to the man who owns the grocery store down the street, to the feminist psychologists — have been telling me that someone should be taking care of my child, and I should be working. So my husband and I agreed to put Joseph into day care. . . .

One morning, I explained things to my son.

"By being in day care, Joseph, you can experience self-sufficiency and confidence," I said, as I pulled on his diaper. "I read about this in one of those books on child-rearing and feminism. You can see role models of women as achievers, and develop specific skills as well. . . .

"You only miss me when I leave you because you are attempting to recreate an idyllic, economically unrealistic model of the 1950's nuclear family," I whispered over my shoulder to my small auditor. Then we got to the apartment where he would spend his morning with three other children who have been sharing the same damned cold for three weeks.

Joseph started to play with the toys, and grunted in greeting to his toddler colleagues. But as soon as I reached for the door to leave, he threw himself to the floor in front of my feet, arms locked around my ankles, screaming.[5]

Modern Motherhood in America

I think I did the best thing I could for my children by putting them in day care. Look, I didn't even go to work until I had my first child. The dishes were piling up in the sink, I was watching soap operas all day, and here was this little baby crying, and I said to myself, "Can I stand eighteen more years of this?" Maybe that makes me sound like a bad mother, but that's honestly the way I feel.[6]

Modern Motherhood in Sweden

Monika Kullman, a Swedish mother of three, in 1985 applied to the court for welfare payments of about $5,000 a year to supplement her husband's low, subsidized-level salary. Mrs. Kullman was told that she could receive such support only if she put herself "at the labor market's disposal." She was told to find a job, and put her children into day care — at a cost of about $32,000 a year to the government. She wished to stay at home, and care for her own children, and she took her case through the courts, but the State position was that it preferred to spend $32,000 a year of taxpayers' money on the two day-care positions rather than give Mrs. Kullman $5,000 a year towards the support of her family in the home.[7]

Is a Three-Story Colonial Worth It?

Dateline — Washington, D.C.

Most weeknights, if she can summon the energy, Cindy Harvey lays out clothing for her 5-year old daughter, Katie, before going to bed at 11 P.M. Five hours later, Harvey is awakened by the squawk of an alarm clock. . . .

The Harveys, who find darkness when they leave for work and darkness when they return home, are part of a weary army. . . .

"There is no alternative," Cindy Harvey said. "You do what you need to do. You make sacrifices. We could probably live in an apartment somewhere with one car, if I didn't work. But then there would be no trips, vacations, no treats." . . .

"Commuting is tough on the kids," said Tim Harvey, an administrator with . . . a computer management company operating out of the Pentagon. "It's tough on us as parents. You adjust your life around the commute. It's just a hard fact of life. . . ."

At 5:00 A.M. on a recent weekday, the upstairs light shone brightly from the Harveys' three-story colonial house. . . . Already there was a stream of cars on Davis Ford Road, a main thoroughfare leading to I-95.

Twenty minutes later, a fully dressed but still groggy Tim Harvey lumbered downstairs to begin his daily duties. . . . By 5:45 Cindy Harvey . . . was downstairs with [year-old] Megan, who was rubbing her eyes. Kisses were exchanged as Tim Harvey darted off to leave his car in a parking lot and catch his van pool to work. There was no time for breakfast. The children would get some food at the day-care center, but the parents would go without. . . .

By 6:15 A.M. the children were dropped at the center, where they would spend nearly 12 hours. And in a few minutes, Cindy Harvey was headed for I-95. . . .

"Five days a week, it's like walking on a 'treadmill'," said Cindy Harvey. She gets an hour with Megan before putting her to bed about 7:30 P.M. and then tries to take a little time to play with Katie. "It'll be 9:30 P.M. before I know it and I'm asking myself, 'Where did the time go?' Sometimes I'll try to read to Katie, and I'll fall asleep or start to doze off."

The family, she said, lives "for the weekends. That's our time to sleep, to unwind, to be together. And to get ready for the next week. . . ."

Jared Florance, Prince William's health director . . . suggested that commuting could be another factor tearing away at the family structure by damaging relationships. "Under these conditions, some county families won't grow properly," he said.[8]

From the Kids' Point of View

I think my mom should set aside a specific time each day to help my brother and me with our homework. She's a teacher and coaches the track team at her school and goes to lots of teachers' meetings, so our homework just gets squeezed in whenever. . . .

When my mom works on weekends, it's really important to me to have a chance to say good-bye to her, but lots of times she's up and out of the house before my sister and I are awake. . . .

I wish my mom could come and watch me swim more at the day-care center. . . .

When Mom and Dad pick me up from the after-school program, it would be nice if they could have dinner ready so we could spend a nice quiet evening at home. Just once a week, if they could do that and not rush off to more meetings.[9]

Who's Raising Our Children? And Why?

The question has to be asked. Why does a prestigious law firm feel so proud of itself that it encourages mothers to join their children for lunch that it stresses the fact in a press release? Why do the mothers need encouragement to be with their children?

In an age in which every newspaper reports on youth promiscuity, drug abuse, alcoholism, and the like, how can parents of adolescents allow them to come home to an empty house after school? What denial of reality is involved in their thinking? Is it because the parents do not hear about the shoplifting and the sex, because the only adult ear around, the neighbor's, hears it instead? Until the phone call from the police comes to the parents' workplace. . . .

Children in America are starving. For love. For attention. For their parents to notice them. Not in a casual way, by buying them more toys. Not with emotion, but with reason. By thinking rationally about what the children really need and then meeting those needs.

And what children need most can't be bought with money.

The children whose mom is a teacher, who can't get help with their own homework—they know what they need. The kid who yearns for a quiet dinner with his parents—he knows what he needs. These children learn early that talk is cheap. "I love you, dear" from your mom doesn't mean much if you have to hang out outside a neighbor's house to find someone who has time to listen to what's worrying you.

I'm sure the Harveys are lovely people. And if they want a three-story colonial home in the suburbs, and vacations and treats, well, who can blame them? That's part of the American dream, isn't it? They have a right to it, don't they, if they're willing to work for it? And they certainly are working hard for it—no question about that. But what price are their children paying? What responsibility do the Harveys have to their children? Meeting material needs is only one part of parents' responsibilities. The children will someday grow up and leave home. Then it won't matter if their childhood address was a three-story colonial or an apartment. It will matter if they knew that they were the most important thing in the world to somebody. When they spend twelve hours a day in a day-care center and the one meal a day they share with their parents is prepared in a rush of fatigue, where are they going to get that fundamental emotional security?

The woman who can't cope with a crying baby because she is so absorbed in the soap operas is right to feel guilty. She has refused to take responsibility for that baby—and the child is the loser. She can change, though, if she makes up her mind to do it. Not that it will be easy, but it can be done. But in a society bombarding women with messages about how irrelevant motherhood is, what is going to motivate her? When "just a housewife" is a joke and the cultural stereotype of a mom is of a brainless, frazzled frump, what self-respecting woman is going to aspire to motherhood as a lifetime ambition? With a "common knowledge" that day care is harmless, even beneficial, to children, how is a mother going to know that she is hurting her children by subjecting them to communal forms of child rearing?

With the opinion-making elite bombarding Congress with rosy pictures of the "progressivity" of the Swedish government's child care system, and the credentialed experts at Ivy League universities using their federal grants to persuade United States government officials to make laws and policies on Swedish premises — what chance does a maternal impulse have? How can a kid's need for Mommy compare with such forces?

Every cultural pressure is against motherhood. Every pressure encourages mothers to pursue "self-fulfillment" instead of their children's development. When our country had a legal code that gave "separate but equal" privileges to one-fifth of the population, cultural pressures encouraged discrimination on the basis of race. Every pressure was toward "knowing one's place as a Negro." It was just the cultural climate. But it changed. People changed it because they saw and sought a higher good, a more sacred principle.

There's a higher good, a more sacred principle, here too. The life of every child to be born in this country is at stake. Every child is at risk of being abandoned by his or her mother if the direction of the culture doesn't change. Don't we already have enough despair, violence, and self-destruction among our youth and young adults? Do we really want more? That's what we're going to get unless we change the course of our society.

This is a free country. But women are not free to be mothers. They used to be. A few decades ago, motherhood was a national treasure. What has happened? Can the trend be reversed?

Can motherhood survive?

2

WHO ARE THE LONELY?

(Only a Mother Away from Death or Destruction)

God sets the lonely in families.
Psalm 68:6

Webster's *New World Dictionary* defines *lonely* as "alone, solitary; isolated; unhappy at being alone; longing for friends, etc."

Loneliness has more to do with unhappiness than with the presence or absence of other people. You can be lonely in a crowd. What the lonely have in common is emotional aloneness, the absence of intimate relationships that matter, that provide order and love in the universe.

The Lord God said, "It is not good for the man to be alone" (Genesis 2:18).

It is, indeed, not good. A puppy left alone in the house day after day will grow wild and destructive. Lonely teenagers resort to alcohol and drugs to cover the emptiness inside, then to promiscuity, and sometimes, finally, to suicide, if the pain becomes too great. Lonely adults are prey to the same plagues.

We are all potentially the lonely, potentially sojourners in a strange land.

Are not married people just a partner away from loneliness? Without a strong relationship, a person can be lonely in marriage. But we can *learn* how to have a good marriage: we can, if we are willing to make the effort, learn to respect, forgive, love, and serve our spouses. Are not teens really just a parent or sibling or friend away from loneliness? By exercise of emotional self-control, if he understands why he should exercise it, a teen can restrain himself from lashing out in adolescent frustration at the person who stands ready to comfort him. Aren't all adults just a few people away from loneliness — as long as they know they need those people? Social skills and friendship skills can be learned, if we are are convinced we need to make the effort to learn them.

But a baby? A baby perhaps has more needs than anybody. He will die without attention, food, comfort, warmth, nurture. But *a baby doesn't know he has any needs.* He cannot do anything — not a single thing — to help himself. He cannot decide to change himself to overcome his loneliness. He cannot reason to himself, "People don't like it when I cry in the middle of the night, so I must exercise self-control and not expect a feeding at two in the morning." He can't figure out why people react the way they do. The baby doesn't speak the language of the people around him: not their verbal language, and not their emotional language either, at least not for a time. He doesn't understand how he affects them. He doesn't know if he pleases or displeases them. A baby is quintessentially what Scripture calls an afflicted person. A baby is only a mother away from death or destruction.

Some babies are more obviously afflicted, of course: a study of asthmatic babies found that 42 percent of them had problems in their emotional attachment to their mothers, while only 14 percent of the non-asthmatic babies in the study had such problems.[1] The babies only did what all babies do, with the added complication of more urgent physical needs. The mothers reacted one way or another to them — some better, some worse.

A baby is afflicted, needy, helpless. How does the Lord call us to respond to the helpless? We are to feed the hungry and care for the helpless (Ezekiel 18:7), to clothe the naked (Luke 3:11), to shelter the homeless (Isaiah 16:3–4). Most of all, we are to love one another (1 John 4:11). When we were needy and neglected, the Lord ministered to us Himself, lavished riches upon us, rescued us from ruin, and set us at

His right hand. God has written His law in our hearts, in our very nature, to care for our own offspring. Even if it were not a spiritual obligation, it is a natural impulse. *Every baby is only a mother away from death or destruction.*

"That's No Fair!"

A feminist may read that last sentence, that every baby is only a mother away from death or destruction, and react with anger: "That's no fair! There shouldn't be such a heavy burden on one woman!"

But a Christian will react differently: "Yes, a baby is a burden. But, Lord, your burden is light." A Christian knows that God made that child. Whatever the circumstances of conception or birth, whether legitimate or illegitimate, whether wanted or unwanted, whether poor or rich, whether sick or healthy, whether in a happy family or in an unhappy family — God knows all that, and He knows more besides. And He called that baby into existence. Either God knows what He is doing or He does not.

Since as a Christian I believe that God knows what He is doing, I consider it a privilege to share in the carrying out of His plan. I know that God has a plan for that baby, has knit him together, has numbered the hairs of his head, knows that baby's whole life. I know that God has predestined that baby for adopted sonship with Him in Heaven. And since I am the mother, I know that God has given me a part to play in carrying out His plans. I know that being that baby's mother is part of God's plan for me.

God may want that baby given to somebody else in infant adoption. And if so, the birth mother's obligation extends only so far as keeping as healthy as possible and nourishing the baby with love (important because hormones produced by the mother's body influence her emotions and affect the child), extra vitamins, and good food. If the child is destined for later adoption, the mother has the responsibility for giving love and care until she relinquishes the child to the adoptive parents. Then the adoptive mother accepts the burden of standing between that baby and death or destruction. Being the birth mother is a noble role to play in another person's drama of life. But most babies are not adopted; most babies are raised by the mothers who give them birth.

None of which necessarily means we have the skills to be good mothers. All it means in practical terms is that we are willing to follow our Lord's leading. Part of faithful following is learning as we go along to do the best job we can.

But is the mother really all that stands between a baby and disaster? No, not all. The psalm does not read, "God sets the lonely with mothers." It reads, "God sets the lonely in families." In God's plan mothers are not alone: they are members of families. Even so, the responsibility of motherhood is heavy, and neither men nor women in our culture find it easy to understand and accept responsibility.

Taking Responsibility for Motherhood

Those of us who advocate Christian values in the public arena — even if we don't call them "Christian" — get accused of minding other people's business; having old-fashioned and anti-woman ideas; being moralistic, oppressive, and totalitarian, and worse. We're charged with wanting to deprive people of happiness. It's ironic that frequently the people who charge us with being moralistic are themselves unhappy, but insist that they know what's best for them and how to achieve their own happiness.

Let me give you an example. Carla Parillo of Rhode Island is a pleasant enough woman off camera. But I met her on a television talk show, and she was a tiger. Her story was this: After her divorce, her ex-husband did not like the live-in boyfriend she soon acquired, and a local court forbade her to allow the boyfriend to sleep over if her three children were home. Carla was so incensed by this interference with her freedom that she took the matter to the U.S. Supreme Court. Carla could not understand why it was anybody's business but hers who slept in her bed.

When I appeared on the *Larry King Live* television talk show with her, I noted that this boyfriend was long since history, so perhaps he hadn't been too committed to her after all. This prompted Larry King attack me for living with my head in the sand — was I really so out of it as to expect people to make commitments to each other before they had sex? Carla's lawyer was lighting into me as well, so I was delighted when the phone calls started coming in. Almost all of them expressed concern about the harm to Carla's children of having different boy-friends parading through their mother's bedroom. Carla insisted that there was no harm to her children in the way she conducted her sexual relationships and that nobody—least of all the children's father—had any right to tell her how to live her life.

That her children might have needs other than hers or in conflict with her desires seemed beyond her comprehension. Or at least, so she sounded. She certainly wasn't about to take seriously any suggestion that what she wanted to do might not be good for her children.

Isn't that rhetoric typical? Don't we hear that kind of rhetoric every time the morality of a personal decision is questioned? But what is really being said is, "I want what I want, and nobody else's needs dare impinge upon my desires." Or, in other words, "I'm not about to take responsibility for anybody else; I want what pleases me, and me alone." The attitude pervades modern culture. To some extent, we are all vic-tims of that type of thinking. And the biggest losers in most cases are children. Their total dependence on us is what makes their needs so compelling. And at some deep-down instinctive level, people know it. It's hard to escape some guilt when we put the children at risk. So peo-ple who are determined to do something that might put them at risk, simply deny the risk.

Why does our society defy traditional teachings about relationships? Are not these the things our society feels guilty about?

"_____ doesn't hurt kids." Fill in the blank. My having live-in boy friends doesn't hurt my kids. Divorce doesn't hurt kids. My drinking doesn't hurt my kids. Day care doesn't hurt kids. Adultery doesn't hurt kids. Pornography doesn't hurt kids. Homosexual teachers don't hurt kids. You can think of some more things to insert. Aren't those assertions really little more than rhetorical masks to cover a posture of defending and excusing what we know—or at least suspect—is wrong?

Carla probably could understand how the example she was setting might hurt her children. She was saying on that television show that she didn't want to admit that having live-in boyfriends might hurt her chil-dren. If you press them on it, few people really mean that divorce doesn't hurt kids; what they really mean is that they don't want to admit that divorce may harm kids. They want to allow divorce, if not for themselves, then in theory for other people, and they are afraid that an admission that divorce harms kids might weaken the case for it.

This book is written to answer the claim that "not having a family life doesn't hurt kids." The theories and the people who can say, "a qualified day-care provider is as good as a mother" are deceiving themselves, and I hope this book will help them see it. The women who say, "My kids are doing fine, and I'm not raising them myself" may be correct. It is possible. But it's more likely that those women have not looked very objectively at their children. I know that I used to say things like that when I was not looking with very honest eyes. Even if I had seen the reality, I was not prepared to accept responsibility for changing my life to correct what was wrong.

Like millions of women of my generation, I wanted to do what I wanted to do, and I assumed that having a family was an optional extra, that having a family wouldn't change the course of my own life very much. I was able to take care of myself, but I didn't accept the responsibility of taking care of anybody else.

What Is a Family?

God sets the lonely in families. He does this in order to change people's lives. He does it because He loves us — and being in a family protects us from the physical and emotional isolation to which we are all subject.

Of course we aren't all destined to get married and have families. Throughout the ages of history, many who wanted to live single for the Lord did so — but they did it in spiritual families. The monasteries of Christendom are not haphazard, catch-as-catch-can, do-your-own-thing environments, like hippie communes. They are disciplined, structured families. And for good reason. Even Christ was tempted by Satan when He was in the wilderness alone. How much more so would we be?

God meant us to be in families. He could have created lots of unconnected individuals in the Garden of Eden. Instead, He declared that it was not good for Adam to be alone, and He created Eve and made a permanent union between them. He could have created lots of couples, who could rotate partners when they wanted a little variety in life. Later, He could have caused Eve to give birth to her children without Adam around to help raise them. He could even have created children who were able, like puppies, to leave their mothers after six weeks. But He didn't do it that way.

He joined man and woman together in a bond that He wants nothing but death to sunder. He designed children so that they come from the union of man and woman and so that they require decades of love and care and nurture before they are mature. God didn't tell His people to separate from their father and mother when they became adults — quite the contrary. Many generations lived together in one household. Grandparents, great aunts and uncles, parents, sisters, brothers, and their spouses and children — these were members of the extended families of the Old Testament. And more besides. Even servants and their families were part of a man's household, and entitled to his protection and care. God did not mean for us to be lonely; He meant children to grow up in permanent families with mothers and fathers and other adults.

What's So Unique About a Family?

What does the family do that nobody else can do for a child? It is the only system that allows motherhood to flourish.

We cannot change the way we are genetically programmed. And we are programmed to bond in infancy with one person and only after that bond is secure to go beyond it. That's dumb, you say: a goose will follow the first thing it sees after hatching. But I'm not saying we're no different from geese. A goose's brain is imprinted when its eyes first see daylight. That's programmed in the brain cells by nature for the protection of geese. A mother goose who isn't around when her eggs hatch has a hard time keeping her goslings around until maturity. The sight of a baby goose following a dog or cat is for us a barnyard comedy, but if the goose were capable of emotions, he would probably be in anguish, unable to comprehend why he didn't fit in, why he didn't sound like the dog, why he couldn't go into the house like the dog, and so on. Whatever the goose is supposed to learn from the mother goose, he would not learn from the dog, and his level of misery would be increased by that much.

The relationship between the infant and his or her mother is the first, primary, most essential, most critical relationship of life. That relationship is the basis for the formation of human personality. That relationship establishes the child's capacity for love throughout life. The quality of that relationship creates the conditions for the development and exercise of conscience. The quality of love between a mother and child is the model for all other love the child will experience, either as a child or as an adult, either as a receiver or as a giver, either in having or in seeking.

There is a basic reality that we cannot "pretend" out of existence: *the quality of love and care that a child receives in the first three to five years of life is the main factor in whether that child will be able to think, to learn, to love, to care, to cooperate with other people—in short, whether that child will merely exist or will thrive and flourish and add to human society.*

Whether we like it or not, that is the reality. Reality is God's gift to mankind. We have no choice but to accept it and take responsibility to order our lives accordingly.

Is this a heavy burden on a mother? You bet it is. Is it more than a mother can be expected to do all by herself? I think so. She was not meant to provide all this on her own, and fend for her own survival as well. The well that fills her emotional bucket does not exist inside her. Her own need for love continues and grows. As she gives love to her children, she needs to be receiving love from others. God did not set the lonely with mothers; He set children and mothers in families.

I've often wondered why most women are so physically exhausted during the early months of pregnancy. It would have seemed more logical for nature to make women strong then so that they could flee from enemies if necessary, thus increasing the children's chances of survival. Then someone pointed out to me that the wife's weakness in the early months of pregnancy brings forth the first protective feelings in the father-to-be, who heretofore may have regarded his wife as a feminine version of himself and not have understood that motherhood would change her drastically. That's an interesting insight, and it graphically demonstrates that God does indeed intend us to depend on one another for love: the baby on the mother, the mother on the husband, and the husband in turn on others. The infant/mother bond is exclusive only for a matter of months; then the infant begins to establish bonds with the father, and these bonds are almost as important as the maternal one. These bonds also tie the father closer to the family and so strengthen the whole unit.

Psychologists universally recognize that there are two main psychological tasks in growing up: first, to attach to the mother and then the father and the world beyond; and second, to successfully separate from mother and father in order to become a mature person who can function in the world. The first task is undertaken in infancy; the second task begins in adolescence.

Those emotional tasks are accomplished most naturally and reliably in a family. Hormones of growth and maturity make the physical aspects of the second stage inevitable, but if the emotional task of attaching was not accomplished successfully in childhood, adolescent separation will not result in a mature person who can function well.

Let me say it another way: *unless you get a lot of love and attention from your mother when you're a baby and a little kid, you won't be happy when you get to be a teenager or adult.* And unhappy teenagers and adults tend to become and to cause unpleasant statistics.

Am I saying that people whose childhood emotional needs are not satisfied are doomed to be plagues upon society? No, I'm not saying that. But I think I could accurately enough say that most people who are plagues upon society did not have those needs satisfied.

Nor am I saying that people are victims of environment. God did not make us to be miserable, but He knew that many of us, left to our own devices, would make ourselves that way. That is why He sent us a redeemer. The love of God for us is incalculable. The power of the Cross to make up for human shortcomings, to heal our self-inflicted pains, to meet all our needs, is infinite. No matter what traumas we suffer in childhood or at any other time, God can overcome them — if we ask Him and trust Him and do our part of the job.

Of course, we will not be the same as if we had not suffered them. Just as wounds may be stitched closed but will leave scars, so harm inflicted on the human mind and emotions may be correctable — at great cost of time and effort and skill. But the scars from the harm will remain, though with God's help they can stay closed.

But we love our children! We want more for them than lives of possibly correctable harm and controllable pain! Of course we do. And that is why we must recognize God's plan for the rearing of children and why we must do all we can to live our lives so that our children may experience God's ideal as closely as is humanly possible. God's plan is for children to grow up in families. "Your statutes are wonderful; therefore I obey them" (Psalm 119:129).

God's Statutes Under Attack

Unfortunately, society today does not obey God's statutes. Many people and groups of people have built their lives around disobeying God's statutes — some deliberately, more without thinking — and their influence affects even those of us who do believe His statutes are wonderful and do try to obey them.

In 1980, the United States government spent millions of dollars to hold a series of White House conferences on families. They didn't call the exercise "White House Conference on *the* Family" — because the political appointees in charge of the fiasco couldn't decide what a "family" is! They held the conferences anyhow and ended up recommending gay rights and legalized abortion, among other things, which hints at the kind of pressure groups controlling that conference. The conference ended up being an attack on the family and on motherhood.

Ever since then, around election time, we hear lots of warm fuzzy rhetoric about "family." Remember when "motherhood" was something no politican would dare be against? But motherhood went out of fashion when feminism came in. Now, the bell-ringing phrase is "family," whatever it means.

And few politicians are willing to say what it means to them. To me, legally, a family is persons related by blood, marriage, or adoption. I suppose I should clarify that by adding heterosexual marriage and legal adoption. There are those who would define family as any group of people who live together and share cooking facilities. Some might include nebulous traits like "share a common commitment to the future," which would make an army platoon a family — after all, they live together, eat together, and have a common commitment to surviving their army days and returning to civilian life.

The criticism leveled against my definition is that it is too "restrictive." What about the woman who has a baby out of wedlock? I'm accused of not considering them a valid family. But the baby is related to her by blood, isn't he? Of course, that's a family—not a full family as God would like it, but a family nonetheless. Then I'm accused of judging or scorning certain people because I say that their families are less than ideal. But that is not to scorn anybody; it is only to warn them that their choices may have made their lives much more difficult than God intended them to be.

The agenda of that White House conference was organized to promote ideas contrary to God's statutes. Tragically, such ideas are common currency today.

Think about abortion. It's a pretty clear-cut violation of God's law. There are people, many people, who make a living promoting abortion, lobbying Congress and state governments to make sure it stays legal, propagandizing for it, and raising millions of dollars to keep the campaign going. To say nothing about the people who perform the abortions and work for the people who perform them. Not to mention the people who have abortions or who help their friends to get abortions. It's no accident that most major magazine editors and television producers approve of abortion; the abortion lobby has systematically cultivated them and propagandized them and won them over. And because it is won over, the popular press treats abortion as if it were okay, and most television programs and shows take the same attitude.

But that doesn't make abortion okay, does it? Of course not. The same kind of lobbying effort has been going on for a long time and is growing steadily on other matters as well, matters that are similarly opposed to God's laws: "gay rights," pornography, and easy divorce are familiar examples.

The valuing of human life is one of God's laws which has been under attack for a long time. The campaign against this one has been couched in various terms: sometimes noble sounding and altruistic, sometimes militant and angry. When it's sounding noble, it talks about "the best interests of the child"; when it's being militant, it talks about "a woman's rights." The demands of this movement have been made to industry, labor, education, and legislatures at all levels, from county boards through state legislatures to Congress. So well has the abortion lobby sold its case that most of us don't even realize how successful it has been, how well it has succeeded in changing the attitudes and habits of our whole society.

The change also goes by various names: child care, child development, and day care are the most common ones. But the underlying philosophy is *social parenting*.

What Is Social Parenting?

Social parenting is the idea that somebody *other than parents* can, or should, raise children. Only occasionally do you hear somebody making a case that somebody besides parents are actually *best* to do the job, but plenty of people do say that among themselves. Articles in law journals discuss whether the state should require all parents to be licensed, for instance.[2] But for popular consumption, the idea is sold on the grounds that "it doesn't hurt kids" and "it fulfills women."

It doesn't hurt kids if they spend most of their waking hours with somebody other than a loving parent. It doesn't hurt kids if they get breakfast and lunch at a day-care center, and their mom fixes dinner on the run. It doesn't hurt kids if the bus takes them from school to another institution to wait for two or three or four more hours until a fatigued, tense, distracted parent can come pick them up. You've heard these views expressed.

If you had a baby recently, you found sections on day care, with advice on how to find day care that you trust in the "educational materials" the hospital gives out to new mothers. But you found no mention of how you may break your heart and your baby's if you use it. You can hardly pick up any of the parenting magazines without reading about "The Day Care Crisis" or "What to Do About Day Care" or "How to Cope as a Working Mother." But few and far between are articles like "I Quit My Job to Raise My Baby and Now I'm Happy."

I hope that by the time you finish reading this book you will no longer be able to sit calmly by when somebody says, "Day care doesn't harm kids." I hope you will be moved to speak truth to that error — truth in love, but truth nonetheless.

Modern society is built around self-gratification. The "me" generation didn't last just a few years. It's not surprising that people raised with contemporary ideas and without an eternal vision find Christian teaching about children and family to be oppressive. Self-sacrifice and service are dirty words to most postfeminist women and even more fearful sounding to contemporary men. And let's be honest (we'll talk about this more later): service and self-sacrificing love are the basis of Christian teaching about family.

A person doesn't have to be a Christian in order to know and practice self-sacrificing love. But it sure does help.

3

OLIVE SHOOTS OR WEEDS UNDERFOOT?

(Love and Obedience)

Children are an heritage of the LORD,
and the fruit of the womb is his reward.
Psalm 127:3

Thy wife shall be as a fruitful vine by the
sides of thine house: thy children like
olive plants round about thy table.
Psalm 128:3

Why do people have kids anyhow? How are parents supposed to respond to their children? Since modern society doesn't really have answers to those questions, it talks out of both sides of its mouth. Certain groups in Washington, for instance, lament that "we don't spend enough money on children" and at the same time insist on a "woman's right to choose" to kill her child.

Occasionally, some public figure laments bitterly that we are "not a child-centered society" and that as a nation we have an obligation to "give our children the best." But then it turns out that public figure is really talking about funding certain programs so as to employ adults who can get paid to be concerned about children between nine and five on work days. And some people use the "child-centered society" rhetoric to justify having government pay the costs of separating children from their families by putting them into warehouses known as day-care centers. Is this concern in the best interests of the children or for the job security of bureaucrats?

On one hand, women's magazines are filled with heartbreaking stories of couples who are unable to bear children, and the National Center for Health Statistics concludes that one in four American couples are infertile. On the other hand, millions of babies go unadopted each year — and not just minority or handicapped ones. Could it be that these thousands of infertile couples are looking not just for a child to love but for a piece of *themselves* to love? Is that love or is that selfishness?

On one hand, obstetrics has been turned on its ear by couples demanding natural births, midwives, Leboyer deliveries, and the like — all so that the mother can have an opportunity to "bond" with the baby. But on the other hand, many of these same natural-delivery babies are put into day care at a few weeks or months of age. And many of these delivery-room fathers find it necessary to end the marriage a few years later in order to "continue growing."

Don't misunderstand me — I'm sympathetic to the pains of infertility. And I'm all in favor of natural childbirth and fathers in the delivery room. (My firstborn and I owe our lives to an alert midwife, so I'm a staunch defender of what was called at the time "alternative childbirth.") I'm just pointing out the inconsistency: we demand the best delivery, yet we farm the child out to day care. How can we be so concerned one month about doing everything "naturally" and then so studiedly unconcerned a few months later? Might it be that women have demanded natural deliveries because such deliveries make birth a more satisfying experience *for them,* but they have not empathized with their infants enough to know that day care is not a satisfying experience *for them?* Might it be that men who find it emotionally satisfying to be present at a birth find it emotionally exhausting to continue to support the wife financially and psychologically and so allow their preoccupation with themselves to justify abandoning their wife and children?

Do we view children as appendages to our own lives? Do we accept them as separate individuals, whom God has assigned to us, to nurture and love and train and raise and bring to Him? Or do we view them as frosting on a finished cake, a nice "extra" but not something that changes the texture of our lives? What is the purpose of having children? To give us satisfaction, ego gratification, contentment, a sense of accomplishment—or to give God glory and to give Him sons and daughters?

One or the other must be the main reason. The answer should be easy for a Christian.

To God Be the Glory? Or to Me?

Either we will worship God or we will worship idols. Either we will be committed to raising our children for the Lord or we will be committed to raising them for us. Either we are committed to doing what is necessary and best for our children or we will live according to our own desires for ourselves. A Christian cannot say, "I love my kids and do my best for them as long as it doesn't interfere with my desires for myself/my career/my love life/whatever."

"I'll love my kids and do what's right for them as long as my spouse is nice to me, but if my spouse gets difficult, we'll divorce, and I'll abandon them." Would anybody say that? And yet how many people live exactly like that?

"I love my kids and put them first as long as I have no job offer that's too good to refuse." And when the irresistible job offer comes, how many people rationalize it: "Well, with the extra money, the kids will be better off because I can buy them more things."

"I love my kids and will do my best for them as long as we don't have to be poor, but if raising these kids means we're poor and my parents criticize me for that, then I'll do whatever it takes to avoid that criticism—even if it means taking a job and putting the kids in day care."

If you have relied on such thoughts, take another look at Psalm 128. In the ancient Middle East, a fruitful vine alongside the house meant you had permanence and stability. The vine gave you shade and food; it comforted you. Olive shoots symbolized everything you needed to enjoy life: food, oil, shelter, and wealth coming from the olive tree itself. Olive shoots are beautiful to see as well: bright green in that parched land. God intended children to be all these things to us: fullness, contentment, satisfaction, wealth — all the things that make men and women happy.

Alas, in our postindustrial society, children do not bring us wealth and are likely to make us poor. They consume food rather than produce it (with the increasingly scarce exception of farm families). They require shelter but are unable to help construct it. And so for us today, unfortunately, that Biblical image does not automatically convey the depth of meaning the psalmist had in mind.

What image might engender a similar sense of hopefulness in our late-twentieth-century society? *Children are CDs in the bank? — Children are a European sports car in the driveway? — Children are a permanently chic wardrobe? — Children are a paid-up mortgage?* Somehow, those images don't work. God doesn't make CDs or sports cars or wardrobes or mortgages. But He does make children. We must not forget that.

And the other thing we must not forget is that God gives us children to raise for two reasons: because He wants many sons and daughters in His kingdom and because He wants to change us. He wants us to raise our children to know Him and love Him and serve Him so that they can be happy with Him — if not in this world, then for sure in the next. And He wants us to be drawn closer to Him by our children. He knows that raising kids is difficult and demanding and that we can succeed at the process only if we get better at loving and serving and making sacrifices. God wants us to die to ourselves so that we might live with Him, and for most of the human race, rearing children is the way we learn to die to ourselves. Pure desire for God should be enough motivation, and it is for some people — for mystics or saints. For most of us, our fallen natures are so strong that just about the only place for any unselfishness to occur spontaneously is in our attitude toward our children; so grace builds upon nature, and God uses our love for our children to draw us closer to Him.

First Comes Love

Isaiah does not lose much in translation when he tells us how to teach children: "For precept must be upon precept, precept upon precept; line upon line, line upon line; here a little, and there a little" (Isaiah 28:10).

This is how "children weaned from their milk, those just taken from the breast" learn, Isaiah tells us, explaining that just so God will teach His people.

"How many times do I have to tell you to wash your hands before you sit down at the table?" "If I had a nickel for every time I've reminded you to make your bed, I'd be rich." Sound familiar? It should: precept upon precept, line upon line, a little here, a little there. "Honey, remember we talked yesterday about why you shouldn't take Sally's toy without asking her first?" "Johnny, remember, you promised me you wouldn't tell me any more fibs?" That's how children learn.

Who but a permanent, loving mother can impart this kind of education? Only a person who is with the child all or most of its waking hours knows what input has been made and needs to be made in order to produce the desired output.

It begins at the breast. The hospital handouts said, "Never put a baby asleep into the crib." The people who wrote those books must have intended mothers of newborns to be entirely deprived of sleep! My experience was that if I didn't put new babies into the crib already asleep, they would never sleep!

Perhaps I spoiled my babies. Perhaps I overindulged them. By the time Caroline was a year and a half old, I couldn't put her to sleep without giving her "mama nursee." Daddy or her big brothers could rock her to sleep all right but I couldn't get by with something that simple. We had an elaborate lovers' ritual to follow. When she was ready for bed, in double diapers and pajamas, I'd ask her: Do you want some mama nursee? She'd nod or say yes and start smiling with intense delight. So we'd say kiss everybody else good night and head upstairs. She'd climb up the steps by herself and then run, literally run, to the rocking chair in the corner of her room. She'd climb up on it and sit over to one side, looking at me with eager expectation, total attention, and that wonderful smile. Then I'd sit down, and she'd arrange herself in my lap. Within two minutes total contentment would absorb her and those blue-gray eyes would close. Calling it a lovers' ritual is not an exaggeration: I was her first love, and the depth and completeness of my response to her taught her about the possibilities of love for the rest of her life.

Contrast this leisurely nursing relationship with the contortions a working mother must go through to nurse her baby. A few minutes when they first wake up in the morning, perhaps putting a sleepy baby to the breast with the result that not much milk gets taken. Then mom has to rush around to do the breakfast and morning chores and to take baby to the babysitter. Perhaps it's close enough to work that she can race there on her lunch hour: "Fifteen minutes there, fifteen minutes back. Hope there's no traffic snarl on the way. Should allow plenty of time to nurse. . . . Hope the baby's not asleep. . . . Hope the sitter didn't give her a bottle earlier this morning. . . ." In the afternoon the mother can go to the ladies' room and squeeze her breasts for fifteen minutes and save the milk: "Hope it doesn't go bad before I can get it to a refrigerator. . . . Seems there should be more. . . . Maybe she didn't nurse enough yesterday to keep the supply up. . . . Is my boss wondering why I'm spending so much time in here?" And then at the end of the day, race out of the building: "Hope the boss doesn't notice how eager I am to get out of here and how little attention I'm paying to what he's saying." If parking isn't a problem when the mother collects the baby, perhaps a quick nursing there at the babysitter's will calm her cries. And then home, to start dinner and evening chores: "Thank heavens for the baby-rocker-seat so I can put her in it and she can watch me fix dinner. . . . What will I do when she gets too big for that and wants me to hold her? . . . Oh well, I guess that's why playpens were invented. . . ."

This is the pattern that many new mothers follow, mothers on career tracks as well as mothers in routine jobs. Why do they bother to nurse? Probably because they know that it is best for the baby, medically and emotionally. Which it is. But is the emotional goal being met? Where is the sense of intimacy in a hectic schedule like this? If the mother is nursing to establish closeness with her baby—a valid reason for breast-feeding—is that purpose served in this scenario?

Well, let me say this: it's better than nothing. At the very least, Mom's persistence in nursing gets baby into Mom's arms several times a day, for more than a minute or two. For a few minutes of blissful union in the otherwise frantic day, Mom can contemplate the universe in her child's eyes and be aware of her love for him and his need for her. These brief moments give baby his best shot at capturing his mother's heart so that when he begins to miss her and protest about being taken to the babysitter, she might be empathic enough to feel his pain. Her empathy might help her decide to spare him that pain. The longer Mom can nurse, the better for everybody. But what will happen when Mom's milk dries up? What pretext will she and baby have then to get close and cuddle each other? Somebody else can always stick a bottle in the baby's mouth, after all, and warn a busy mother to save her own energy and beware of "spoiling" the baby.

Mother Nature is very clever: she has her ways of making us want to do what is good for us, like nursing our babies. The more we nurse, the more we cherish the tender intimacy . . . and the more we want of it. And the more we want of what is good for us, the better off we are. The more of ourselves we give our children, the more of themselves they will be able to give as they mature.

In fact, the very first, most fundamental essential for motherhood is *time* (well, really, God's grace and the disposition of the mother's heart to want it—but I'm talking practical logistics now). The mother who wants to nurse needs *time* with the baby in order for nursing to achieve its dual purpose. If a mother spends time with baby, it doesn't matter whether the baby is nursed or bottle fed. The biggest difference is that nursing helps to ensure that the time will be taken and the attention will be devoted to the little nursling.

"That ye may suck, and be satisfied with the breasts of her consolations; that ye may milk out, and be delighted with the abundance of her glory . . . as one whom his mother comforteth, so will I comfort you" (Isaiah 66:11, 13). If we have not been comforted by a mother so that we know what it feels like at a deep, preconscious, subconscious, unconscious level, how will we understand God's promise to comfort us like a mother?

From Love Comes Teaching

Little by little, a child grows. A little here, a little there, precept by precept, rule on rule. A child's development is unpredictable in the short term. Sometimes you'll have a good routine going; other times no two days will seem the same. Some days the child is "teachable"; some days she isn't. One day she may be attentive, relaxed, pleasant, and seem to be trying to talk. Then that night her teeth may hurt, and she'll sleep badly, and the next day it seems she does nothing but fuss and want to be held. It might be days before she evens out again.

You never know which day is going to be a good one and which a difficult one. But she's your child, and you know how to read her, and you can learn to adjust your plans to her abilities. Maybe you were planning a big grocery shop today, but it's obvious she needs a morning nap. So you borrow the milk you need from your neighbor and defer the grocery until evening when your husband can stay home with her. You don't force the unhappy baby to endure an hour-long tour of the grocery store (and the other shoppers to endure her protests!).

Imagine how a day-care worker feels when confronted with a toddler having a bad day on the day for the outing to the zoo. Or even worse, suppose it's several toddlers. The day-care center has planned the outing, rented the van, made the arrangements. Rested or weary, cheerful or crabby, the kids must go. Where is the flexibility? It isn't there. How could it be? Managing groups of people, children or adults, is a task that has very limited flexibility — especially if the children involved are not trained in obedience.

> Jesus was an obedient man. He wasn't obedient "for the most part."
> He wasn't "sort of" obedient. He was perfectly obedient. Jesus was
> characteristically obedient. It wasn't simply something he could do
> from time to time; it was his characteristic response to godly author-
> ity. That is what we are aiming for in our children — not simply chil-
> dren who can be obedient and respectful from time to time when they
> are in the mood, but children who *are* obedient and respectful.[1]

What a wonderful distillation of wisdom in Ken Wilson's *The Obedient Child.* Ken's years of experience training his own children and counseling other parents has led him to conclude that obedience is an absolutely essential prerequisite to bringing up children in the training and instruction of the Lord. And, he says, there is no mystery to raising obedient children: "A reasonably healthy home + clear standards for obedience and respect + consistent training in and enforcement of those standards = obedient and respectful children (more often than not)."

But notice the second and third part of that formula: clear standards and consistent training. Spending a portion of life in a day-care center or with a babysitter who does not have the same standards and consistency means that two of three essential conditions for learning obedience are not met. And children who are put into day care very young have less opportunity to learn obedience; and they (and their parents and society) suffer the consequences.

Recently we tried to teach Caroline to obey the command "come." It was an essential thing for her to know, so it was one of the first we deliberately set out to teach her. She was fifteen months old. We began at Easter, when we happened to have paska in the house. Paska is a delicious, rich, Russian Easter cheese made with farmer's cheese, eggs, sugar, and heavy cream. You know, the two-thousand-calories-to-a-spoon kind of treat; absolutely irresistible. This was Caroline's first taste of it. I stood in the kitchen and called her from the living room: "Caroline, come." When she came to me, I gave her a bite of cheese. Then Bill took her back to the living room, and I called her again and gave her another bite of cheese. After a few times, we switched positions and repeated the process a few more times. She liked the cheese so well that before we gave up the exercise she was coming before she was called.

I think she at least got the idea that "come" had something to do with going to the parent who said it. (For a while I think she thought it had something to do with cheese because the next night I noticed her walking by herself back and forth, back and forth, between the living room and the kitchen, looking a little puzzled, as if trying to figure out what she had to do to get the cheese again!)

But a good beginning is only as good as its follow-up. In the next days and weeks we had to say "come" in different circumstances, and we had to take the time to make its meaning clear. There were times when I'd say "Come, Caroline," and she'd look at me with a twinkle in her eyes and a naughty smile on her chubby cheeks and turn around and toddle off in the opposite direction, with her arms flapping and her padded bottom swinging from side to side. It was so cute that if Grandma had been around to see it, she'd have roared in laughter and delight and said to me as I went off to firmly bring the baby to me, "Oh, Connie, she's so cute! She's just having a little fun! Don't scold her! She was just playing."

But I had a plan for teaching her this simple thing, and I knew I had to carry out the plan. And after a certain number of those cute naughty defiances, when I was certain she understood and was deliberately not complying, I had to get very stern and administer a little spanking to that cute little bottom. I could do it because I was essentially her only teacher, and I knew she understood what I meant. If she didn't take me seriously on this, she wouldn't take me seriously on the next thing I tried to teach her. And day after day the teaching has to be practiced and reinforced, sometimes easily and sometimes not so easily, depending on her receptivity on different days.

But suppose she went to day care eight hours a day? Even if I told the day-care worker that I was teaching her "come," the worker might or might not follow up. After all, with four, five, six, or more other toddlers to look after, she couldn't pay special attention to just one. Or, if she did follow up and happened to have a foreign accent, Caroline would not realize she was saying the same word.

Or supposing Caroline understood and still chose to run off? What could the day-care worker do? Maybe she could chase her — if another child was not demanding her attention at that moment. But she wouldn't scold her — after all, it might make her cry and that would create a commotion. And she wouldn't dare spank her; somebody might see that and shout "child abuse." Furthermore, in order to keep the day-care activities going smoothly, she couldn't risk Caroline's starting to dislike her, which might well happen if she tried to force compliance. After all, children don't love their day-care workers, and they don't have an internal motivation to please them. Besides, most parents would probably object if the day-care staff tried to discipline their child.

Let's imagine the best case day-care scenario. Say it's just Caroline and a babysitter with a couple of other children. And the sitter does follow through, and Caroline learns that "come" from Mrs. Adams means the same thing as "come" from Mommy or Daddy. But then Mrs. Adams gets very sick and has to stop taking care of children. And Caroline goes to Mrs. Bailey. Maybe Caroline misses Mrs. Adams, or maybe Mrs. Bailey doesn't expect Caroline to obey, or maybe Caroline doesn't remember what it means the first time Mrs. Bailey says it, and Mrs. Bailey doesn't really expect her to obey, so Caroline gets the idea that "come" doesn't mean the same thing from Mrs. Bailey as it did from Mrs. Adams.

It wouldn't be long before she would ignore my command to "come." After all, if she ignores Mrs. Bailey, she'll establish that habit. Then, if I were to try to enforce obedience, and Mrs. Bailey didn't, I would be confusing Caroline. No wonder most parents, if they are aware, decide to spare themselves the uncertainties and the potential guilt and to rationalize: "Well, kids aren't capable of obedience until they are school age anyhow."

Suppose I weren't like that, though, and really wanted an obedient child. If the different expectations went on for a period of time, with issues other than "come," Caroline might get pretty unhappy at not being allowed to do at home the fun things she was allowed to do at day care. And she might start liking day care better than home because that's where she gets her own way. Her infant heart would have grown a few roots of self-will, a few roots that perhaps could have been avoided or at least delayed, roots that would later grow into thorn bushes of barriers between her and the Lord. And meanwhile, instead of being a tranquil, pleasant place for all of us, our home would have become a stage for a battle of wills between a child and her parents — as far too many American homes already are.

Neither the Lord nor we would be pleased by the results of the day-care experience. We would have a disobedient child, a confused child, one whom we wouldn't be comfortable taking to visit Grandma for fear her behavior might embarrass us, and my husband and I might argue over her behavior. Caroline would ultimately suffer the most. By failing to learn obedience to human parents, she will be handicapped in learning obedience to her heavenly Father.

"Increased Parent-Child Conflict"

This hypothetical story is not as far-fetched as it might sound. Not too long ago the *International Journal of Psychology* carried an article by researchers from the University of Maryland and the World Bank who looked at the child-rearing beliefs of mothers and day-care providers.[2] They found strong differences between mothers and caregivers. Compared with mothers, caregivers "more highly valued the development of individualistic skills . . . and deemphasized the importance of obedience." Caregivers were more likely in discipline to use "strategies that accommodated the desires of the child." In other words, the day-care workers in this study take the path of least resistance, give the child what he wants, do not demand obedience. What reason is there to think any other day-care worker would be different?

And what effect does this have on the child? Social scientists are extremely cautious about drawing conclusions about the effects of anything. The conclusion that "exposure of the child to outside influences may result in increased parent-child conflict" is a monument of understatement.[3]

Creating parent-child conflict is one risk of day care to the raising of a godly child. Another risk is engendering confusion: the child will not learn that words mean something but rather will become distracted with too much context. If "come" does not mean the same thing from everyone who says it, the child will suspect that other words mean different things depending on who says them. And then the child will spend precious time trying to interpret what is said and deciding whether it must be taken seriously rather than simply obeying. Totally apart from this confusion is the emotional upheaval of a change in babysitters or caretakers, which in itself interferes with development.

Now the usual response from someone who wants to justify day care is to say that "kids learn to adapt." Mothers who use day care like to hear the reassurance that their children will not suffer any permanent effects. I used to tell myself that every time I saw my boys suffering the ill effects of being raised by someone other than their parents. And, indeed, they were: they were adapting to a different set of more lax rules and growing in their dissatisfaction with home, which they found stern by comparison. I too was "adapting" to tolerating their discomfort and the domestic discord that conflicting authority was producing.

Actually, there is medical evidence that even when children seem to be "adapting" on the outside, they are not really even physiologically adapting. In a study at Stanford University a mother monkey was removed from her baby for half an hour. The baby monkey screamed the whole time. A blood sample showed that the baby's adrenalin level was very high. Then the experimenters put in a different female, and the baby seemed to calm down, but another blood sample showed the baby's adrenalin to be just as high. A human study has also suggested the same result: adrenalin in the blood is significantly higher while children are in day care than it is when they are at home.[4]

Adrenalin is the body's "fight or flight" hormone. When we're frightened, adrenalin gives us that extra boost of energy to fight off an attacker. High levels of adrenalin interfere with learning, however, which may provide a biological clue to why children under prolonged stress often develop learning difficulties.

Let's return to my hypothetical story of Caroline trying to figure out the rules of obedience among Mrs. Adams, Mrs. Bailey, and Mommy. The same process of sorting out goes on all the time with children. Children whose whole lives consist in figuring out whom they have to obey and whom they don't, who's going to give me consequences, and the like, live under a continuous stress, don't they? Teachers may say, "They're not learning." But they're learning, all right: they're learning how to interpret commands, how to test limits, how to make some sense of different people who behave inconsistently. What they eventually learn, if this state of affairs continues, is how to be independent in the worst sense of the term because eventually they figure out how they can ignore just about everybody. With all that going on, no wonder they can't figure out reading and arithmetic! The next step, of course, is to figure out how to change rules and, beyond that, how to ignore them without consequence.

Isn't it really kinder to the child for Mom and Dad to give a clearly understood set of rules that apply in all places and all times with clear and certain knowledge that Mom and Dad will administer consequences for violation of those rules, no matter where the violation occurs. Such a clarity gives the child security; he knows what is expected of him. It takes the burden of figuring out the world off his immature shoulders and frees him to relax, to learn, to grow, to develop freely. Failing to give children such order in their universe is really to invite their exasperation, and we have been taught to avoid that: "And, ye fathers, provoke not your children to wrath: but bring them up in the nurture and admonition of the Lord" (Ephesians 6:4).

Godly training of a young child is almost impossible if a consistent caregiver is not present all the time. Is that a radical statement to make?

I make it. If you have agreed with me that God gave us our children so that we can lead them to Him, then you understand how serious this statement is.

Rules to Grow By

Ken Wilson has distilled from the teaching on love in 1 Corinthians 13:4–5 several guidelines for obedience in young children. There are a few things, he advises, that parents should teach and insist upon. I think it's a very reasonable list, but it's a list that no day-care center on the face of the earth is going to follow.

- Children should do whatever they are told to do, when they are told to do it, without fuss or resistance.

- Temper tantrums should not be allowed.

- Children should obey parents and other trustworthy adults.

- Children should not interrupt adult conversation.

- Children should relate to the physical environment of adults with respect.

- Children should not yell around adults who are engaged in adult activities.

- Children shouldn't answer the phone until they've learned how to do so competently.

- Children should learn to greet adults.

- Children should respect the dignity of others.

Most people feel their house can't hold more than one or two children because too much noise and confusion arise. An ordinary house can contain quite a few children who live by Ken Wilson's rules and still leave the adults feeling like human beings. Rearing children according to these rules goes a long, long way toward making children pleasant to be around. Parenthood is a calling of service, and children who follow these rules are far more pleasant to love and serve than children who are rude and obnoxious and willful. These rules make life easier with young children: they make life with older children actually enjoyable! Disobedient children are like weeds underfoot; obedient children are like olive shoots in a parched land.

Obedience and Self-Esteem

In light of life's ultimate purpose, rules of obedience are indispensable. An adolescent who hasn't learned obedience as a child has a poor foundation for self-esteem. If he has never really known what was expected, how can he know if he has met expectations? If he doesn't really know if he is accepted by his parents, how can he really accept himself? If he has grown up deciding for himself which rules he is going to obey, when he chooses to obey them, he is approaching adulthood with a faulty conscience: "If I get caught and the punishment is serious, it must be wrong. Otherwise, if I want to do it and can get away with it, it's okay." I can't think of a greater handicap for successful living in society. Or, far more gravely, few attitudes are greater obstacles to achieving conversion and submission of a life to the Lord.

By passing our children to somebody else, we are removing from ourselves the challenge that God meant for us to have. Yes, it requires patience not to fly off the handle at a kid who has just annoyed us. But the answer is not to get the kid out of the way; the correct response is to change ourselves so that we learn to control our tempers. By not raising our children ourselves, we deprive ourselves of growth opportunities that God meant for us to have.

Social parenting subjects children to care by different people, who all have different expectations, standards, and enforcements. These things are enormously important to children because the expectations of significant adults are the framework of reality for a child. What we learn in the first few years of life never leaves us, however we overlay it with other things. Victims of a stroke, as they return to normalcy, begin first to learn to feed themselves, just as children do. The first names they will remember will be those of their mother and sister and brother. They will remember something that happened when they were two years old; the anxieties of childhood will be experienced all over again.

The childhood experiences of a stroke victim may have been consciously forgotten, but they were all still there in the mind. All of our children's experiences remain in their minds, reposing in the memory, and are a part of them. And that goes for absences too. What children lack in their early years may be covered over as they grow up, but the hole remains, an unpredictable spot of vulnerability in years to come.

If social parenting deprives children of the primary experience of mother-love, and of learning obedience, and of accepting parental authority, Christian parents must give serious second thoughts to using or approving day care.

TIME, GUILT, AND STRONG FAMILIES

(The Pleasures of Family Versus the "Pleasures" of Career)

Cooking and cleaning can wait
*   til tomorrow*
For babies grow up, we've learned
*   to our sorrow;*
So quiet down cobwebs, and dust go
*   to sleep,*
I'm rocking my baby and
*   babies don't keep.*

Author Unknown

T his little verse conjures up a pleasant image: a young mother in a rocking chair, cuddling a cooing baby, each taking delight in the other. What could be more natural? Nothing. But the point of the verse is that such a tender moment does not come easily, what with all of a mother's chores and errands. It may be natural to love and enjoy our children, but like many other natural impulses, that one is often overwhelmed by our technological, materialistic society. Love and enjoyment take time to grow, and time is the first casualty of technology and materialism.

The mother cuddling the child in the rocking chair is no ordinary phenomenon; she is a heroine, standing athwart the powerful influences of her age, making a political and moral statement by taking time to enjoy her child. She is saying no to social parenting, saying yes to mothering. She is daring to enjoy her baby.

There is a lost phenomenon: enjoying our children. Americans seem to be afraid of children (we fear their temper tantrums, so we lose control of them early), may worship them (we turn our lives inside out to satisfy their whims, thus spoiling them and rendering them intolerable), may feel guilty about them, may be proud of them, may use them as pawns in power plays against ex-spouses, and may experience a whole range of other emotions—but delight, simple enjoyment in their presence, is more the exception than the rule.

And yet simple enjoyment in the presence of each other is what family life is theoretically all about. Olive trees, after all, are enjoyable for many reasons in a parched land, and Psalm 128 compares children to olive shoots. Home should not be the place where exciting things happen; it should be the place where we are enjoyed by other people just because we're who we are. I remember a popular song a few years back by a female vocalist, which had a theme that went something like this: "I want someone to love me just for being me," she sang, "just for being me, just for who I am. . . ." In a world that teaches us to value other people for their utility, for what they can do for us, that sentiment is poignant.

Even Benjamin Spock, the guru whose permissiveness toward children I regard as one cause of the disenchantment my parents' generation experienced with family life, is now trying to turn back the clock: "We should be trying to bring back the pleasures of family life. Parents should make family life fun, enjoyable, and expect kids to be part of it, instead of this barbaric lack of ceremony and formality," he urged an audience in Boston. That's fine for him to say, but unless children are trained in cooperation with their parents and each other, it's not realistic to expect them to be a willing "part" of the family. When kids are whining and disobedient malcontents, it is most difficult for family life to be fun, no matter what the programmatic agenda is. When children have never been taught to set a table or clear it without complaint, when they won't eat what is served without griping (unless it happens to be their favorite food), family meals understandably will lack formality.

Dr. Spock also picked up on a common theme today: "We should bring up our children to believe that their families are more important than work."[1] Such ordinary common sense is far from the reality of postindustrial, postfeminist America. Postfeminist America is full of women who have been taught that unless they fulfill themselves they are wasting their lives; these women are living to work. Postfeminist America is also full of women who are raising children without male support. And these women are working to live — to live, often, on a shoestring budget in a climate of tension and acute fatigue.

Seventeen Hours a Week to Make Life Worth Living?

According to pollster Louis Harris, in 1973 the average American had twenty-six hours per week of "leisure" time.[2] By 1989 that figure had fallen to seventeen hours. Seventeen hours a week is two hours and a few minutes per day. Two hours a day is not very much to spend in unstructured activities. If you're a mom with young children or teenagers, two hours a day of unplanned activities might seem like sheer heaven — if you can steal one hour a week to soak in the tub, you think it's been a week of high luxury living. And if Dad has any time left over on the weekend, once he does his prayer time and finishes mowing the lawn (which involves first fixing the lawn mower) and reviewing those reports from the office, chances are he needs a nap — and is not thrilled with the idea of going strawberry picking with the boys. Well, perhaps Lou Harris would not agree: chances are, he would consider prayer time to be strictly a leisure activity. So subtract another seven hours from the leisure time available to a Christian in 1989.

That leaves a grand total of ten hours a week of "leisure" in which to build the personalities of our children. It's bad enough if this is Dad's schedule. And that makes Mom all the more indispensable as the architect of the human personality. But what if Mom is working too, and has just about the same schedule? Worse yet, what if Mom is the only parent?

Shortage of time may be the biggest enemy of family life today, with simple fatigue running a very close second.

Behavioral scientists call this "role strain," and research repeatedly finds "a high degree of vulnerability among working parents both at home and at work." Boston University recently concluded a study of the job-family strain among 711 employees of a large northeastern corporation. Its findings were typical: the mother usually is worse off because of her more than eighty hours a week of work, home chores, and child care, and the strain shows up as "decreased physical and emotional well-being as measured by depression, life satisfaction, health and energy levels, and days absent." And men are not exempt: the husbands of working wives experience more strain than the husbands of unemployed wives: "Employed wives may not be as available to provide emotional support for husbands," surmise Bradley Googins and Dianne Burden.[3]

Now let's take that scholarly language and translate it. I give you Sophie, a mother who is under pressure to perform on the job. She feels obligated to stay as late as she can, and to bring work home. The detour to the day-care center consumes a precious thirty minutes; she's anxious to get home; the traffic is bad. She hurries the kids up and doesn't stop to talk with the woman who has spent the last eight hours with them, so she doesn't have any idea what kind of day her children have had. Wishing she didn't have to fix dinner, she cuts corners on it and cuts conversation short at the table so that she can pack the kids off to bed as soon as possible. Then, finally, she can spread out her work on the dining room table and stay up past midnight poring over it. Oh yes, there is perhaps a goodnight peck on the cheek for her husband. She may wonder why he sighs as he heads off to bed without her, but she quickly returns her attention to where she feels it more properly belongs.

As this sort of evening becomes the norm rather than the exception, Sophie soon begins to suffer the ill effects of no time to herself. And her children soon begin to suffer the ill effects of an inaccessible mom. And her husband begins to suffer the ill effects of the lack of attentive wifely companionship. No doubt the husband is pleased with the income since it means he can stop trying so hard to get a promotion. And the kids are probably quite enchanted with what the income can buy for them and are so occupied by their electronic games and new toys that they don't realize what's going on with the emotional climate. A moment of truth comes sooner or later, however. A study conducted at Memphis State University followed the marriages and careers of twenty-seven hundred women for fifteen years. The conclusion by Julie Heath, the assistant professor in charge of the study? "Among those women with jobs, the more they work, the more likely they are to divorce."[4]

Now let's translate Sophie's life into the experience of a child, seen through the eyes of a teacher:

> I stood before my class of third graders, eager to get on with the activities of the day. As we opened our spelling books I noticed great drops of tears falling from Mike's eyes. His efforts to hold back the flood were in vain. Giving the class an assignment, I stepped outside the classroom with Mike. His silent tears had progressed to full-fledged sobs. He managed, however, to tell me that a very special aunt who had been living with his family had just moved away. He obviously felt he had been deserted and deceived by someone who had claimed to love him. Mike needed a large dose of emotional first aid that morning. But I, his teacher, was not the one to give it to him. Before he left for school his mother should have seen a flashing red signal of distress. *She* should have applied the emotional bandages that would have freed Mike to perform that day, healthy and strong, to his fullest capacity.[5]

With evenings like that described above as the pattern of life, how can Mom be expected to notice the signs of Mike's distress? Perhaps she let him eat his cereal while she was getting dressed herself. Or maybe she was long gone when he got up and let himself out of the house in time to catch the bus. Or maybe he did bring up the subject, weepily, and Mom said impatiently, "Oh, for heaven's sake, Mike, we talked about that last weekend. People have their own lives to live." Or maybe she was off on a business trip, and Dad had all he could handle with fixing breakfast, planning dinner, and keeping everyone on schedule, so Mike knew better than to try to talk to Dad.

Beware Bad Advice

You get the picture of how everyone suffers when we lack the time to pay attention to each other. Most people who are living without enough time couldn't put it into words, but they know something is wrong. In fact, people living this frenzied life often are seeking a way out of it. But their impulses in the right direction are headed off. Consider this item from a Question-and-Answer section of *Parents* magazine.

> Q: I am 25 and have a nine-month-old baby. My goal in life always was to get married, have children, and take care of my family and home. The problem is that I also have a full-time job. I know that we could make it solely on my husband's income. But he and my mother both believe I should keep my job so that we can live better. I find myself feeling inadequate as a wife and mother because of this situation.

What a wonderful woman! She has all the right instincts! Congratulations to her! But she is young, intimidated by her mother, and not yet confident enough of her motherhood to defend her instincts against her husband's materialism. If I were writing the advice column, I would commend her for her instincts, encourage her to stand firm, and give her some ammunition she could use to convince her husband that what she wanted was best for his child. Instead, what kind of answer does Cynthia Deutsch, Ph.D., give on behalf of *Parents* magazine?

> A: . . . the problem of accommodating career and family . . . must be worked out by each family in terms of its own best interests and needs. You do not indicate whether you enjoy your work . . . and whether, therefore, your current conflict is basically the problem of the guilt you feel about not following your long-term expectation of being home with your baby. If that is the case, then the solution is to be found in working through your guilt feelings. On the other hand, if you are not particularly committed to your work . . . improvement in your situation will rest with coming to terms with your family about your multiple roles. . . . To do this, you might begin by avoiding the view of your situation as an "either/or" choice. It may be that part-time work could give you a stable schedule and some income. . . .[6]

"Whether your current conflict is basically the problem of the guilt you feel about not following your long-term expectation!" As if the guilt she is feeling is because she is a spoiled child not getting her own way! In this entire answer, there is no mention, not even a hint of a mention, of what is good for the baby! It never occurs to Cynthia Deutsch, Ph.D., that the mother's guilt might be real and justified and quite healthy in its recognition of her baby's unmet needs.

This kind of nonsense is not what the young mother needs! She needs encouragement to make motherhood her priority. Her good instincts are in that direction. They should be reinforced. One would think that a magazine that labels itself for parents would be sensitive to what is best for children. But, alas, it is simply in the business of making money, and to do that, it has to say what the world seems to want to hear. After all, if the magazine encouraged too many mothers to be full-time mothers, they might not have the discretionary income to continue to subscribe. Besides, chances are that most of the editors of the magazine cut their teeth on feminism and really believe that a woman without a paying job is incomplete.

So, on the cycle goes, career women giving advice to mothers, encouraging careers. *Parents* doesn't invite successful mothers to write advice columns. They've been too busy raising children to have established reputations as "experts." (This aspiring "expert" is writing these words at half past one on a night when I know my husband will be able to fix breakfast in the morning—and writing this book is even slower than reading it because such mornings are rare!)

As a mother of teenagers and toddlers, with an infant on the way, I read about others with seventeen hours of leisure a week and wish I could get a couple of them for myself. Every mother I know has the same kind of schedule, but the happy ones accept it as part of their state in life as mothers just as they accept the fact that fathers, no matter how willing, simply cannot comfort a crying baby the way a mother can. It's not the father's fault; it's just the way life is. Being up at two in the morning doesn't prevent us from being "fulfilled" women, because our attitude is adjusted to it.

Having the right attitude toward family life is something that our age has to learn. I don't know whether our grandparents absorbed it by living it or whether they were taught it explicitly. But I'm sure that the children who are growing up as we enter the twenty-first century will, at some point, have to sit down and think about what makes family life successful—if they have the time to think about it.

Characteristics of Strong Families

Common sense may tell us a great deal about what makes families strong, but it takes a behavioral scientist to get it published.

Nick Stinnett, professor of human development and family life at the University of Alabama in Tuscaloosa, and John DeFrain, a professor in the Department of Human Development and the Family at the University of Nebraska-Lincoln, investigated what makes families strong. By running ads in almost fifty newspapers in twenty-five states, they identified thousands of families that considered themselves strong. Questionnaires were sent to all those families, and here's what emerged among the over three thousand families that responded.

Strong families have six traits in common:

- *Commitment.* The parents simply make the decision to invest time and energy in family relationships. Sexual fidelity is a fundamental first premise, and the decision to spend time with kids rather than office work is almost an absolute.

- *Time Together.* The strong families spend lots of time together — working, eating, attending church, and so on. They don't allow their members to drift into their separate private universes of work, amusement, and separate social life. And they don't fall for "quality time" cop-outs, either.

- *Appreciation.* Strong families learn to look at what they (and their individual members) have accomplished — not what they have failed at. When Dad gets home, he notices out loud that a delicious dinner was prepared — and fails to mention that the car didn't get washed for the fifth day in a row since he asked for it to be.

- *Communication.* Lots of conversations, casual ones, are the prerequisite to good serious ones. Without lots of talk, sharing the trivial and the ridiculous and the inconsequential, a person isn't ready or able to share the tremendous when it comes along.

- *Spiritual Wellness.* They have a religious affiliation, and they live up to its expectations. And they practice in everyday life the values they believe in: honesty, helpfulness, and care for others.

- *Crisis Handling.* They realize that this life is not perfect, that it is full of suffering and difficulty, and they don't expect it to be otherwise. So a crisis does not bowl them over.

Now, I suppose there is nothing intrinsically, inherently, mutually incompatible between these traits of strong families and social parenting. Theoretically, I suppose, it should be possible that a child can spend three-fourths of his waking hours in the care of strangers and still understand his parents' commitment to him, feel appreciated, have good communication, be able to cope with crises, and all the rest. Theoretically, maybe . . . but in practice?

The Distracted Mother

Lack of time is probably the greatest enemy of family life today. And the first victim is the mother. I once read a Romantic poet's description of the mother as the "angel of the hearth." I've also read some pretty brutal vilifications of mothers from the pens of some contemporary feminists. But I believe that the mother is the soul of the family. All members of the family look to her to set the spiritual, emotional tone for the family.

Remember Sophie? For a career-oriented mother like her, even if she spends several hours a day in the physical company of her family, she might still be emotionally elsewhere. On weekends she may take the kids to the pool, but instead of splashing around with them, she'll sit by the side and think her own thoughts. The kids may enjoy being at the pool, but it doesn't bring them closer to Mom. A career-oriented mother lives in a state of constant distraction.

First, of course, are the long hours on the job and the demanding problems that may absorb her there—problems which cannot be put aside until tomorrow because they're most likely people problems, idea problems, or management problems—infinitely variable, infinitely adjustable, infinitely "improvable." The job will have firm deadlines: she has to solve this problem by this date because she has a meeting scheduled to tell somebody else what solution she proposes. Deadlines focus attention on things. At the job is a boss, who can get by with being a whole lot less tactful than her husband, since he signs her paycheck. Paychecks are powerful focusers of a person's attention.

Families have few deadlines: perhaps school registration has to be done by a certain date and vaccination by a certain date before then, but there are no deadlines by which Maximilian has to learn to tell the truth or Josephine to iron clothes. Those things happen as they happen, which is fine, since it makes the process of learning relatively free of pressure and hence more enjoyable. But the very freedom from pressure also means these things can slide . . . and they will if Mom doesn't preoccupy herself with their accomplishment. I found myself repeating a thousand times: wipe up the floor after your shower before you leave the bathroom, and I got annoyed every time. But once I thought about it enough that I captured the boy in question on his way out of the bathroom, presented him with a special sponge I had remembered to buy, showed him how to do it, and then disciplined *myself* to go upstairs to check the bathroom floor after every shower he took for two weeks; then he began to wipe up the bathroom floor. When I did, what in management would be called "prioritizing" the problem, it was on the way to being solved.

But doing that meant I was thinking about that boy's shower-taking habits when I was doing other things. When I was working five or seven days a week (depending on travel schedules) and my aunt was raising my children, I didn't prioritize home problems. I simply couldn't keep track of them. Oh, occasionally, if something got really noticeable, I would deal with it. Pearse had five ear infections one semester, for example, so I made the effort to find an ear specialist, agree to have the adenoids removed and tubes put in, made the hospital arrangements, took time off from work, and got the operation done. It all took a great effort, however, and the only time I could be home long enough after the operation for his recuperation was over the Christmas holidays, so it put a damper on the entire family's Christmas.

At least his ear infections stopped. But contrast that story with this. After I quit working, I began noticing that Michael complained about stomachaches frequently. So I took him to the doctor about it and spent the next six months finding out what was going on. As we drove to the pediatrician for the very first appointment, I said, "Mike, I want to find out why you have all these stomachaches all of a sudden." Mike looked at me. "Mom," he said, "I've complained about stomachaches for three years." And when I thought about it some more, I realized he had. During those years, I hadn't had any problem with intermittent deafness. I had just dismissed or ignored or rationalized what Michael said to me . . . because I didn't feel I could take on another problem.

But that's not my worst horror story.

There was an even bigger picture I overlooked because of the distractions of working. When I took Mike for his four-year-old checkup, the pediatrician recommended some specialized testing to investigate developmental lags. I called the recommended clinic, but they didn't have weekend hours, and I was working full time. I feared I couldn't take time off work to take Michael for several treatments a week forever, so instead I consulted family, and heard what I wanted to hear: "Don't worry; he's just a late bloomer. The doctor doesn't know what he's talking about." So I convinced myself they were right.

Four years later, when the kindergarten teacher had real reservations about promoting my seven-year-old to first grade, I couldn't escape the reality, and I got the testing done. It turned out that Mike had serious perceptual-motor dysfunction (learning disabilities). He also by now had emotional difficulties because for seven years he had believed he was stupid because he couldn't do what his big brother did. Some remediation was possible — but it took two years to find a treatment that really worked, and by then the therapy was much less effective than it would have been if he had received it at, say, age four or five.

Was I a worse mother than other moms with demanding careers? I don't know, but I don't think so. There are so many hours in a day and so many responsibilities and problems a woman can handle. A woman has to make choices about what problem she is going to handle when. Do I still feel bad about how I "handled" this one? Yes.

Cynthia Deutsch, Ph.D., might say that I feel guilt about not meeting my expectations as a mother — but she'd be wrong. I had real guilt because I had done real wrong in ignoring a real problem. I thank the Lord for the grace of real repentance and the mercy of real forgiveness. But Michael has a burden for life . . . and now I pray that some day he will have the grace to forgive me.

These are relatively tangible medical examples. The same thing happens with emotions. With so little "prime time" to devote to relationships, they either never develop or they deteriorate. The communication skills don't grow; the appreciation does not get expressed; the religious commitment doesn't develop; and so on. Net result: the family doesn't become strong.

How the Family Weakens

Many two-career families in effect live as married singles — separate interests, separate schedules, separate preoccupations, sometimes even separate budgets. Occasionally they share sex, but they're not living as lovers pursuing life's greatest adventure and carrying out God's calling. And if there are children, conversations between husband and working wife can sound more like management meetings than like conversations with a beloved.

It's often cited as a positive aspect of working mothers that men now spend more time doing child-rearing duties. Indeed, they do, but guess what? Spending more time with the children does not bring more harmony to the family. One study found that among men whose wives were employed, the greater their involvement with their children, the greater their unhappiness with their marriage.[7] That's not surprising to me — men are just as involved in their careers and just as tired at the end of the day as women. And they are a whole lot less skilled with children and never expected they'd be doing child care, so it's predictable that they would be tense and disenchanted with having to do household chores in addition to their own jobs. Similarly, I might add, a woman who did expect to be doing child care, but finds herself expected to support the family financially as well, becomes disenchanted with having to do her husband's job in addition to her own.

The nature of work itself today also weighs in against the skills that nurture family life. The woman with a career (as opposed to what is called the casual worker) is more likely to be tempted to continue the career after the children arrive because the financial and other rewards are greater. But it is the very involvement with career that makes her life more stressful. A nine-to-five job on an assembly line can be left behind pretty easily; an eight-to-six job at a desk demands homework and preoccupation all the waking hours. Friendships sometimes fade away for career mothers because precious time is channeled into "old girl networks" which are more mutual-exploitation societies than friendship networks. Time does not permit new friendships because friendships require time to spend together, and time is the missing ingredient.

A successful career today is most likely to be in management, and management is all about getting people to do what you want them to. Another word for this is manipulation. Women are naturally better than men at getting people to do what they want, which is why women excel at management and are greatly desired by employers. Alas, manipulative skills may be an asset on the job, but what happens when you start treating your husband and children the same way? If you're a good manager, they won't even realize what's happening . . . until one day your husband asks himself why he's not getting emotional satisfaction out of his marriage anymore . . . until one day your children, no longer three and four but now thirteen and fourteen ask themselves why they should do what you want anymore. Over the years, in order to survive the juggling act, you have been so organized that there was a niche for everything . . . except time-consuming relationship building. You may have had power over your kids when they were small, but when they develop minds of their own, you may find you do not have authority.

Do I paint a grim picture? Yes. But ask yourself: isn't it all common sense? Perhaps it hasn't been said very clearly for the past twenty years. But the American Medical Association knew all this in 1960. Listen to this passage from an article in the January 1960 *Today's Health* magazine:

> If working means that you have no time to listen to accounts of the day's triumphs and problems, to give counsel where needed, to hold the baby in your arms or read a bedtime story, then — unless the family couldn't possibly do without your income — it's not worth the sacrifice. If the household is to have a sense of unity, parents must place before everything else the needs of the family as a whole.[8]

Doctors then were not afraid to call a spade a spade and to describe the adverse effects on children of working mothers. Imagine if new mothers today were given articles to read that included this kind of information:

> . . . certain kinds of behavior problems seem to occur frequently among children whose mothers work. The child seems to be on edge,

fidgety, easily irritated, or brought to tears. He may have difficulty conforming in a group situation. His attention span may be short and he has difficulty sticking to his school work so that his achievement is below his capacity. He may bite his nails or nibble excessively between meals. He may be reluctant to go to sleep at night and seek repeated excuses for getting up once he is in bed.[9]

The tragedy is that now, the child described is almost so typical as not to be noticed anymore. When researchers today do a big study and find that children who were put into day care before age one are not as well liked by their third-grade teachers and classmates, it is headline news (see chapter 13). A generation ago, it was what conventional wisdom expected. And conventional wisdom was correct.

Contrast it with today's "wisdom" of T. Berry Brazelton, sometimes called America's favorite pediatrician: "If a mother is to be free emotionally to realize her potential in the workplace, she must be confident that her baby is in good hands."[10] Brazelton accepts that mothers want to find fulfillment in the workplace; all his writing is built on the premise that they will make career or job a higher priority than baby; and within those parameters, he devotes himself to suggesting ways to minimize harm to baby.

To his credit, Brazelton observes one sad effect of a mother's decision to put career first: "I have found that, in a prenatal interview, when both parents anticipate the pressures of having to return to work 'too early' [in their own words, 'before three months'], they guard against talking about their future baby as a person . . . perhaps they already are defending themselves against too intense an attachment to the new son or daughter in anticipation of the pain of being separated prematurely from their child."[11]

This is a painfully frank admission that if a mother anticipates separation, she never falls in love with the baby in the first place. If she doesn't fall in love with the baby, "maternal leave policies" don't make much difference.

Does It Pay (Anybody Other Than the IRS)?

Yesterday's conventional wisdom (and we can assume that the AMA in 1960 was voicing conventional wisdom) also had this sound advice:

If the increase in the family income is the motivating factor . . . the
salary should be considerably more than the cost of domestic help or
day-care service, transportation, extra clothing, etc. It ought to be
enough to really make a difference in the family's standard of living.
Otherwise, it isn't worth coming home tired, harassed with responsibilities, and often irritable with the ones who mean much more to you
than all those persons you've had to be polite to throughout the day.[12]

It does sound radical, doesn't it, in an age of self-gratification, to
dare to say that children will suffer when mother is distracted and husband will suffer when wife is irritable? Somehow, modern secular society has come to regard children as the distraction from the real work of
fulfilling one's ambitions and husband's emotional needs as so much
more baggage for an ambitious woman to have to tolerate. But even in
1960 today's attitude was rearing its head: ". . . the young college graduate who finds homemaking confining may have some moments of guilt
and anguish, but will probably be a better mother if she is permitted to
fulfill her compelling need for the ego satisfactions of achievement in
the competitive fields of business, science, or the arts."[13]

Let's go back to that sensible question: How much do you have to
earn before it's enough to pay to keep life livable? Most women can't
earn that much.

What do I mean by keeping life livable? I mean keeping the work
load on a mother to levels that one woman can handle and still be able
to enjoy life. Most working mothers take on employment in addition to
cleaning, cooking, laundry, managing family accounts, grocery shopping, gift purchasing, holiday entertaining, family correspondence, and
all the usual errands, not to mention all the child-related jobs such as
health care, wardrobe preparation, homework supervision, teacher visita-
tion, child-and-friend social direction — and these are only some of the
indispensable tasks! And most mothers do it without any additional help.
Back in 1960 when the AMA was warning women about going too
readily into careers, it was assuming that hired domestic help was available to women who took on careers outside the home. I don't know if
that was true in 1960, but I know it is not true today, not in most places
and not for most working mothers or even most career mothers.

What will happen is that, in order to focus attention on the most
important, you simply eliminate certain other items. You ignore the

child's complaints about school, for instance. Or you decide "I'll clean the house only before we have company, period. If that bothers my husband, he can clean it himself." Or "I'm sorry that my neighbor/aunt/mother is sick, but I can't fix her a meal/call her up/go visit her because I haven't got the time."

Of course a woman cares if her mother is sick, but if she knows that making one more time-consuming phone call (in which Mom will lament for the thousandth time that her only daughter never has the time to come visit her) will put her over the emotional edge of the balancing act of supervising homework while fixing dinner, while doing laundry, while planning a report for the office, all in the remaining two hours before bedtime—who can question her decision to omit that one more stress-inducing item?

One woman can only do so much. It is folly or worse to pretend otherwise.

The bitter sorrow of the mad dash of women into the paid work force of this day and age is that very few women earn enough to make it worthwhile . . . although if you ask them, most would say they are working for money. Money indeed! But at what cost? The cost of order in their lives? The cost of their happiness, their satisfaction with life, their marriages? The cost of their children's enjoyment of childhood? The cost of peace and quiet at home and good extended family relationships seems to be the least most working mothers pay.

Let's talk just money for a while.

Karl Zinsmeister of the American Enterprise Institute points out that "working wives are earning 28 percent of total family income at present. That's just about the size of the average family's total federal tax bill. In other words, the wife is working just to pay off Uncle Sam, no more." In 1948, he points out, in contrast, a married couple family with the median income, two children, and average deductions paid less than one-third of 1 percent of their income in federal income taxes.[14]

Never mind the bitter, bitter unfairness of a tax system that builds a welfare state on the backs of parents trying to raise children. Just consider the insult to motherhood in that fact: mothers are encouraged, propagandized, forced, whatever, into the work force, at great cost to themselves, their marriages, their children, the happiness of their whole lives—and why? *So the government can collect more money.* This is outrageous! Wars have been waged over lesser insults. But in the name of "liberation" women today have fallen over themselves to be victimized by this system.

For now, let's look at microeconomics: a family budget. Then and now. The November 1957 *Better Homes and Gardens* magazine had an article titled "Can Working Wives Make it Pay?"[15] "An increasing number of salaried wives frankly prefer working to staying at home," stated the article. The article is an intriguing glimpse down memory lane. "Today, the average wife has her last child when she is 26," is one sentence that brings a chuckle in today's era of "last-chance babies" for career women. And back then, the child care deduction phased out at a joint income of $5,100. It is interesting to observe that even then, though tax policy punished wives, the trend toward working wives was going strong.

Assuming a wife earned $3,600 a year, the article estimated extra expenses due to wife's working at $1,040 a year. Taxes; child care; more expensive, quicker-cooking cuts of meat; bakery goods rather than homemade; lunches instead of leftovers; more clothes; more laundry and cleaning bills; beauty shop; meals out; cleaning help at home; taxi rides on late mornings — these were the expenses assumed to be $1,040 a year. The amount contributed after these expenses to the family income was projected at different levels of husband's income:

Husband Earns	Family Net Pay from Wife's Work
$4,000	$1,880
5,000	1,860
7,000	1,820
15,000	1,460

The pattern continued at all levels of wife's and husband's income. As the article put it, "The increase in the number of working wives from upper-income families provides dramatic evidence that the dollar sign isn't always the greatest charm of the paid job." Interestingly, as wife's income went to $6,000 a year or beyond, it was assumed her expenses went up only modestly: to $1,500 a year. If we can assume that the typical woman's earning was close to $3,600 a year, it seems that it was expected that her cost of working would be at least one-third of that.

Does that pattern hold true for thirty years later? *Woman's Day* recently ran a similar article.[16] This article took a more particularized approach, analyzing two families with different circumstances and needs. Greg Napier made $34,000 and Jan earned $20,000. However, they figured the monthly cost of Jan's working at $1,210 (child care, household help, extra children's and Jan's clothes and extra Jan's dry cleaning, transportation, eating out, and convenience foods). Not even included in that calculation is the $119 a month social security tax she paid (even though paying it would probably not increase her own social security benefits in later years). Her expenses of working, therefore, were $1,329 — and her take-home pay was $1,100. This meant that her expenses of working, unlike the 1957 woman's, were not merely one-third of her pay — but more like 120 percent! Annually, it was costing her $15,948 per year to bring in a $20,000 income. And the extra $20,000 no doubt cost the family another 20 percent on its total federal tax bill.

How many families with working mothers are in the same circumstances, if they stopped to analyze it carefully?

I don't doubt that there are many families with actual financial circumstances like the Napiers. But probably most do not sit down and figure out costs ruthlessly. Jan Napier quit her job when she realized that the whole family was, in essence, subsidizing it. Had she been more dedicated to her job, when confronting the same figures, she might have cut out the domestic help instead (she was one of the lucky ones) — $200 a month can seem pretty attractive, especially before the cost in fatigue and stress is experienced. But that would not have changed the total family budget much, and it would have changed life for the worse.

Since quitting work, Jan seldom buys convenience foods, and the family has cut entertainment costs "to the bone." They haven't been able to save much, either, and Jan does miss the social life of working. "The good part," she concludes, "is that I'm enjoying my children at a special time in their lives. And I have the security of knowing that I'm doing what's best for them."

In the other case study, the Robertson family, the mother earned about $1,300 a month, with expenses of $521. The expenses are little less than a third of her monthly pay. But since her husband, still in the early stages of starting his own business, was bringing in only about $1,200 a month, without Fran's income the family could not meet their $1,758 total bills. So Fran, despite the fact that a baby is on the way and her five-year-old is in day care, is continuing to work. "It's really difficult when your child begs you to stay with him and you have to leave for work," she says.

What strikes me as discordant is that *Woman's Day* operates from the premise that it is perfectly appropriate that economics should control a mother's decision to work. As the article concludes: "Though both feel some regrets over what's missing in their lives, each has the satisfaction of knowing she's doing what is best for her family at this time. And who can argue with that?" What's best financially for the family may not be best in other ways. But nobody dares say that aloud.

The Big Lie of the late twentieth century is that day care doesn't matter much: of course it should be available and abundant, but it's fine to accept or reject it; it doesn't matter much either way.

PART 2

THE MENACE OF SOCIAL PARENTING

5

WHAT IS DAY CARE, ANYWAY?
(On Definitions and Nannies)

*". . . and the Devil hath power to assume
a pleasing shape."*
Shakespeare, Hamlet, II.2

Hamlet was right. Satan does have the power to assume a pleasing shape. Social parenting is not in accord with God's plan for the raising of children. Social parenting also has the power to assume a pleasing shape.

Day care is one of those pleasing shapes. To this point, I have talked about day care as if it were interchangeable with social parenting. Actually, social parenting is far broader than day care.

Social parenting includes, for instance, the attitude that it is the schools' responsibility to provide children with medical care and psychological intervention. It also includes the notion that it is society's obligation to remove the children of the poor from parental influence. Look around and you'll see lots of examples of the idea that "we" can raise kids better than parents can, "we" usually being professionally credentialed members of the so-called "helping professions."

If you're reading this book, I'm not afraid that you're one of those whom social workers feel are unfit to raise their own children (unless perhaps you believe in spanking and do it in public). Chances are, if you're reading this book, you're a conscientious parent who wants to be better and wants to protect your family from the many arrows that modern society aims at it. You probably don't use day care for your own children. But you probably do have friends, sisters, and other relatives whose children are in day care. It's likely that your children will date and possibly marry children who spent some of their childhood in day care. So you want to know a little more about day care. Hopefully, also, your concern for your friends and relatives will motivate you to warn them about the risks they are inviting for their children.

Also, you're probably aware that "child care" is one of the hot items on the agenda of the United States Congress and most state legislatures. Pressure is strong on government to "do something" to "solve the nation's child-care crisis." Since you want to be an informed citizen, you need to understand what they're talking about to be able to read between the lines of what the politicians say. Day care is the opening wedge of the campaign for social parenting, after all, so we need to be informed about it.

What Is Day Care?

Some people use the term *day care* pretty loosely — to mean anything other than Mom with kids. Actually, there is quite a gradation of non-mother care arrangements, some of which are old and some new, and not all of which have the same merits (or demerits).

Let's begin with the general term: is it child care or is it day care? It used to be that arrangements made to provide for children so that mothers could work was day care. But for historical reasons, day care has a slightly pejorative tone; it sounds like a parking place. So the fashionable term today is child care.

Also, the term day care assumes that mothers will need their children cared for so that they can work during the day. Yet many of the service-sector jobs that are most populated by women (e.g., nursing, cleaning, waitressing) are done at night or around the clock. Indeed, some 16 percent of the nation's work force works hours other than seven in the morning to six at night. It's not surprising that one hot new trend in the child-care industry is "night care." Another hot trend is for "sick child care."

The Washington, D.C., area has more working women than any other area of the country. So it is not surprising that Washington should pioneer this trend. In the District of Columbia, some fifty-eight family day-care providers are licensed for evening and some night care. And the city's Office of Early Childhood Development is trying to figure out how to encourage more.

It also happens that there is now a trend to provide day care for the elderly, more and more of whom share a similar fate with the young in our hectic society: namely, being parked somewhere for the day. Everyone says it's good for them, of course, but what is certain is that senior day care enables grown daughters to pursue paid employment while paying somebody else to give care and nurture to their flesh and blood. I have long maintained that the two groups at the opposite ends of the age spectrum could be good for each other and that their problems could be solved in tandem, but such proposals do not get very far with the senior citizen lobby or the child-care lobby: the former wants subsidized idleness for its members while the latter wants to create a whole new job category of semiskilled workers.

But back to our terminology.

"Play School"

Most people are familiar with "play school," sometimes called "nursery school." Many children begin experiencing it at about age four. Often what is called a "mother's day out" program is actually a "nursery school." Its essential features are these: it is a part-day, part-week program. Not every day is "mother's day out," but mothers do need some time without little laplanders constantly present: how are you going to get your hair cut with a two-year-old on your lap, for instance? How are you going to do Christmas shopping with a three-year-old in the cart?

The main goal of play school, despite the name "school," is not academic at all but social: parents think it is good for their kids to get to know other kids and begin to learn how to act around groups of other children.

"Preschool"

"Preschool," or "early childhood education," on the other hand, has as its main goal what educators call "cognitive development," the intellectual and cultural enrichment of children. In the late 1960s it became quite the fad among social planners who saw it as a solution to welfare dependency and/or crime among the lower classes. Head Start is one ongoing result of this fashion, and as the impoverished become more embedded in unemployment and social chaos, the tasks of Head Start keep expanding: not only is it early learning (since now children are eligible from birth until full-time school attendance), but now it is used as a vehicle for parenthood education; for physical, emotional, and mental screening of children; and for similar social work functions. Currently, Head Start programs nationwide include about 450 thousand children, but liberals are constantly reminding Congress that only one in five of the children who "need" it are receiving it. Interesting, isn't it, that these liberals do very little to remind Congress that these same children need mothers and do absolutely nothing to try to ensure that these children have fathers? Perhaps that is because the liberals have concluded that somebody other than mothers and fathers is best for needy children.

Preschool begins as young as age three and is envisioned as a full-day experience whether mother has a job or is at home. Since the main purpose is enrichment, a preschool environment will offer lots of activities designed to teach the alphabet, numbers, and the like. Following the theory that "if it's good for the underprivileged, think how good it will be for the privileged," preschool is now quite the thing among upwardly mobile people too. The children of professionals go to preschool, period. Some exclusive private schools boast of teaching their students to read even before kindergarten.

I should mention that there is considerable difference of opinion about whether early cognitive training is good or bad. Tons of paper have been generated on the question of whether children do gain any advantage, and if so, whether the advantage persists as they get older. As I read the evidence, here's how I interpret it: children in Head Start do gain an early advantage over similar children not in Head Start. They can read sooner, for instance, and count. But by fourth or fifth grade their school performance is not much different.

An important reason for their doing better earlier is not only that they went to preschool but that they got a lot of attention from their mothers for going. A fuss gets made over them because they can read, for instance. They're called upon to show off to visitors, you know, things like that, which makes a child feel very proud and very motivated. But this attention does not persist, and as it fades, so does their motivation and their achievement.

Home Start

There was a program called Home Start, which sent preschool teachers into homes with educational toys to lend, to teach mothers how to play with and interact with their children. This program had better results than Head Start. That didn't surprise me. I was encouraged that the mother's influence was shown to be stronger than a preschool's. It's what I would have expected.

I have problems with the very idea of Home Start, however. It is really a sobering example of social parenting at work! The premise of the program is that poor mothers do not know how to raise their children and that therefore the government needs to send people into the home to teach them. Now, it may be that after several generations of dependency on government and victimization by an incompetent public school system, many poor mothers indeed do not know how to raise a child. Since many of the mothers in the target area of Home Start are little more than children themselves, it is easy to see that their own immaturity and ignorance and hopelessness ill equip them to form the personality and character of another.

I agree that a problem does exist. But is the federal government the one to solve it? This is where I turn pale. I have always believed that the level of government closest to a problem ought to be the one to address it. And, better yet, before government gets involved at all, let the natural structures of human society — the family, the community, the church — work on the problem. If anybody is going to intervene in the home, let it be the church rather than government.

There are competent mothers even among the underprivileged and in the underclass of our society. These are the women who should be running such programs. They know the problems; they may have been in the same circumstances themselves; they speak the language; they can relate to the young mothers who need instruction. Ah, but they do not have the college degrees in early childhood education. So they are not deemed worthy of administering government money. Instead, college-educated, middle-class people are given the job, probably mostly young graduates who couldn't get other jobs, who don't know and don't like the people they're supposed to be "helping." And the result is a lot of money spent for very little result.

The church, by contrast, could do a very effective job of training young mothers. People concerned about the eternal spiritual welfare of the mothers and their babies would feel an intensity of concern that paid bureaucrats can't even begin to feign. The local church, with local people, would actually know the mothers well enough to be able to help them. If the woman who visited once every two weeks to bring a new toy and see how things were going also saw the mother hanging around by the laundromat talking to the drug dealers, she could speak to the real problems. The real task is the character development of the young mother; by comparison, handing out toys and instruction in "interacting effectively with your toddler" is very, very superficial. This mother needs her life changed, and a government program is not going to do it. The church—through its practical ministry and its preaching of Christ and Him crucified—can change lives; government programs cannot.

Am I saying it's okay for the church to do social parenting, but not for government? Well, of course, not as its primary job. The primary job of the church is to preach the gospel. But the church ought to inspire and lead laypeople in helping each other with the problems of their lives, and those jobs ought to be carried out under spiritual direction. This is what the church used to do. In Roman society, for instance, it was considered normal for people to put unwanted babies out on the hillsides for the wolves to eat. Christian families didn't do that; in fact, Christians went around taking in babies that had been left on hillsides. Christians treated their children differently from the way the world around them did; they taught others to raise their children differently. In the latter days of the twentieth century we don't expose our children to four-legged, howling wolves, but we abandon them nonetheless, in more prolonged and more brutal ways to the neglectful wolves of day care. The church needs to be a witness again, to stand against these trends.

I agree that people today need help in learning how to be parents. But our help is in the name of the Lord, not in the name of Washington, D.C.

Meanwhile, back to terminology.

Everything Else

Of course, parents and the public come to view both nursery school and early childhood education as interchangeable with each other and with day care. And if the purpose of the program is simply to allow the mother to work on a regular basis, it probably functions like day care.

To add to the verbal confusion, there are different types of hired care. Family child care does not mean what it sounds like: it does not mean families taking care of their own children, although family day-care providers often do care for their own along with their paid charges. Family day care is the most popular form of day care: it's taking a child to another mother, who earns money by taking in children. Family day care can be licensed or unlicensed; only a very small percentage is licensed, which is why nobody really knows how much of it there is, although estimates are regularly attempted.

The kind of day care that is most often licensed is "institutional" or "center-based" care: the day-care center, the nursery school, and so forth. Back in 1960, when times were different, 64 percent of licensed day care was used by children whose parents were definitely upper middle class; that was when nursery school was a privilege of the well-to-do. Today, most people prefer the informal family day care for their children.

The final category of day care is what statisticians call "in-home" care. This means that someone, a nanny or a maid, comes to the child's own home to care for the child while the mother works.

What's Most Popular?

In the spring of 1989, the Philip Morris Companies commissioned a survey by Louis Harris and Associates on the topic of child care. Re-

garding "organized day care or group care facility," 25 percent of respondents said it was "very effective." And 32 percent considered a
"nursery school or preschool facility" to be very effective. Another 45
percent rated "a kindergarten or grade school" as "very effective" —
which suggests to me that large numbers of Americans do indeed regard
early education as day care. No wonder some states are considering
lowering the kindergarten attendance age to four.

"Very effective" at what, you wonder. And well you might. The
actual question read to the people surveyed was this: "How effective are
different types of care when it comes to giving parents peace of mind
and the confidence needed to do their jobs?" That's so revealing! These
parents were saying that their child-care arrangements are good for
them, the parents! Practically the entire national debate on child care is
being argued on the same basis: namely, what is best for parents. And
that is the basis on which mothers are flocking to the work force — day
care is good for them because it allows them to work. Nobody asks what
its effect may be on children.

Most people, given the choice, would prefer a relative to a stranger.
The survey asked: "If you had to choose, other than a day-care center,
which one of the following would you choose for your child. . . ?" And
75 percent chose "having a relative care for the child." Perhaps we can
conclude that most people consider relatives to be quality people because — guess what the respondents to this poll cited as *the most important* factors in choosing a child-care facility! "Staff quality" and "staff
reliability."

The Historic Nanny

I was surprised that "at home by a non-relative" received such low
marks on the Philip Morris survey. I would have thought more people
would at the very least imagine that having a nanny would give parents
peace of mind and confidence needed to do their jobs. But of course a
nanny is only as good as her quality and reliability, and therein may lie
a clue.

When we hear the word *nanny* most of us probably get mental visions of Mary Poppins: full time, fully attentive to the children, full of

love for them, great fun for them, absolutely supportive of the parents and parents' goals for the children, wonderful problem solver, emotionally very sensitive . . . shall I continue? Or have I said enough to make it clear that such a person belongs in a novel?

Still, I think the image of Mary Poppins hovers about in the minds of our age as the vague image of what day-care workers ought to be, or are, somehow like. It's worth spending a few minutes talking about the historic nanny to dispel some misunderstandings.

The nineteenth-century English nanny figures in many a novel, but that reflects reality: during the Golden Era of the Nanny (1850–1939), there were from one to two hundred thousand nurses and nannies in service at different times.[1] It was not just an upper-class privilege. A growing population and a growing national wealth created conditions for an abundant servant class, and a stable and class-conscious society made domestic service an honorable and enjoyable profession. The system had its pros and cons, of course.

The most obvious advantage was that the nanny was able to devote her entire mind and emotion to the children. Unlike a mother, she did not have to also worry about other aspects of the family or household. She incurred the expenses she deemed necessary, and she didn't have to worry about pinching pennies. Unlike a mother, she did not have to worry about doing laundry or buying groceries or running errands. She was there to give her full attention to the children. What mother does not wish she were so fortunate as to have such singleness of mind? No wonder so many nineteenth- and early twentieth-century British memoirs dwell so fondly on the nanny. Any child could have tons of fun with the full attention of another adult, especially one whose purpose in life was to make the experience enjoyable.

Jonathan Gathorne-Hardy, who seems to be a contemporary expert on the nanny as an institution, says that nannies were "able to devote themselves to their children to a degree perhaps never possible before or since" and that their "love produced not just a Churchill but thousands upon thousands of secure and happy human beings."[2] Nannyism was rather informal in its early days, but by the heyday of the institution, there were regular training programs for nannies, and the experiences of people raised by nannies bear remarkable similarities. Two moral imperatives seemed universal, and, indeed, the combination of them is almost synonymous with the Victorian age in which nannies thrived: 1) authority must be respected and obeyed; and 2) it is wrong to indulge the self; the best actions are those directed toward the good of others. "This morality made, in some respects, for a great certainty in private life. It also . . . underpinned (and underpins) whole areas of English behavior: the incorruptibility of the Civil Service, the respect for the rule of law, the acceptance of an obedience to the State. It underpinned the British Empire."[3]

Not a bad list of accomplishments for nannies. Sad, though, that those accomplishments cannot be attributed to the mothers of the era.

The downside to nannyism is also obvious: the situation could be great *if* the chemistry between the nanny and the parents and the children was right *and* as long as it lasted. Mothers were inclined to jealousy, and nannies were prone to getting married (or, if the jealousy got bad enough, to getting fired). In such cases, the emotional trauma to the child could be considerable, depending on how great the attachment was. Gathorne-Hardy cites instances of people whose nannies departed when they were aged two or three, and who, fifty-five years later, still feel the grief—and still remember their nannies' faces. Many loving children became insecure adults because of the disappearance of a beloved nanny. Members of the English upper class during the nanny era were known for their reluctance to commit themselves emotionally, for a certain shyness or coldness toward other people. That is exactly the result that could be expected from breaking the crucial emotional bond with the beloved mother figure. For nannies were indeed emotional surrogate mothers.

Sometimes a nanny could be advantageous: there's the story of one boy who, at age five, heard arguing and shouting outside his parents' door. The nanny promptly marched him back to the nursery and, in response to his question, told him his parents were going to be taking part in a play. From his child's perceptions, he wondered why he was never taken to the play and why the rehearsals continued for many years.[4] During World War II, children evacuated from the Blitz suffered considerable anxiety, but less so upper-class children than the rest: "They simply moved out of the cities with their Nannies and were as emotionally secure as though they had remained at home."[5]

Love also worked both ways. Gathorne-Hardy interviewed not only the former charges of nannies, but also former nannies. Out of eighteen in-depth interviews, one-quarter of the nannies had suffered nervous collapse on leaving a child they loved.[6] Since the nanny had responsibility for discipline and training of the child, winning and keeping the child's love was not only a matter of emotion, but a matter of job facilitation: a child who loves is more willing to obey the person whom he loves.

The phenomenon of divided loyalty was not unique to England, although England raised nannyhood to the level of a profession. Wealthy New Yorkers might vie with each other to obtain English nannies, as did the royalty of all Europe, and the South had its own version of the nanny. Scarlett O'Hara, remember, was mightily concerned with Mammy's astute observations of her behavior toward Ashley Wilkes — as far as the movie viewer of *Gone With the Wind* knows, Mrs. O'Hara was oblivious to the infatuation.

The Nanny Today

Few upper-middle and upper-class mothers had demanding, independent careers outside the home during the era 1850–1939 in England, and few indeed in the earlier part of those ninety years. Yet they had other women to rear their children, primarily, but not only in England. The children of contemporary women with demanding full-time careers would probably be better off in many cases if their mothers could somehow reproduce the institution of the nanny.

But history cannot be repeated. According to the U.S. Department of Labor, only 6 percent of working mothers nowadays hire somebody who is not a relative to come to their homes to care for children under five. Among women with college degrees, 14 percent do, and that figure is growing. Professional women want professional women like themselves to take care of their children. But they're not to be found.

Norland Nanny College in England is still operating, and its graduates are hired at high salaries even before their training is completed. Some are successful in the United States, but most American women are not comfortable with an English nanny's expectation that she will take over the whole household.

If all the rhetoric about the massive and irreversible trend of American mothers into the work force were true, American nanny colleges ought to be an idea whose time is about to come. But the nanny is not catching on in a big way. Nannies, after all, are more surrogate mothers than social parents. They are under the authority of the real parents; they do not fit the trends.

There is an American Council of Nanny Schools, and some community colleges are developing nanny programs. But in 1986 George Washington University and Georgetown University, both in Washington, D.C., capital of the working mother, abandoned plans to create a nanny training program: "We only got calls from people looking for nannies — not from anyone who wanted to take the course," lamented a university official.[7] Perhaps there is a demand for trained nannies, but the demand is not perceived by prospective college students.

American women are likely to regard themselves as superior to the job of raising other women's children. One Washington, D.C., woman reported that as a result of an advertisement she ran in the *Uptown Citizen,* a community newspaper of posh northwest D.C., she received ten calls from Latin Americans, seven from Africans, seven from West Indians, and one each from a Lebanese, a Chinese, a Sri Lankan, a Pole, an Indian, and a Dane. Only two U.S. citizens were interested in the job of being a nanny. Tragically, in our postfeminist society, any task having to do with the care of children has been downgraded socially and robbed of all prestige. In former generations it was not only socially acceptable but socially approved for women to help other women with their domestic needs — but not today.

Several cottage industries in Washington thrive on providing child care for working women from the farm belt states: ads run in farm communities for young women to come to Washington, D.C., to do live-in child care yield some responses. One service, Potomac Nannies, Ltd., for a "minimal" fee of $225, will even go to a family's home for a personal training session, to teach parents how to correctly and safely hire an "in-home child care provider"!

Numerous programs have been launched to provide *au pair* arrangements for young European women to come for a period of time to live in an American household in return for child-care services. The process was once illegal because an *au pair* had to have a student visa and be registered at a college, but the demand for live-in child care was so strong that the State Department created a special *au pair* exemption for certain organized programs.

But the institution of the nanny does not lend itself to contemporary America. Young professionals want child-development expertise, and they also want housework done — but a young woman with two years of early childhood education in college considers the latter beneath her dignity. If a mother insists on having the housework done, she is likely to settle for a foreigner. Then the risk is the nanny will be so concerned not to make herself needless housework that she will not allow the child freedom to explore or be creative, which mothers believe limits their intellectual development.

The emotional situation is far from ideal. A class structure exists in America, but we pretend it doesn't, and so the professional woman feels guilty about hiring the unskilled woman, who may resent the fact that she has to take care of someone else's children while neglecting her own. Without experience, young professionals are not comfortable giving orders or checking up on them or enforcing them. The inevitable love triangle of mommy/child/nanny and the inevitable guilt/dependency/jealousy are exacerbated by language barriers and social discomfort. Few grandparents understand the pressure on a young professional mother; in one family, the wife's mother was convinced the only reason the foreign-born nanny was there was to be a concubine to her daughter's husband!

When nanny reports bad behavior, who does the mother believe and back up — her child or the nanny? The cultural differences subject discipline, already difficult enough, to tremendous inconsistencies. What Mom doesn't even notice might provoke howls from the babysitter, and vice versa. Very quickly, children figure out that they're smarter than the nanny and devise infinite ways of circumventing her rules. When that happens often enough, she quits — and the kids have won that round, leaving their work-weary mother to start all over again.

The fact that a child is in his own home may reduce some commuting difficulties and perhaps some anxiety connected with being around large numbers of other children. But being in a familiar environment does not make up for the absence of the mother. Psychiatrist Peter Barglow of Michael Reese Hospital in Chicago has studied the emotional development of children raised by nannies. Upper-middle-class one-year-olds cared for at home by nannies have weaker attachments to their own mothers than do babies whose mothers are home full time, he has found.

There also are problems with cognitive development in children with foreign-born nannies. Melissa Stevens does admissions testing for Washington-area private schools. Over the past nine years, she has seen a downward trend in the schoolreadiness of nanny-reared children. "Parents assume that if they're educated, that if the child's environment is enriched, that if they provide extra enrichment activities for the child, the child's intelligence will be at the level you might expect. But if the person the child is around all day is undereducated and doesn't speak the child's language, you see the effect. . . . Nobody has the intense interest in a child that the parents do. If they want their child to develop along lines parallel to their own level of accomplishment, rather than by someone else's, they need to find a way to share the benefits of their own education and of themselves," she urges.[8] In other words, it isn't enough to require the nanny to take Susie and Billy to Gymboree and the zoo and the National Gallery of Art and the public library read-aloud story hour; Susie and Billy need more interaction with Mommy and Daddy.

And then there's the problem of references. All Washington watched with horror the unfolding of a headline story in 1989. "Live-in Nanny Charged in Death of District Official's Infant Girl" was the first headline.[9] "Ex-Nanny Had Record Before Girl's Slaying" was the headline a few days later.[10]

Assistant D.C. Corporation Counsel Amy Schmidt had hired a woman she knew as Linda Pearl Amos, after carefully checking her references and talking to women she believed were former employers. But Linda's real name was Linda Johnson, and her work record was fabricated. Two weeks on the job of looking after Jamie Banker, only child of Amy Schmidt and her husband Dr. Lawrence Banker, the nanny slammed the baby four times against a wall because she would not stop crying. The infant, nine months old, died of blunt force to the head. Before her arraignment, the nanny tested positive for cocaine.

It turned out that Linda Johnson had a two-page list of arrests and convictions in Louisiana, and had served eight years of a twenty-year sentence for forgery and attempted distribution of heroin. What about those references? The woman Amy talked to was the next-door neighbor of the people Linda actually worked for. All Linda ever did was periodically clean the neighbor's house.

Most nanny stories do not end this tragically. Amy Schmidt and Lawrence Banker have a great grief to carry with them for the rest of their lives, and perhaps Amy wondered privately whether keeping the prestigious job of assistant corporation counsel was worth the price of her daughter's life. Publicly, the day-care advocates used the wave of news stories to issue new demands for federal regulation of child-care providers.

For various reasons, the nanny is an idea whose time is not now. It is no excuse to say, "Well, I'm not with him myself, but we have a devoted nanny, so he's not suffering." Maybe today you do, but what about next year?

Does Washington Lead the Nation?

Still, I can't help but wonder if a nanny arrangement might be better for many children than the patchwork quilt of day care that tends so often to be the case.

Here's an example from my hometown. As I mentioned earlier, Washington, perhaps because of the presence of the federal government, has America's highest percentage of two-income households. And the trends are following suit around the country. Does Washington lead the nation, I wonder, in the way its working parents treat their children?

> Frank and Frankie Davis drop off their 4-year-old son Franklin at a day-care center about 9 A.M. But the Davises, busy Capitol Hill professionals, often work past the dinner hour and well beyond 9 P.M. . . .
> On the days when the Davises have to work late, they expect to pick up their son from his daytime baby sitter and drop him off at the evening center. Those days, Franklin is away from home about 12 hours. "He'll probably enjoy the interaction with the kids," his mother said. ". . . I don't think he'll be terribly tired, going from one day care to the next."[11]

I weep for Franklin; if his parents could get him a good nanny, his future, even at this late date, would be brighter. At least, one surrogate adult at a time is better than the vast numbers he has. The day-care center probably has two shifts — that's two people, the night-care center would be another person. And that's not accounting for the new faces he has to accommodate when the usual ones take vacations or change jobs. Poor Franklin! It probably took him two weeks to learn all their names. And you can be sure they all have different accents, different tolerances for disobedience and naughtiness and temper tantrums, and different ways of expressing disapproval (if they even bother to disapprove).

I suppose it would be uncharitable to ask why the Davises bothered to have Franklin at all. Maybe they really believe he will enjoy being shunted from pillar to post. He's only four years old, has probably never known a different life, and can't articulate his objections very well. If both Frank and Frankie Davis are such high-powered congressional staffers that they are needed until nine in the evening, their joint income could be into six figures. Some day Franklin, whether he knows it now or not, will probably wish the family had traded part of that income for one more parent.

And if Frank and Frankie are not congressional staffers, but instead work for the gaggle of pressure groups and cause-related groups that cluster around "The Hill," one has to wonder what cause means so much to them. Perhaps it is saving whales or protecting the environment or trying to advance the civil rights of the poor . . . or it could be even less idealistic, like getting tax breaks for a particular industry or reducing international trade regulations. Who knows? One of them may be involved with day-care legislation.

Maybe Frank and Frankie truly believe Franklin is not worse off for spending twelve hours a day in different day-care arrangements. But I'll wager that Frankie was back at work within months of Franklin's birth, which might explain her lack of empathy for him now. I'd also be willing to wager that if Frank and Frankie were more emotionally involved with Franklin, they would have reservations about what they're doing. But with the kinds of jobs they have, the impending vote and preparation for it consumes all available mental, emotional, and physical energy.

There isn't time to be lonely . . . or to realize that somebody else might be.

6

IDEAS AND CONSEQUENCES
(Beware the Visionaries and the Politicians)

The LORD knoweth the thoughts of man,
that they are vanity.

Psalm 94:11

The lifestyle of Frank and Frankie Davis, who work from nine in the morning until nine at night regardless of the needs of their young children, is typical for influential Capitol Hill staffers.

After all, if you're out to change the world, you have to be prepared to devote your whole mind and heart and soul to doing it. Washington, D.C., is full of people who burn with a hard gem-like flame, squandering the hours of their lives and the years of their youth in a passionate effort to remake democracy or redesign human nature or save the country from one or another real or imagined threat.

The campaign for the federal government to lead the way in social parenting is one such effort. Rarely has there been so carefully orchestrated or expertly managed a campaign. I can say that with some authority since I worked on Capitol Hill for sixteen years and had a hand in designing a few campaigns myself.

You're reading this book because you're wondering whether motherhood can survive. But I have to take a little digression here. Whether motherhood can survive or not depends in part on how a few current political wars end. I know, you're interested in motherhood and not in politics. But bear with me as I try to explain the political battle. It matters to you; it matters to your children; it matters to motherhood. Besides, you're a citizen, and you vote. You may as well take a few minutes to think about the forces at work to shape your thinking and your voting.

The first thing you need to know to exercise your right to vote is whether you're being manipulated.

I said the child-care campaign was well organized. How do you know a well-organized campaign when you see one? For one thing, you can tell by the results: public discourse undergoes a sudden change. One day, nobody has given a thought to federal day care; a couple of months later, everybody's talking about it. One day, congressmen are wary of something, don't know much about it, and haven't got anything to say on the subject. A little while later, they have a ready answer to a question on the matter and have form letters in their computers to crank out responses to constituents who ask them their position. When you see this happen, you know something is making it happen.

Another way you can recognize an orchestrated effort is by watching the media. Articles suddenly start popping up in the *New York Times* and the *Washington Post*; then the news magazines pick up the same theme. Next thing you know, network news is doing features on the topic. Then you hear documentaries on National Public Radio. If the pressure groups are really well organized, one or two nights before a crucial vote is to take place in Congress, you will see a public television special devoted to the issue. That was the case with the Act for Better Child Care, a federal social parenting proposal.

A Closer Look at the Propaganda Campaign

Throughout the propaganda campaign, the same themes will be repeated over and over. Sometimes even the same phrases will be used over and over by different people. Rarely will more than three different aspects of a problem be talked about. Remember, the goal of propaganda is to tell people what to think, and if you inject too many ideas into the discussion, people might get confused and start thinking for themselves. Then they might not reach the conclusions the organizers desire.

When the Act for Better Child Care was launched, a massive press conference was held by the Alliance for Better Child Care, the group that had essentially written the legislation and assembled the supportive coalition. Dozens of people participated. That meant they read printed statements of support for the legislation. Listen to a few of these statements. See if you can identify the major propaganda themes of the campaign.

The American Academy of Pediatrics: "The United States is one of the only industrialized countries in the world that does not uniformly regulate and promote quality child care," Dr. George Sterne, chairman of the AAP's Committee on Early Childhood, says.

Senator Tom Harkin (D-Iowa): "The United States is the only developed country with no federal child-care regulations or policy."

Service Employees International Union, AFL-CIO: "There are almost 15 million children in the U.S. under the age of fifteen with working mothers, yet affordable, accessible child care remains a significant problem, especially for lower-income families."

United Church of Christ, Office for Church in Society: "A dollar spent through the Act for Better Child Care is probably the best dollar which could be spent fighting poverty. . . . Ending a two-tier system of child care in which the poor have to accept inferior care because it is all they can afford would be a major step toward social justice. . . . The ABC bill is an immediate tool for fighting poverty and will help the United States catch up with other nations."

One theme is guilt based on national pride—we're the only industrialized nation with no federal child-care policy. How can we tolerate such lack of social conscience? Actually, the only industrialized nation with which we have serious competition problems does not follow a policy of social parenting. But more about that in chapter 7. The phrase, however, popped up in practically every media treatment of the issue for the next year.

Another theme is guilt over poverty. The Service Employees Union speaks mildly about helping lower-income families, but the United Church of Christ is explicit in ringing all the bells intended to produce guilt in affluent hearers: "two-tier system," "step toward social justice."

After all, what good American can tolerate a two-tier system for any-body? And doesn't everybody favor steps toward social justice?

But did you notice the similarity of themes? Doesn't it figure that when all the press secretaries were preparing those statements, they had in front of them "fact sheets" thoughtfully provided by the Alliance for Better Child Care? This is the way propaganda works: a couple of major ideas are restated and rephrased just enough to sound as if they were the creation of many different minds united in one single idea.

We are all the victims of propaganda because when we hear the same thoughts coming from many different sources, we are supposed to feel left out if we don't agree with them. There is seemingly spontane-ous pressure to agree with the new ideas, especially if the mouthpieces for them are such unimpeachable sources as the American Academy of Pediatrics. After all, if the nation's most expert doctor in matters of early childhood says the country needs a national day-care policy, who am I, just a housewife, to disagree?

Coalition: The Illusion of Consensus

Getting Congress to do something requires two levels of action: one for the real world, outside the Capitol Beltway, and one for inside the Belt-way. The propaganda campaign, which of course begins in Washington, percolates through the entire nation, creating an awareness throughout the land of a "national crisis." But inside the Beltway, the name of the game is coalition building.

Take a look at just a few of the organizations listed as "members" of the Alliance for Better Child Care:

- Amalgamated Clothing and Textile Workers Union

- American Academy of Child and Adolescent Psychiatry

- American Federation of Teachers, AFL-CIO

- American Home Economics Association

- American Public Welfare Association

- Association of Junior Leagues, Inc.

- Bakery, Confectionery, and Tobacco Workers International Union
- Business and Professional Women/USA
- Camp Fire, Inc.
- Catholic Charities
- Child Welfare League of America
- Children's Defense Fund
- Christian Children's Fund, Inc.

All these already, and I'm only at the third letter of the alphabet! The list goes on for four pages. A few more highlights:

- Church Women United
- Communication Workers of America, AFL-CIO
- Food Research Action Center
- General Board of Church and Society of the United Methodist Church
- Lutheran Office for Government Affairs
- Mexican American Women's National Association
- National Association for the Education of Young Children
- National Association of Community Action Agencies
- National Association of Social Workers
- National Child Abuse Coalition
- National Congress of Parents and Teachers
- National Council of Jewish Women
- National Council of La Raza
- National Council of Negro Women
- National Education Association
- National Organization for Women
- National Urban League, Inc.

- Society for Research in Child Development
- Union of American Hebrew Congregations
- United Auto Workers
- United Way of America
- YMCA of the USA

What is the point of assembling this long laundry list of endorsers?

Inside the Beltway, the goal is to create the impression that the campaign is broadly based, very popular, and so universal that no congressman in his right mind would disagree with it. Take a moment to think about the pressure groups represented in this list.

- Churches: many different denominations
- Minorities: Black, Hispanic, and Jewish organizations
- The Rich: Junior League
- The Poor: Urban League, Children's Defense Fund
- Yuppies: Business and Professional Women and others
- Feminists: National Organization for Women and others
- Working Class: labor unions
- The "Helping Professions": social workers, Child Welfare League, and others
- The Experts: Society for Research in Child Development, National Association for the Education of Young Children, American Home Economics Association, and others
- Organized charity: United Way and others
- Educators: NEA and AFT
- Mental Health Professions: pediatricians, psychiatrists, and others

Impressive, isn't it? A hometown newspaper editor reading the list will scratch his head and think, Wow, this must be everybody who matters in Washington. He won't stop to notice that all the groups have one thing in common: they're all what would be called political liberals. He doesn't know that many of those organizations are on the list not because their membership agree, but just because the Washington staff happen to agree. The hometown editor won't wonder who's left out. For sure, the Alliance for Better Child Care won't tell him who's left out. After all, the list includes even a consumer group, the Food Research Action Center, though what its interest in child care can be is beyond me. For such is the purpose of assembling massive coalitions: to create the impression that the issue is one whose time has come, that a mighty, unstoppable river of public demand is sweeping through the land, that the people are speaking.

I'll tell you who's left off the list: some of the largest Christian denominations in the country, that's who. Any organization with a conservative approach to public policy. And all the employers in the country. Not a single organization on that list represents the productive, private economy. Every single one, religious lobbies excepted, is a service organization or a consumer of public money. The people who produce the nation's wealth are not in this coalition. You and I are not represented in this coalition.

Inside the Beltway, then, this coalition creates a sense of awe and guarantees a good kickoff to the propaganda campaign. What purpose does it serve outside the Beltway, where you live?

Outside the Beltway

If people are convinced there is a national problem, they want their congressional representative to do something about it. Sooner or later, enough people will write to their representative and senators and give them a nudge. And if the representative gets enough mail on one side of the issue, unless he's exceptionally highly principled to the contrary, that's going to influence his vote. I should, of course, say, "his or her" vote. But you know that's what I mean, so let's just simplify the syntax.

The organizations that participate in the press conference and put out support statements publicize their support among their own members. The members read the newsletters and say, "Hmmm, this sounds important." Some organizations will urge their members to write to Congress to speed up the pace of action. Labor unions, for instance, are particularly adept at prodding their members into action. When a congressman comes home for a visit and gives a speech locally, a few labor union members may be in the audience for the sole purpose of asking him questions on the issues the union leader has talked about recently.

These efforts are calculated to make an impression on the congressman: "Gee, my constituents are really concerned about this. I'd better get on top of it and give them what they want."

There's a phrase my political mentor taught me: In politics, perception is 90 percent of reality. All the efforts of the coalition, the press releases, the propaganda blitz, are calculated to produce one thing: a perception of real need, of real demand, of real public concern.

Is the public concern real? Ask yourself. How concerned are *you* about a national child-care crisis? How concerned were you before you began hearing about it on TV and reading about it in women's magazines? If an issue requires the orchestration of massive, well-funded efforts by many different organizations to "make" it "real," is it genuine? You answer that question.

Understand, however, that in Washington it doesn't matter that the whole issue has been artificially created. So have most of the crises Congress is daily called upon to deal with. Congress lives from crisis to crisis. It was not always so. Even twenty years ago Congress was a far different place from what it is now, with pressure groups and lobbyists controlling its agenda. But that's the way the game is played now.

And the fact of the matter is that right now the nation has been led to believe it has a child-care crisis and that the answer is for the federal government to put its authority and its money behind bigger and better schemes of social parenting.

What Do They Want?

Since the pressure is coming from an identifiable group of organizations, let's ask the question: Why? Why are they doing it? What do they hope to get out of it?

Forgive me if I sound cynical. I admit right now that I don't believe the heart-rending rhetoric about concern for children. Very, very few people who operate in Washington have such a concern in their hearts.

But many have mastered the rhetoric of concern because they know it makes good propaganda and provides instant credibility for what they say.

It's easy to see what the yuppies want: help with their child-care expenses. By getting the federal government to commit to help, they'll have more disposable income.

It's easy to see what the labor unions want: help with child-care expenses for their members, many of whom truly do live hand to mouth.

It's easy to see what the feminists want: help with completing the feminist liberation of women. It's no secret that women's liberation cannot be complete as long as mothers are responsible for raising their children. Social parenting is the answer—and always has been. Feminists will support anything that diminishes the importance of motherhood.

What do the professional poverty lobbyists see in the bill? More federal programs, some of which will employ their constituents, some of which may provide services to the children of their constituents.

What's in it for medical and mental health professionals? Business. After all, federal day-care programs will have to have psychologists and psychiatrists and doctors on staff. Lest I be too cynical, I should add that these are the people who see the harm inflicted on children by casual day-care arrangements. Many of them no doubt are sincerely concerned and want to prevent children's suffering. But they have been told that "women are going to work and that's that," so it wouldn't occur to them to urge something radical like a return to motherhood. The professionalization of day care seems like as good a means as any of reducing the chances of harm to children in day care.

What's in it for organized charity? Things to do, government help with programs that will justify the charity's continued existence. At the local level many United Way people sincerely do want to help the children of working mothers and think that running or financing a day-care center is a good way to do it. With the federal government in the act, more money will be available, and they just might capture some of it, especially if their Washington representative is in on the ground floor of writing and lobbying for the bill.

And now we come to the educators. Why would teachers want federal aid to social parenting? Teachers already suffer more than anybody else the consequences of the social parenting epidemic already raging. Children growing up emotionally unstable, without learning obedience or having consistent discipline, are the problems in the classroom, the ones who might beat up other kids or assault the teacher. They're the ones most likely to be behavior problems in the classroom. Poll after poll of teachers' concerns show fear of physical violence from students at the top of the list.

So why are teachers lobbying for more social parenting, for more of what causes their biggest problems? For educators, the issues are survival and employment. That's right. Take a look at population projections. The American population is declining. We have been at below-replacement levels of fertility for a decade now. More and more working women means fewer and fewer babies. Fewer babies today means fewer students tomorrow. And that means fewer jobs for teachers. Remember, a teacher is expected to handle many students in a classroom. It's common for teachers' unions to complain if there are more than twenty-five students in a class. But in day care — ! Ah, there, a teacher could be expected to handle no more than three or four toddlers. The proportions are considerably more favorable to high employment. Never mind that some mothers regularly handle more toddlers than that at a time. Once child care becomes a "profession," strict ratios will be imposed.

There's more to it too. And here the "experts" come in. The experts are the dangerous ones, the visionaries.

Beware the Visionaries

One of the chief visionaries of social parenting is Edward Zigler, director of Yale University's Bush Center in Child Development. A founder of Project Head Start back when Lyndon Johnson was president, Zigler has all along been a shaper of the whole social parenting agenda. He is a practical visionary. Having directed the federal office of child development, he has some sense of what is achievable, and his ideas have tended to be achievable ones.

Nonetheless, it's difficult for him to reconcile his scientific knowledge with his political agenda. In 1988 he admitted in an interview, "I have no hesitance in saying that hundreds of thousands of children are experiencing care that is compromising their optimal growth and development."[1]

But for the rest of the interview he talked about long-term plans for government to provide more money for child care. He didn't urge mothers to rescue their children from these compromising care arrangements. As he had said earlier in another interview, "They thought I was saying that mothers of infants were not to work. What I'm saying is that mothers are working, and they will continue to work, and we have to make sure that we have infant day care of good quality."[2]

He had already reconciled the seeming contradiction in his own mind. Zigler has already decided that the empirical data on how children are harmed by day care is "interesting but irrelevant" for several reasons. "We will not know the ultimate effects of infant day care until these infants have grown up and become parents. We have a whole generation that we should be watching."[3]

He wants to "watch" the whole generation with total dispassion, from a distance, with his mind already made up about what they need. Zigler's vision for the twenty-first century is for public schools to be the linchpin in a nationwide system of social parenting. Public schools would operate networks of licensed infant-care providers. They would themselves provide day care for children from age three on up. They would provide after-school care for children through junior high school. Parenting classes would be operated out of the public schools. The schools would be community centers for civic organizations and youth groups.

Nor is this all mere vision; all over the country public school districts are already offering after-school care and toddler care. Parent education for teenage parents is becoming commonplace as well. Zigler would have it be universal, however. He estimates that quality child care for every child in America under age fourteen would cost $90 billion a year.[4] He'd like to see that entire cost covered, like public school costs, by local, state, and federal taxes.

Now there's bitter logic: already many mothers have to go to work in order to pay the family's tax bill. If the tax burden were increased by another $90 billion a year, hardly any father could support a family on one income, and then every family would need this comprehensive child-care system.

I don't know about you, but I don't think the schools can handle all the jobs they already have. They're already required to perform too many social services and not enough educational functions. Whatever happened to the idea that schools were the places where children were taught how to read and write and figure and to understand and appreciate the best ideas in our civilization? I guess that idea worked only as long as families provided love, security, discipline, and breakfast.

The Infinite Industry of Social Parenting

Another influential visionary of social parenting is Jule Sugarman. Sugarman, who is currently secretary of social and health services in the State of Washington, was also one of the directors of Head Start and head of the federal office of child development back in the 1960s and '70s.

In recent testimony before Congress, Sugarman offered what I think is a valid insight: a new child development industry is emerging, a combination of public and private sectors. He thinks it's a great industry. I think it's a tragedy. This industry includes most of the activities focused on children and their families from before conception through age seven. Until recently, nobody would have thought of activities focused on small children as an industry since most such activities were conducted by people known as parents.

In Sugarman's vision, parents are superfluous. He never mentions them in his testimony. He seems to assume that they cannot provide the services he considers necessary and so they don't matter. The industry's job is to get to the kids, and that's as far as his concern extends. What sort of things are included in the industry?

> Good prenatal medical and nutritional services are an essential ingredient of early childhood along with a full range of pediatric services. There must be good dental, mental health and other specialized health services such as optometric, audiology, and speech therapy activities. A full and effective program of immunizations must be included. I think it is essential that periodic developmental assessments be conducted, first at birth, then at six to nine months and at least once more at the ages of two and three.[5]

Sugarman estimated that by 1994 there would be 55,242,000 children aged zero to fourteen. Then he calculated the number of children in full-day child-care programs, part-day child-care programs, school-age day care, Head Start preschool; then the number of children in poverty and in single-parent homes. Since he assumed that every child in poverty and in a single-parent home would be in need of services, he ended up estimating that by 1994 there would be 84,000,000 children who should receive services.

Did you catch that? Did he calculate more kids needing services than exist? He surely did because, you see, "some children will receive more than one service." Oh yes, he estimated that this new industry would be worth $101 billion by 1994. Sugarman quotes from his testimony before the Subcommittee on Education and Health, Joint Economic Committee, U.S. Congress, December 14, 1988, lamenting that right now nobody is in charge of this industry. He declared, "Some public institution needs to have the responsibility for seeing to it that services are available and accessible to those who need them."[6]

There you have it. Right there, in those words, is the definition of social parenting: *a public institution making sure that every child, even those not yet conceived, receives certain medical, dental, and psychological intervention, diagnosis, and treatment.* Not *parents* — not *family* — responsible for providing for children's needs. A *public institution* responsible for providing for children's needs.

Such a vision of society as parent can only exist and advance if parents themselves go along with it. If parents fail to provide for their children's needs — and dual working parents are barely capable of providing for all the needs simply because their time and energy are limited — the fires of social parenting will be fueled. If parents see themselves as the center of their family, this social parenting vision will die. But if parents accept government (or "service providers") as the center of their family, Sugarman's vision is not only accurate, it's inevitable.

Yes, of course, families need help. I'm not saying they don't. There is no shame in admitting that your extremely hostile teenager might be helped by a psychologist. And of course all children need doctors and dentists. And so on. My quarrel with Sugarman is over his emphasis. I say parents should be responsible for meeting these needs in their children, and service providers and government should cooperate with parents. That's the way it is in God's eyes, and that's the way it should be in government's eyes. Sugarman would have it the other way around:

that the public institution is responsible and parents are to cooperate with it.

Can motherhood survive? Only if parents are militant in opposing the vision of themselves as mere conduits for medical, dental, and psychological services to their children.

The Social Parenting Think Tanks

Jule Sugarman and Edward Zigler are far from unique in their vision of a future in which government agencies, not parents, are responsible for children's every need. Indeed, many of the behavioral scientists who advise the government share the same kind of ideas. And they are typical of the academics, the experts, who are relied upon by the likes of the Alliance for Better Child Care to provide ideas for legislation.

Ideas have consequences. Social science ideas are no exception.

Congress, you know, has science advisers, experts who advise on everything from weather patterns to the behavior of diseases. In 1963 Congress created the National Academy of Sciences to respond to the requests of any department of government for information on any subject of science or art. This was necessary because often government has to make laws on scientific matters. The whole AIDS debate is a recent example. Deciding what drugs ought to be controlled substances is another medical science example. Military policy today depends increasingly on science advisers: what scientists say is possible and what they say is not are matters of enormous debate. Geological policy is another area: what science says about the likelihood of oil being in certain kinds of rocks can be very important politically, for instance.

Scientists, of course, have their ideologies and political biases just like anybody else. Their private views can color their public pronouncements. In physics and other physical sciences, objectivity is a little easier to maintain simply because everyone agrees on the laws of physical science, at least for practical purposes. Unfortunately, social science is far less precise.

Congress has social science advisers as well. The National Academy of Sciences Committee on Child Development Research and Public Policy is a key shaper of our nation's official policies toward the family.

But social science is a subjective area. How do you interpret behavioral science data? At least, if you're looking for oil and ten experts look at the same data, most of them are likely to agree on the cost-effectiveness of drilling at a particular site. But you can get ten experts to look at a dozen studies of the effects of day care on children, and no two will agree on whether the effects are desirable or undesirable or on what to do about them. Further complicating the situation is that for several decades now the behavioral sciences have been the preserve of a cadre of visionaries who would like to remake the world in the shape of their hearts' desire.

Thus when social scientists are called upon to give advice, the only way to get one voice as an end product is to make up a committee of people who think the same to begin with, people who have the same political worldview and happen to be sociologists or psychologists or child developmentalists who will tend to draw the same conclusions from the same research. If you throw in a political conservative and they all examine exactly the same studies and articles, they won't agree on what the problem is or what caused it or how it could be prevented.

So how do you think the problem of seeking consensus is usually handled? Do you imagine that the National Academy of Sciences conscientiously puts scientists of differing personal political persuasions onto the same committees, just to make sure all viewpoints are heard? Are you kidding?

As David Goslin, executive director of the National Academy of Sciences Assembly of Behavioral Sciences, so delicately put it, "The translation of scientific information into prescriptions for public policies . . . divided the Committee on essentially non-scientific issues about matters of politics and social philosophy [which] are not always fully supportable by scientific evidence."[7]

Goslin was referring to a 1976 report of the National Academy entitled "Toward a National Policy for Children and Families." This report was in some ways the beginning of the current national debate on the government's policy toward the family. The report was actually inconclusive because the authors did not all share a similar political worldview. After that experience, however, the new Committee on Child Development Research and Public Policy was formed to get a group of credentialed experts to agree on what government ought to do.

That Committee has been setting the tone for the translation of behavioral science information into public policy ever since 1977. This elite group of social scientists, it so happens, have been very taken with the Swedish example of government policy toward the family. Motherhood is not doing very well in Sweden.

ON SWEDEN AND THE UNITED STATES

(We're Not Immune to Social Parenting)

For my people have committed two evils; they have forsaken me, the fountain of living waters, and hewed them out cisterns, broken cisterns, that can hold no water.
                                                    Jeremiah 2:13

I have seen child care's future, and it works."[1] With these words the education editor of our most influential national newspaper gave a glowing endorsement to the Scandinavian social parenting system. Fred Hechinger of the *New York Times* defines and sets the tone for what the nation's intellectuals think about education and therefore about children and families. To call him progressive is perhaps a mild observation.

What did Fred see in Scandinavia that sent him into such ecstasies? Essentially, he saw a society in which motherhood has ceased to exist, and he was enthusiastic about the replacement institutions.

In Denmark, he said, "you hardly ever hear a child cry. . . . A typical day-care center includes a section for children from two months to age three, a kindergarten for three- to six-year-olds, and a 'club' for youths up to age 18. The clubs are open from noon to 10 P.M. . . .

Typically the centers are open for a full working day and provide breakfast, lunch, and an afternoon snack. Youngsters up to age 3 are arranged in groups of 10 or 12, with two or three adults. In kindergarten, the groups grow to 20 or 30. . . . Bulletin boards with staff members' names and pictures inform parents daily who has taken care of their children. Parental contact is encouraged."[2]

So Denmark has government-funded institutions that take care of children from two months to eighteen years of age. Parents are even told what adults have been with their children every day and are actually encouraged to talk to them. And Fred Hechinger thinks that's wonderful.

I think the whole thing is sad. I think it's sad that the caretakers shift around so much that a child never knows from one day to the next who will be taking care of him. At least in American day-care centers, parents and children generally know that much. And why? Why? Why? Where are the Danish parents? I know where they are, working, both of them, to survive in their socialist economy. And you know what? I bet children cry in day-care centers in Denmark just as they do in day-care centers in America. Starry-eyed journalists just aren't around to hear them.

Sweden: The Parental State

The subhead on Hechinger's article reads: "In Scandinavia, where a strong democratic society is the goal, child care is an answer." No it isn't. It isn't any answer. It's merely a part of a vicious circle: a socialist state is so expensive to maintain and its taxes so high that it demands the employment of all adults, including mothers. So the care of children becomes part of the responsibility of the state, which of course raises the expenses of government further, which raises taxes further. . . .

But people who believe in socialist societies—"strong democratic society" is the current code phrase for the same thing—also have to believe in social parenting. There is no other way to make the system work.

Liberals have always admired Sweden and held it up as a shining example of an ideal state. Back in 1962, when the celebrated Sherri Finkbine in Arizona wanted an abortion, she went to Sweden. That was the beginning of the campaign in this country for abortion, and Sweden was hailed as the example for us to follow. Today, Swedish policies on children and family are particularly beloved by child development professionals and by feminists and have been since the 1930s when Gunnar and Alva Myrdal, the principal gurus of the modern welfare state, began their careers.

- About ten years ago spanking was outlawed in Sweden.

- Swedish women have the highest employment rate in the Western world.[3]

- And the private lives of Swedish men and women are about as unsatisfying and chaotic as you can imagine.

Whether Swedish women want to have the highest employment rate in the Western world is not much examined. But they have it because their government told them they were going to have it. In the words of a 1971 Commission on a New Marriage Law, the national policy became "to shape a society in which every adult takes responsibility for himself without being economically dependent on another and where equality between the sexes is a reality."[4] The consequence of these developments is that in most Swedish families, both parents work outside the home or are engaged in studies.[5] Remember Mrs. Kullman, whose story was told in chapter 1?

Now where have we heard that kind of talk before? "Equality of the sexes"? Away with "being economically dependent" on another person?

Sweden decided to make men and women equal and began by saddling women with the same financial obligations as men. It is called the "working family" model. The country decided, as a matter of principle, that every nonhandicapped adult should be financially responsible for him or herself. The tax laws were simply changed to punish any family that tried to keep a wife "dependent." In the rare case in which a family tries to live on one salary, the couple pays 62 percent of the husband's income in taxes.[6] So of course mothers have to work; and of course government has to take over the mother's role. Social parenting is the inevitable next step. The Swedish government subsidizes day care as much as nine thousand dollars per year per child.[7] But of course, nobody who raises her own children can get an equivalent tax rebate.

Thus it should come as no surprise that the Swedish marriage rate is now the lowest in the industrial world. The divorce rate is the highest in the industrial world — four divorces for every seven marriages in 1984.[8] And the living together without marriage rate is the highest in the industrial world.[9] Among people aged twenty to thirty, more than 50 percent of the population living with partners is unmarried.[10] After all, why bother to get married? If you both have to work anyhow, what difference does it make?

Not only do almost 25 percent of pregnancies end in abortion, but 46 percent of births are out of wedlock (illegitimacy no longer exists in Sweden).[11] But of course! A husband can't "take care of" a wife in any meaningful way under this scenario. If government is going to take care of the kid anyhow, who needs a husband? In a socialist state, when government provides housing and medical care and child care, what difference can a father make? A father can't "take care of" a child. Government is already providing everything material.

With no material or financial incentive to get married and no opportunity to bond with children, it's not surprising that Sweden's birth rate is so low that the Swedish Information Services doesn't publish it. As one of the fact sheets from the Swedish government so delicately states the matter, "Given the thought of study and the need for a foot in the labor force, women choose to wait to have children. Having more than two children is considered both too costly and too much of an occupational barrier."[12]

The government, however, does fund the Riksforbundet for Sexuellt Likaberattigande — the RFSL, the national gay organization. RFSL has quite a lavish headquarters, which includes a restaurant, offices, and a gay radio station.13 Don't be surprised: If government destroys the relationships between men and women, what do you expect is going to happen?

Ah yes, a great place, Sweden is. Maybe progressive education reporters think that kind of future works, but I don't. Right now, Swedes think they're doing fine and are quite proud of their progressive reinvention of human nature. But I predict that twenty years from now the chickens will come home to roost. By then, Sweden will be suffering acutely from the effects of children growing up without emotional attachments and from the effects of a generation of impermanent interpersonal relationships among adults. Right now, the state can cushion the blows. But that can't last forever.

"Working Family" Policies in America

Thanks be to God, the United States lags far behind Sweden in its response to demands for full equality for women and to demands for full state responsibility for child rearing.

But we are not as far behind as you might think. Did you realize that the federal government has been undermining and attacking motherhood for decades now? It's not surprising that so many women are giving it up; government incentives are in the other direction.

Traditionally, every ten years the president called a meeting of the nation's experts on children. They discussed current problems of children and made recommendations. Not only would these recommendations find their way into legislation, but, more importantly, they set a tone for the national consciousness about children. The White House conference on children of 1909 had the right idea: "Home life is the highest and finest product of civilization," it said.[14]

The climate had changed by the 1930 White House Conference on Children, though. That conference began to pave the way for nonfamily child rearing by endorsing an early form of day care: "If the grouping of little children for a few hours each day for educational activities and for habit-training through nursery schools is found to be desirable in itself, then this service should be extended on behalf of children generally, regardless of the economic status of their family," declared that conference.

Through the thirties, experimental day-care centers and child development centers began to pop up on university campuses. So did charity day-care centers for the poor and immigrants and privately owned ones for the middle classes. With the Works Progress Act of 1932, over fifteen hundred government-run nursery schools were established.

And then came World War II and the restructuring of the WPA nurseries to meet the needs of working mothers. The Lanham Act allowed the establishment of 3,102 day-care programs for mothers employed in the war effort. The Farm Security Administration opened day-care facilities in rural areas. The U.S. Maritime Commission set a new standard at two Kaiser Corporation shipyards: day-care centers operated twenty-four hours a day, seven days a week, and offered food service. Mothers could pick up both children and dinner at the end of their shift.

This explosion of federal child rearing was related to the war effort, and it disappeared shortly after the war ended. The years after the war were the heyday of motherhood. The Aid to Dependent Children program (now known as Aid to Families with Dependent Children, AFDC), established itself squarely on the principle that mother was best, and therefore subsidized mothers so that they could stay home and rear their children. At the time, 60 percent of the mothers qualifying for benefits were widows. Day-care centers shrank—except among the upper-middle class. By 1960, 64 percent of all licensed day-care centers served working mothers in the upper income range. In that year, the decennial White House conference on children once again was resoundingly in the corner of motherhood; it recommended "alternative methods" of child care only when the "understanding, loving care best provided by mother" was not available.

On the surface, all looked smooth. If you watch the television comedies of the day, Mom was at home, Dad was at work, and the family was intact. The prevailing psychological currents were dominated by the work of John Bowlby, who had convincingly demonstrated that a continuous, warm relationship with Mother was the basis for the development of character and mental health. Sociologist Talcott Parsons praised the modern nuclear family and the mother's elaborate role as the emotive, nurturing, and managerial center of the household.

But it was the calm before the storm.

The War over the Family

Even after the war, married women were staying in the labor market. Ever since 1946, labor force participation of married women has gone steadily up. At the same time, the phenomenon of fatherless households began to appear. First noticed in the early 1950s among urban blacks, the trend spread: among the white population, illegitimacy jumped 50 percent between 1957 and 1963. The 1963 rate looks low compared with today, of course, but it was significant because at the time it was a radical departure from recent history. All of a sudden, AFDC was being received primarily by children with fathers absent through illegitimacy, divorce, desertion, or separation. No longer was it an honorable benefit accorded to orphans.

The intellectual climate shifted again. Anthropologist Margaret Mead began the debunking of motherhood by claiming that cultural anthropology showed that children found security in large numbers of nurturing figures (a necessary premise of social parenting). Others followed. One social worker argued that "day care can offer something valuable to children *because* they are separated from their parents."

Ideas have consequences. Public policy follows intellectual currents. For years the U.S. Senate Subcommittee on Education had been trying to figure out how to get federal funding of education into law. Now, suddenly, there was an opening: as the War on Poverty was gearing up, motherhood was no longer sacrosanct. And so "child development centers," later known as the Head Start program, was in that "war" from the beginning. Once again, but this time without a compelling national emergency, the federal government was in the day-care business.

Poverty was the camel's nose under the tent. "Early childhood intervention can help end existing poverty and prevent new poverty" was the slogan. The implication was that mothers had to be replaced if kids were to be kept out of poverty. But of course it didn't work out that way, and as the family in poverty has become weaker and weaker, the programs have increased and increased.

In 1967, Congress provided funds for the day care of AFDC children. What an irony! AFDC had been created so that fatherless children would at least be assured of a mother to raise them. By 1972, AFDC mothers with school-age children were supposed to register for work or work training—not that the provision amounted to much in practice. AFDC's costs were already out of control, on a wild escalation that has continued to accelerate.

And then came feminism.

The House Special Subcommittee on Education gave feminists their first major public platform in some 1970 hearings on "Discrimination Against Women." Back then, the head of the National Organization for Women was still called a chair*man*, and her name was Wilma Scott Heide. Her testimony blew the antibaby trumpet loud and long: overpopulation, she said, threatened the quality of people and the total environment. And the way to solve the overpopulation problem was to give women "expectations of, and preparation for, a viable significant alternative to motherhood."

That same year, NOW's annual conference asserted that "child care must become a political priority." The New Democratic Coalition in the same year demanded that government provide child care to all children whose mothers needed it.

The 1970 White House Conference on Children was a weather vane; it articulated a statement of principle for the new generation: "Society has the ultimate responsibility for the well-being and optimum development of all children." What an enormous departure from tradition. *Society,* not *parents,* is now, according to an official document of the U.S. Government, responsible for children. The basic premise of social parenting was made official in 1970.

The conference went further: The awesome power of day care was fully recognized, giving those who ran it "over 8,000 hours to teach values, fears, beliefs, and behaviors." But such power was needed, this conference decided, so that children could learn things their families could not or would not teach them. Indeed, these were radicals, full of themselves and their notions that human nature could be changed. Unfortunately, they were carrying the majesty of the law, the weight of federal authority, behind them. Considering what happened at the 1970 White House Conference on Children, and its subsequent fallout, it was probably just as well that there was no such conference in 1980. President Jimmy Carter had a White House conference on families that year, which could not agree on what a "family" was and essentially argued over how to implement principles of social parenting and feminism. But the White House conference on children was postponed until the next year. And then President Ronald Reagan, deciding that feminists and the social welfare lobby did not need another platform at the government's expense, canceled the conference.

The parting shot of the 1970 White House Conference on Children was to call for a comprehensive federal child-development program. By 1971, such a measure had passed both the United States Senate and the United States House of Representatives. A senator from Minnesota named Walter Mondale sponsored the measure, and it was presented as an antipoverty program. But it was far more than that: it was a blueprint for social parenting.

Mondale's Comprehensive Child Development Bill would have committed the federal government to establishing child advocacy programs in any locality that had more than five thousand residents. The programs would have delivered a full range of health, educational, and social services to all children—not just poor ones, but all children, on a sliding fee basis. The rationale was that Congress had recognized that such services were essential for all children to reach their full potential and therefore Congress was going to assume its responsibility to ensure that all children had what they needed. Parents were out of the picture.

Social Parenting as Federal Policy

The Mondale bill was vetoed by President Richard Nixon on December 9, 1971, the birthdate of the profamily political movement. But it was a hollow victory. While the totalitarian, social parenting nature of Mondale's bill had been discredited, ordinary day care for working mothers had become respectable. Both sides in the congressional debate had made it abundantly clear that that was just fine.

In the same year, Congress gave NOW half of what it wanted: liberalized tax deductions for child-care costs. In 1976, that deduction became a 20 percent tax credit for work-related child-care expenses, to be raised again in 1984. With this, the attack on motherhood escalated. Motherhood would, in effect, be taxed at higher rates than social parenting. Parents who raised their children themselves would pay higher taxes than parents who hired somebody to raise their kids.

In the name of helping the poor, the attack on motherhood continued. In 1977, Congress approved the measure that has created the most enormous federal support of child care, Title XX of the Social Security Act. Then there were Head Start, child care associated with most federal welfare and job training programs, and the Child Care Food Program. All of these were couched in rhetoric of "enabling the poor to achieve self-supporting status," and together they add up to $2.7 billion a year of federal subsidy of the destruction of motherhood. And that was only Fiscal Year 1987's figures.[15] You can be sure it's more now.

In the name of equality for women, the attack on motherhood continued. In 1981, the U.S. Commission on Civil Rights, no less, declared that women's responsibility for child care "constitutes a significant barrier to equal opportunity." Now the obligation to take care of one's children had become a violation of a woman's civil rights!

Somewhere along the line, as feminism was gaining clout, feminists handed motherhood what has since proven to be perhaps its biggest body blow. It used to be that when a couple applied for a mortgage to buy a home, the bank or mortgage company would compare the husband's income to the cost of the house to decide whether the husband could afford the house. Unless a wife was past childbearing age, her income was generally not factored into the equation. "Discrimination!" charged feminists. "Don't assume that women are going to quit their jobs just because they have babies!" And so the policy was changed, eventually by federal law — the Equal Credit Opportunity Act. By the late 1970s, mortgage lenders were required to consider the wife's income. All of a sudden, real estate prices began to go sky-high — same number of houses, almost twice as much money to pay for them. Within a few years it became clear that the "antidiscrimination" policy of considering a wife's income had in fact been a sentence of doom for motherhood; in practice, it means that wives now must bear their share of the cost of home ownership. Nothing keeps so many mothers in the work force as the cost of buying a house.

Can you see the pattern? First, ideas change, and then policy follows. First, what the academics say changes the intellectual climate, and then Congress follows suit. As long as the various *-ologists* were defending motherhood, motherhood was safe. Once the *-ologists* began attacking motherhood, government began replacing it — with more government.

A Case Study of Swedish Principles in Practice Here

And the trend continues. The fact that feminists have become respectable does not mean their antimotherhood ideas have lost their power. The fact that the country has had a few years of conservative Republican presidents does not mean the attack on the family has stopped.

True, nobody in the administration is explicit about establishing a "working family" policy here and now. But even without any debate, many ingredients are already in place to put such policies into practice.

The pressure is strong for the United States to wake up to the modern world and admit that motherhood went out with the crinoline.

Remember that propaganda theme of the day-care lobby? "The United States is the only industrialized nation in the world that does not have a child-care policy." Just which other industrialized nation do you suppose is hailed as the shining example? You guessed it: Sweden.

Remember the dangerous visionaries? There are plenty of them around, and they know how to make their radical ideas sound like soothing, practical analgesics. Bear with me while I document one example of how the Swedish "working family" model of day care became the reality of government money and government program . . . without anybody ever debating or voting on it and without the public being aware what was being done.

Many academics and experts in the opinion-making elite of the child development profession are quite explicit about their admiration of the "working family" policy. The National Academy of Sciences Committee on Child Development, for instance, advocates the Swedish "working family" model.[16] And these experts are well connected to influence government programs and action. They are well funded by friends in the federal bureaucracy as well.

Wellesley College in Massachusetts is a particular seedbed of this kind of thinking. And now the ideas from the intellectual hothouse at Wellesley are affecting the lives of millions of ordinary Americans in Fairfax County, Virginia. How did this come about? The Wellesley College Research Center for Women sponsors something known as the School Age Child Care Network. This project, SACCN, receives and distributes federal funds for implementing "working family" initiatives. SACCN received funds to establish a local model of a Swedish-style system of day care from the Department of Education's research arm, the National Institutes of Education (NIE), in conjunction with the National Academy of Sciences. SACCN chose Fairfax County, Virginia, for this experiment.

It was a natural choice. Just outside Washington, D.C., with its highest proportion of working women in the nation, Fairfax County is home to more yuppies than you can shake a stick at. The decision was shrewd: if you can get the working women to depend on the county for their child care, they'll be willing to vote more education bonds to keep the programs going when the funds for the experiment run out. Working families, too, will come to like the convenience of government responsibility for child care.

And the idea was guaranteed to spread. Because all the commuter counties around Washington, D.C., are linked together in a service-coordinating body known as the Washington Metropolitan Council of Governments, it was only a matter of time until the other counties began to use the Fairfax County program as a standard. All this began in Fairfax County in 1985. At the time, that's where I lived. When we moved to Montgomery County, Maryland, another commuter-belt county, in 1989, a similar program was just beginning. No wonder Congress is looking favorably at federal child-care legislation. For half a decade now, many of the government workers and congressional staffers have been enjoying the fruits of government child care!

Here in the United States we won't do anything radical like declaring an explicit government policy that all nonhandicapped adults are responsible for their own economic support. That would never happen. Too many sleeping Christians would wake up and growl about that. But through the network of academic experts and federal funds, the same types of programs can quietly be put into effect without anybody's noticing. And you know how it goes . . . once government puts something in place, nobody can ever get rid of it.

THE MOST DANGEROUS ENEMY OF MOTHERHOOD

(Hint: It Doesn't Come from Japan)

*Walk worthy of the vocation wherewith
ye are called, with all lowliness and
meekness, with longsuffering, forbearing
one another in love; endeavouring to
keep the unity of the Spirit in the bond of
peace.*

Ephesians 4:1–3

Here you are, just about in the middle of a book on motherhood. And you realize the last two chapters you have read have been about the inner workings of politics and the making of government policy.

Well, I had to put that in because I feel you ought to know it. You are a citizen, and you need to know how to evaluate the hot air and fancy words that come at you every time there's an election around the corner. We get the kind of government we deserve, after all. And if our government is going to abolish motherhood, we need to know exactly how it is happening.

You're right if you think that government isn't entirely to blame. Cultural trends are also battering away at motherhood. I'm getting to those. But don't forget, culture acts upon and through the system of government. And every government policy either encourages or discourages something. Laws concerning children either support traditional families or weaken them. There is no neutral ground.

Speaking of children and culture, I want to ask a question here: Whatever happened to childhood?

You know, the kind of childhood that you can get a glimpse of by reading a children's book that's fifty or more years old. The kind of childhood implied in what nineteenth-century adults wrote about. The kind of childhood in which a kid played with other kids and invented games and was free to think great thoughts about being a hero and protecting the innocent and doing perilous and holy deeds. The kind of childhood in which a child admired adults and wanted to be like them.

You and I both know that this kind of childhood has been replaced by one in which the kid has to worry whether his parents are going to get a divorce and what's going to happen to him then, how he's going to defend himself against the big bullies at school, whether Mom will be home in time to fix dinner or not. And if he doesn't have those concerns, he worries whether he's too fat and whether his clothes are stylish and whether the girls find him attractive. Beginning around grade four, most children seem like anxious imitations of neurotic adults. The standard fare of "contemporary children's literature" and the "children's specials" on television reflects these neurotic concerns. It used to take until seventh or eighth grade to reach that sad state. Gone are carefree adventures; gone is carefreeness altogether. Gone is the security of routine, the basis of happy childhoods and noble dreams.

For children to be free of cares, somebody else has to be structuring their lives and worrying and making decisions for them, shielding them from worries. Adults make childhood possible by accommodating children and their natures. When adults don't have time to accommodate childhood, it ceases to be pleasant and carefree. Worse, sometimes adults lack maturity themselves, so they are driven to "share with the children" things—usually emotions—that are inappropriate. Everybody has seen this happen in a divorce. But it happens plenty outside of divorce too.

Whatever happened to the idea that we should shelter our children? Have we forgotten how to keep their lives pleasant? Or is it that we simply don't care about how they feel? If Dad is facing unemployment, why make the child worry about it beforehand? If life changes when Dad loses his job, Junior will find out about it soon enough and have to deal with it then. Why saddle him with worrying about it for interminable weeks before it happens (and to a child, even dread-filled days can be interminable)? Why do we have to teach our kindergarteners that there are diseases that could kill them and where these diseases come from?

And yet, as childhood absorbs adult worries and problems, political rhetoric about the preciousness of childhood seems to increase. Maybe it's just because politicians, remembering their own happy childhoods, see that children today do not have such experiences and figure that their knowledge or program will restore childhood innocence and happiness. And maybe the rhetoric succeeds because of our guilt over not spending enough time with our children or paying enough attention to them, and we like to think we can "make it up" somehow by setting up some new government bureaucracy or new program for "children."

Raising children is labor-intensive. It takes lots of time and has to be done one-on-one (or close to it). How much time does it take to get one toddler into winter gear, into the car seat, out of the car seat, into the stroller, into the store, out of the winter gear, through the store and the shopping, and then back into the winter gear, into the stroller, out to the car, into the car seat, home, out of the car seat, into the house, and then out of the winter gear again? Now, how much time does it take to put two toddlers through these paces? Compare that with the time it would take one woman to do the errand herself, and you have an idea of why child rearing is labor-intensive.

Economists would tell us that as economies advance and become capital intensive (like stockbrokering) or technology intensive (like Silicon Valley computer industries), labor-intensive work becomes less economical and less attractive. People invent robots to assemble gizmos on gadgets because employees don't want to do such a labor-intensive job. And then, the robot is cheaper. But there's no way to invent a robot to put snowsuits on toddlers. Inventing social parenting could, I suppose, be looked at as a way of taking some of the labor intensity out of child rearing. After all, day-care employees handle more children than most mothers. As the mother is earning more money by working than she has to pay in day-care expenses, her labors become more capital-intensive as well. And so a purely economic analysis would doom motherhood.

Consider Japan

Speaking of things economic, allow me one more refutation of the propaganda saw that "America is the only industrialized nation in the world not to have government day care. . . ."

I don't see why any politician should be the least bit moved by that charge when the nations being held up as models are the likes of Sweden, France, or Canada. Let's face it, all those nations have limping economies, even compared with ours. None of them is an industrial giant. Industrial nations can strangle themselves in more ways than one, and a nation's choice to commit economic hara-kiri is no reason we should feel guilty about not imitating one of its strategies.

However, there is on earth one nation which is an industrial giant, one which is giving our economy a run for its money now. I just heard on TV that more Americans now are afraid of this country's economic competitiveness than are afraid of nuclear war. Wouldn't you like to know how this country handles the problem of its working mothers? Does this country have social parenting? I refer, of course, to Japan. Even if you never read the business pages of the newspaper, you know that Japan is our biggest industrial and economic competitor and that we are not faring too well in the competition.

Since the day-care lobby makes sweeping statements about "all industrialized nations," I decided to look into Japan's policies with respect to working mothers, government or employer day care, and so on. Guess what? There's not much written. Feminists do not like Japan. This piqued my curiosity. Even so, had it not been for the assistance of a friendly librarian at the U.S. Department of Education, who knew how to access all kinds of unpublished papers on Japanese early childhood education, I could never have found out anything at all.

Women are very much in the Japanese labor market, and labor regulations require paid maternity leave. It is true that the Japanese government supports day nurseries and has since 1918. It is true that most Japanese children are in some kind of preschool education. It is true that day-care centers, known as *Hoikuen*, accommodate children of working mothers from age zero to five for up to eight hours a day and include "baby hotels" for night care.

But there the similarities end.

No wonder feminists do not like Japan. Labor regulations are so discriminatory as to prohibit women being employed between ten at night and five in the morning, except for the entertainment trades! Imagine, regulations which actually protect real, live women, not just the abstract rights of women! Only 7 percent of managers in Japanese business are women, although 53 percent of office workers are.[1] Although 40 percent of the national labor force is female, only half of them are married, so only about 20 percent of the total labor force is married women. No wonder feminists don't like Japan; it's not a role model for the kind of society they want.

Japan, almost entirely a middle-class nation, is a stable society. Adolescent disaffection and crime, as we know it here, hardly exists in Japan. Barely one out of ten families will experience a divorce, compared with our almost one out of two. Fathers support the family; mothers raise the children. Just 6 percent of Japanese families have single parents as head of household—this amounts to about 4 percent of Japanese children. Compare that with the United States, where 25 percent of families have single-parent heads of household and it is expected that up to 60 percent of children will live with only one parent at some time in their lives. In Japan, one family in six includes three generations.

Could it be there's some connection between the stable social order and the economic success of the nation?

There are few similarities between the Japanese day-care/preschool system and ours. In Japan, the purpose for child care is clearly defined and understood. Rather than some vague gobbledygook about children achieving their full potential, which can mean anything anybody says it means, Article 78 of the Japanese School Education Law is very precise about the objectives of kindergarten:

- to cultivate everyday habits necessary for a sound, safe, and happy life to effect a harmonious development of the physical body;

- to make children experience in the kindergarten a group life and to cultivate willingness to take part in it as well as the germ of the spirit of co-operation and independence;

- to cultivate the germ of right understanding of and right attitudes toward the surrounding social life and happenings around themselves;

- to guide the right use of the language and foster an interest in fairy tales and picture books; and

- to cultivate their interest in expressing themselves through music, dances, pictures, and other means.

A similar set of guidelines, issued by the Ministry of Health and Welfare, includes these principles for the nursery schools:

- to nurture basic habits and attitudes for health and maintain a safe everyday life in a fully protected environment;

- to teach them the right use of language with a rich vocabulary;

- to nurture their independent and co-operative attitude;

- to arouse their interest in natural and social phenomena; and

- to cultivate their sentiments and the base for thinking and the seeds of morality through various phases of life.[2]

Imagine if any government body in the United States, no matter how local, attempted to urge a nursery school to plant in children's minds the "seeds of morality!" Why, the ACLU would be down on them so fast their heads would be spinning.

Day care that works like a parking lot for children is going to treat children like vehicles parked for a certain time, deny it how they will. Children who are parked for their parents' convenience will know it too and respond accordingly. No wonder there are as many adverse effects connected with day care as there are (see chapter 13 for more details). In Japan, children are not parked and abandoned in day-care centers.

While the working mothers' day care may be as long as eight hours a day, most Japanese kindergarten is only five hours a day, accepts three- to five-year-olds, and requires much investment of a mother's time. Teachers are responsible for the cleaning of their own rooms, and mothers express their appreciation to the teacher for the many things she does.

Perhaps the main thing she does is to bond emotionally with her charges. Caregivers feel their responsibility keenly. Nap time, for instance, is not the "shut the kids up so I can have a break" sort of affair it is here. The futons (folding mattresses which are the universal bedding arrangement of Japan) are assembled side by side on the floor. The teacher settles between two children; soothes them to sleep, then moves on to the next set of two children, stroking their backs, speaking affectionately to them. There is a climate of intimacy and affection. In a space fifteen feet wide, eight five-year-olds will sleep. In New York City, by contrast, the Department of Health requires the cots in nursery schools to be at least two feet apart![3]

With the emotional bond established, the day-care teacher can relate to the child on a deep level. One professor of infant education from New York City spent a year observing Japanese nursery schools and kindergartens and noted the teacher's "fine sensitivity to children's capabilities." This showed up in such areas as encouraging children faced with frustration, embracing and praising for persistence, and encouraging prolonged attention to certain play so as to develop attention span. A group of three-year-olds spent twenty minutes playing creatively with a bunch of large cardboard boxes; the American observer was impressed at both the length of time and the variety of creative uses for the boxes.[4]

Unlike Japan, America is very mobile. We don't worry too much if our children don't get along well in one day-care center because we can transfer them to another one if we need to. It is common for families to move several times during the elementary school years, even if within the same metropolitan area. In Japan, however, people are more stable.

That stability enhances the prospects of identification with the group. In Japanese preschools, thirty children to one teacher is not uncommon. Can you imagine that ratio of three-year-olds to a teacher in an American day-care center? Impossible! The American teacher would go mad. The situation would be chaos. But in Japan the teacher encourages the class to function as a group, and the children expect to behave that way. In America we all want to do things our way, and most children are allowed from infancy to have their own way, so naturally they are not able to conform to a group. Japanese preschoolers wear uniforms to their schools. Imagine how Americans would react to that. Certain inner-city schools on the East Coast recently have urged voluntary uniform policies lately, to respond to the designer label madness among school children—but even those voluntary policies were challenged in court as violations of constitutional freedoms.

Not only do American children not learn to behave or to conform; they are not even given the chance to learn!

Imagine if you lived in a society where your children were expected from age three to have self-control and compassion. Wouldn't you make sure that your children knew self-control and compassion before they started school? If you expected that your child would remain lifelong friends with the kids she met in her first day-care center, wouldn't you treat the other mothers accordingly? Wouldn't the kids treat each other accordingly? Of course. Not only are children specifically and explicitly taught how to get along with each other and taught pride in being a member of a group, but the very fact that they are members of a group will make an impact upon their attitudes and behavior.

When you know you have to get along with somebody forever, you work harder to conquer your pride and your anger. You are less concerned with attracting attention to yourself and more concerned about the other people. In a stable, nonmobile community, there are such differences in the way people treat each other. Such traits are, in essence, a turning away from Self.

Interestingly, Christian nursery schools are popular in Japan—there are about fifteen hundred of them, although supposedly most people do not want their children to become Christians, but merely to take advantage of the superior education.

Imagine how a society based on these principles could be fertile soil for the development of a Christian spiritual life! Evangelization aside, the social organization alone of Japanese nursery schools is something that American Christians would do well to think about.

Kyoiku Mama

It's a shame that evangelization of Japan has not been more successful because Japanese mothers have an attitude of service that is an example to all mothers. The Japanese mother does not tear herself apart with doubts about whether she will be able to find fulfillment as a full-time mother; she knows that she will devote herself to her children, and she does. From the time of infancy, when she carries the baby around on her back in a sling, through the early years, Japanese mothers rarely use babysitters or resort to playschool. Their goal is not to create children who are independent of them; their goal is to raise children who are close to them.

The object of this single-minded devotion is often education. The achievement of children's educational success is the goal in life for *kyoiku mamas,* or education mothers.

> She studies, she packs lunches, she waits for hours in lines to register her child for exams and waits again in the hallways for hours while he takes them. She denies herself TV so her child can study in quiet and she stirs noodles at 11 P.M. for the scholar's snack. She shuttles youngsters from exercise class to rhythm class to calligraphy and piano, to swimming and martial arts. She helps every day with home-work, hires tutors, and works part-time to pay for *juku.* Sometimes she enrolls in "mother's class" so she can help with the drills at home.[5]

All of this is necessary, in the mother's opinion, because without such vigorous enriching, a child attending public schools simply will not get into a good college. (*Juku* are after-school classes, but not casual once-a-week, half-play, half-learning affairs. They are serious—six days a week, $500 a month, with homework every night.) Organizing all this is also obviously a full-time job for a mother.

Mothers accept educational involvement as their job. "My wife couldn't come tonight—my son has an exam tomorrow," is a legitimate dinner party excuse.

Feminists, needless to say, find such selfless devotion appalling. There is a feminist movement in Japan, and like our domestic variety it is strong on college campuses and in educational and literary circles.

In Japan, the custom is for the whole family to sleep together. But since fathers work late, mothers usually get the nighttime cuddling with the children. Writes the dean of early childhood education of Seiwa College and Graduate School in Nishinomiya, of this custom: It "produces the phenomenon that the mother cares too much about her children, and she cannot live without thinking about them. . . . The mother is so lonely she comes to love the children too much. This is one of the biggest problems that Japanese society has today."[6]

Mothers who love their children too much are a problem we could use a little of here in the U.S. of A.

Our Own Worst Enemy

Leaders of America's dying industries may point fingers at Japan and label it the "real enemy" of America's economic well-being. I think that is, as the slang saying goes, a bum rap. Japan is not an enemy. We are our own worst enemy.

Let's face it: Japan has no land, few natural resources, and great distances to cover to compete with us. But it's competing very well, thank you. We, on the other hand, have vast land, vast resources, and generations of ingenuity and inventiveness behind us. But we're not competing very well.

Obviously, something other than material resources is involved here.

Something makes the Japanese people willing and able to work hard, to work well together, to cooperate with one another, to apply themselves to a common task and achieve a goal. Americans used to be like that, but something has changed. Businessmen cite the unwillingness of labor to cooperate with larger goals in mind. Teachers note the unwillingness of students to cooperate with each other, from kindergarten on up. Community leaders lament the unwillingness or inability of people to cooperate with their neighbors. And so on.

I think there's a clue to be found in comparing how Japanese children are raised with how American children are being raised.

The Japanese mother defines herself in terms of her children: it is my responsibility to see that my child fulfills his responsibility. Mothers whose children are successful are admired by the community; those whose children do not succeed are pitied. Now, I can see how a little of that can go a long way. If a child is rebellious or unsuccessful, for instance, the mother could be devastated, thinking it was her fault when it wasn't. A child could become an idol, if a mother's own self-esteem is so tied up in him.

But contrast this with what is increasingly the standard attitude here: "Well, it's his problem, not mine, if he doesn't learn/won't behave/won't obey/doesn't do homework." "I tried, but I have my own life to lead, after all." We know where this attitude leads—and it's certainly not into good colleges. It's not into good family life; it's not into successful maturity; it's not into economic productivity. In short, it's not anywhere good.

But the attitude is common among American parents. And not just in this generation, either, although it is becoming more common as time passes. Single parents can barely cope with just the burdens of survival: it's understandable that they relinquish concern for the external accomplishments of their children. Understandable, but tragic. And the same indifference can be found in two-parent families as well. Mothers intent on self-fulfillment find ready excuses to relieve themselves of responsibility for their children's success in life.

Multiply that attitude by millions of mothers, and you have millions of children who know their parents don't care intensely and who know they're going to be allowed to do what they feel like. Naturally, then, they don't even bother to make an effort to learn what is difficult or hard to master, whether it's calculus or self-control. And the results speak for themselves.

The Enemy of Motherhood

That casual and even indifferent attitude is the worst enemy of motherhood in our society. What government may do wrong, what misguided notions the opinion makers and "experts" may spew forth, can be changed. If the climate of the country doesn't accept nonsense, nonsense won't have a very long life. But indifference to our children will allow greater and greater nonsense to be perpetrated. Indifference not only accepts social parenting, but invites it and justifies it.

"We have to provide hot breakfasts because parents send kids to school without any."

"We have to provide after-school care because otherwise kids would be going home to empty houses and TV sets."

"We need government to immunize kids because so many parents are neglecting to have it done nowadays."

"We have to offer sex education in schools because parents don't bother to teach it at home."

"We need more counselors because so many of these kids can't get their parents to talk to them."

How many times have we heard fundamentally the same old reason for yet a new incursion of public authority into areas previously reserved to the family? And yet the "because" clauses are not untrue. Some parents do neglect their children. Some parents do abuse their children. Some parents do not do their jobs as parents.

But do even these failures justify the establishment of institutions and agencies that further deprive the family of functions to perform? Do they not rather call for turning the hearts of parents toward their children?

Private actions have public consequences. If enough people are poor parents, however privately so, the public consequences eventually will be measures that give the state more control over everybody's life. A hundred years ago enough parents let their children play hooky that truancy laws had to be written. If today enough parents send their kids to school without breakfast, school breakfast laws will have to be written — and school breakfasts will have to be paid for by the parents who do feed their children breakfast.

The cycle is vicious: the less parents do their jobs, the more government will take over the parents' functions. And the more distracted government gets with running the ordinary lives of its citizens, the less attention it can pay to economic productivity and competition. And the more government takes over the parents' functions, the more government costs, and the less parents *can* do their jobs. Where does it end?

The businessperson who thinks Japan is the enemy because of tariff policies and trade laws and so on sees only part of the picture. Japan is winning the industrial competition because Japanese mothers are more involved in their children's success than American mothers. The businessperson who thinks that social issues are silly and doesn't see any harm in social engineering that would push more mothers into the work force is shortsighted in the extreme. Business does not operate in a vacuum — what is going on in society is going to affect business quite directly and quite promptly.

It is a vicious cycle: indifferent parents, incompetent employees, incompetent government, inefficient business. If the family is strong, the nation is strong. If the family is weak, the nation will be weak.

The only real way to break the cycle is to turn the hearts of parents toward their children. That is not something that government can or should do—not that our government is inclined to do it anyhow. But it is something you and I can and must do. Do you now see why I am taking the time to explain the threats against motherhood and to show the impact of global attitudes on our personal lives?

We need to explain to women why it hurts not only their children but themselves if they fail to develop a close relationship in the early years of their children's lives.

We also need to explain why they do not find support for motherhood in modern society. One place to begin is to ask the question, Whatever happened to the family?

DEPENDENT IS NOT A FOUR-LETTER WORD

(Say *No!* to Independence)

*The eye cannot say to the hand, I have no
need of thee; nor again the head to the
feet, I have no need of you. Nay, much
more those members of the body, which
seem to be more feeble, are necessary.*
                    1 Corinthians 12:21–22

There used to be a social institution that fostered and supported motherhood and took care of all things pertaining to the rearing of children. It was so fundamental that people didn't talk much about it and didn't pay much attention to it. They didn't try to improve on it; they just built on it.

Even the Bible doesn't talk much about it; Scripture just *assumes* family as part of creation.

Family begins with marriage: Adam and Eve were united before the Fall, so we can be sure that marriage was part of God's original intention for His children. It was the first human covenant relationship. Later, it was the model for God's own relationship with His people (Ephesians 5:22–33). Marriage is fruitful. As the love between the Father and the

Son brings forth the Spirit, so love between husband and wife brings forth children, a trust from God (Ephesians 6:4). As the Trinity dwells in mutual relationships of perfect love with each other, so we are to dwell in relationships of love. Being fallen, we cannot have perfect relationships, but we have the model to follow, and, being redeemed, we have the grace to follow it.

Love Is a Relationship

Social parenting is an abomination because it strikes at the root of the human personality. The very basis of the human personality is the interaction of human beings. With social parenting, there may be informed, concerned, knowledgeable interaction; there may even occasionally be affectionate interaction between the child and the caregiver. But it will be "according to the book," it will be formal and limited, and it will be transient. On the other hand, true love, enriching love, the kind of love that models the love of our Savior for us, grows from continuity, from constancy, from repeated experience.

It is the interaction between parents and children (line upon line, precept by precept) that builds a covenant relationship between them, that builds honor and love and caring. Maybe it would be more charming if children could know their mother loved them simply by hearing her say it . . . or receiving lovely new toys and gifts from her after every business trip. But, as it is, children come to sense their mother's love only through the building of the relationship: through laughing and playing while changing two-and-a-half years' worth of diapers; through kissing and comforting bumped knees; through making up games with the mashed potatoes and peas; through answering a trillion questions; through discipline and repentance and forgiveness. These are the opportunities for building relationships between parents and children that social parenting destroys. Children don't understand protection, nurturance, care, or love as abstract principles — but they understand that Mommy will reassure them when they're afraid and that Daddy will take care of them. When they become grown up, they can put words to these experiences, to these relationships.

When children finally are old enough to give their hearts to the Lord, it will either be because of, or in spite of, the love they have experienced in childhood. Whether we want to or not, whether we intend to or not, either by action or default, we are going to shape the personalities of our children, and that shaping is going to either open their hearts to God or put obstacles in the path to God. Social parenting puts obstacles; proper upbringing can inculcate good habits and protect against trauma so as to maximize children's openness to God.

I was thirty-five years old before I was able to say "God loves me" and know that the statement means a relationship with God. Oh, I had known my doctrine since I was five. I had known all along that God loved us so much that He sent His son to die for us. That's what I thought love was: a bitter duty. My mother was not happy being a homemaker, and more than once I recall her saying how much she loved me, often joining the thought with a dire reminder of "You'll never know how much I sacrificed for you." Don't misunderstand me — my mother did love me. But I suspect that for her, love was actions, duties, and sacrifices. That's what I grew up thinking love was, especially God's love for His creatures. I had some hope that human love might be a little more enjoyable, but I feared that I was a romantic for allowing myself such an illusion. For years and years when I occasionally heard people talking about how God loved them, I would dismiss their talk as childish. Now I wish I had known such "childishness" myself! And a lot earlier than age thirty-five.

Love is more than feelings, of course; indeed, love is primarily a decision and actions flowing from those decisions. But underlying the choices is a relationship. Without the relationship, the choices are dead and dry. A man who hates his wife can be faithful to her out of a sheer sense of duty; but the faithfulness will turn his heart to flint. If he loves her, the same decision to faithfulness, even if painfully made because it means renouncing another love, will give life to his heart. The duty is the same; the choices are the same. What is different is the relationship.

Only through family life can children experience profound relationships. And social parenting deprives children of this profundity.

Family Functions

Motherhood thrives within the nest of the family. If the family is not functioning, motherhood will not do well because, by its nature, it needs support from other members of the family. How was the family meant to function? Turn back a few centuries in history, so we can get a good clear view of family in a traditional society. By traditional, I most emphatically do not mean the 1950s; I mean the pre-modern, pre-industrial, pre-technological era. I don't think America ever was a traditional society in the sense in which I am now talking.

In former ages the essential relationship-building job of the family was reinforced by the family's practical functions. Parents didn't spend much time analyzing their relationships with their children; they were too busy taking care of them. But that very care was based on a presumption of certain covenants and obligations, and the children grew up to feel love and obligation in return.

What were some of the functions the family performed?

The family offered personal care. If you were born into a family, you had a name; if you weren't, you didn't. The rest of your life depended on that. If your father did not claim you, you just might starve to death. If you were in a family, it meant someone would nurse you when you were born and feed you as you grew up. When you were sick, someone would take care of you. You would be nurtured. Your father shaped his life around providing food and shelter for your mother, so she could nurture you. Someone cared whether you lived or died. In your old age, someone with a blood connection to you would offer you food and a seat by the fire.

The family offered the means of survival. Your father taught you how to farm; your mother taught you how to milk. The family taught you how to react when the lord of the manor spoke to you (in certain eras the wrong response might cost your life!). The family also taught you which mushrooms not to pick. It gave you your livelihood and your religion and your politics. Later, survival skills became more complicated, but your family still taught them. Up until the age of government loans to students, imparting survival skills remained the duty of the family.

If you were a girl, your family was a key decider of your future through its responsibility to find you a husband. Arranged marriages do not mean that love cannot grow; love grows from respect, after all, and respect grows with time. The wisdom of your elders would know what young man would be capable of earning your respect and also taking good care of you. They could protect you from your own mistakes. If you were a son, your family had less power to protect you from mistakes but still had more influence than it has in America today.

In a traditional society, when your parents died there would be things that belonged to you, tools with which you could eke out an existence — perhaps the continuation of the lease from the landlord, perhaps the land itself. If your family disowned you, you were penniless, and your survival could not be taken for granted.

In short, the family was the provider of health, education, and welfare. It ensured survival, it nurtured, it taught morality, it formed character, it met emotional needs. It was not small; it was built around the nuclear marital unit, but it usually included lots of relatives and hangers-on of all kinds. It was the economic center of most people's lives up until nearly modern times. With all this activity embedded in it, naturally the family was the main source of self-fulfillment. Since the important things in life took place within the family, their emotional significance was inseparable from the emotions attached to the people known as your relatives. It was easy to have a relationship with members of your family, if for no other reason than because of your proximity with them.

Now, think about these functions of the modern family. Your existence need cause your father no change in his lifestyle, and in many circles, thanks to acceptance of social parenting, it changes your mother's as little as she can possibly arrange. In your old age or ill health, government will pay for you to be put into an institution but won't help much if you stay home with relatives. But chances are your grown children are two-career families anyway; they might be able to hire a stranger to look after you, but couldn't spend much time with you themselves.

Your wealth does not depend on your keeping faith with your ancestors. Oh, a few people inherit some, but most people today acquire their wealth by their own efforts. Your education depends on your family only if you are sent to private schools.

Notice how in one area after another, functions formerly performed by the family are now provided by institutions or government or by people themselves. Not for everybody and not in all cases, to be sure. But the pattern is clear. In some cases the depersonalization stems from technological change — you can get better medical care in a hospital than at home, for instance. Sometimes it is culturally induced, like the expectation that children will choose for themselves what training and career they will pursue. Often, however, it results from pressures and incentives, intended or not, of government policies aimed at "helping the family" — such as laws stating that parents who don't send their children to educational institutions are guilty of truancy.

Families are strong when they have functions to perform. When the important functions of life are performed by the people who love us, their very performance strengthens our relationships. Common experience is the greatest builder of relationships. When the functions of survival are performed by strangers or institutions or ourselves, their performance doesn't build our relationships; it may even isolate us from the people who love us or reinforce our reliance on ourselves. When that happens, our relationships are reduced to artificial experiences like holidays together or to the exchange of material things to make them meaningful. Modern people are the losers in such a situation.

Do I make family sound too terribly ideal to be believable? I hope not. I'm not describing an ideal; I'm describing, in general terms of course, what family meant for most people throughout the ages of human history — and what it still means for people in the third world or living under oppression. The affluent, modern, technological societies are the ones that have removed functions from the family and thereby altered the emotional climate beyond recognition.

Of course, any individual family, even in the most traditional society, was not perfect. What I have described is the structure of family life in society. Every family provided its own emotional content, as it does today. A family is a psychological hothouse. Whatever is in the hothouse has ideal growing conditions. If there are love and humility and gentleness and sharing in the family, those qualities will grow and thrive. If there are distrust and selfishness and hatred and individualism and materialism, those too will have ideal growing conditions. This is why having teenagers is so sobering: we see in them all our own faults that we thought didn't matter, and we realize that in our particular hothouse, these weeds have been growing along with the flowers. In a family in a traditional society, the hothouse would be full of all kinds of things, so no one plant would matter too terribly much. Nowadays, when the emotional hothouse has relatively few plants growing in it, every plant matters enormously.

Let's Rethink Self-Reliance

What single thing has done the most harm to the family? I wouldn't blame it on technology — that is morally neutral. I wouldn't blame it on industrialization — that too only changes us as much as we allow ourselves to be changed. No, the family is weakened most by the same trait that fosters social parenting and which is undermining motherhood: our emotional independence.

Because of our fallen human nature, our emotions tend to follow our self-interest. When our worldly self-interest is the same as our spiritual self-interest, conditions are most ideal for virtue to thrive. When society praised a woman if her children were virtuous and successful, she naturally put tremendous effort into rearing them. When society praises a woman if she earns as much as a man, then, naturally, she will put tremendous effort into increasing her income.

There's a trait missing from the modern world. And the lack of it destroys marriage, motherhood, and the family. It has been replaced by another trait, one that we all recognize and claim and even honor. Our ancestors in the faith knew that the first trait was the mark of a noble character, and they labored their whole lives to achieve it as their own, struggling to root out the second trait when it raised its head. Today, our society glorifies the second trait and teaches it from infancy onward, explicitly ridiculing the first trait and castigating those who would nurture it. The new trait goes by several names: self-reliance and independence are its best-sounding ones; selfishness and me-first are less pleasant names for the same thing. The old trait goes by names like humility, submission, trust, dependence.

That's right: dependence is a virtue. Had you ever thought of that? Americans are in love with independence. It's supposed to be our national virtue. The pioneers who carved out new states because they wanted elbow room, because a neighbor fifty miles away crowded them — this is the kind of self-reliance we have all been raised to admire. When the job at hand was conquering an empty continent, at least self-reliance helped to get the job done.

I wonder what the human cost was, however. Today just about everybody recognizes that we as a nation lack effective relationship-building skills. Even Christians, who are highly motivated toward successful relationship-building, realize they need help to build relationships with their spouses, their children, their coworkers, their relatives. But we grew up in families, and our parents grew up in families. Why didn't we learn by osmosis how to build good relationships? Didn't we have them?

I suspect we didn't, as a rule. I suspect that the happy families were the exceptions rather than the rule in our generation and in previous generations. Our American forebears were so busy carving out the wilderness or building empires or otherwise inventing a new nation and a new society that they forgot how to build relationships — if, indeed, they ever knew. I wonder . . . for centuries, wasn't the frontier where people sent the kids they didn't know what else to do with? Weren't the sons who went west the ones who had argued with their fathers back east or behaved improperly in some relationship? Going back further, weren't the ones who came to America to begin with for the most part those who were willing to break their home ties? What can we infer about those ties if they were so readily broken? Later immigrants, we know, were reluctant to leave or brought their ties with them, as when entire villages emigrated together. But it's the independent, self-reliant Anglo-Saxon model that we've made our national icon. Have we perhaps found our national models among those who are the least skilled to build proper human relationships?

Just for the sake of the nation alone, isn't it time we started reevaluating what kind of characteristics we are going to value? Do we still have an empty continent to settle? Or has the time come to live together now? When your nearest neighbor lives thirty feet away from you, doesn't it require a whole different mind-set than when the nearest neighbor lived thirty miles away? Half of the country's population lives in urban areas of a million or more people.[1] Many live in townhouses.

Have you ever watched the summer pass in a row of townhouses? Each house has a postage-stamp lawn and very little storage space. Yet each townhouse has its own lawn mower, despite the inconvenience of storing it. So independent are we, so unable to share, so reluctant to ask our neighbors for help, that we would rather tolerate the hassle of storing the darn thing than try to work out an arrangement with a neighbor. Is our pride in doing things our own way perhaps beginning to boomerang on us?

The isolation of mothers in the suburbs is legendary. But when the suburbs first started spreading, mothers for a while continued to have a system of social support because they relied on each other for certain vital things, like transportation. Most people didn't have two cars, so mothers planned to share their activities. Even if a mother did have her own car, she had to have another woman to help drive the baby to the doctor, to sit beside her in the car and hold the infant.

I remember my mother's story of a crisis of her early motherhood: one day, my two-year-old sister fell down with a glass in her hand and severed the artery in her wrist. Mother had to get her to a hospital immediately. Thirty years later, in retelling the story, Mother would still add, "Thank God for Irma. She drove while I held Alyce's wrist so she wouldn't bleed to death." The bond between my mother and Irma was cemented in many such instances of mutual need and aid. Twenty-five years later, without even Christmas cards in the interim, when my parents happened to be in the area again, they called up Irma and visited her, and it was as if only yesterday they had been young mothers living next door to each other. The invention of infant car beds and car seats destroyed this last vestige of interdependence among suburban mothers. The modern career mom could not exist without the infant car seat. But, oh, how we love our independence. We would rather "do it myself, thank you" than have to rely on anybody else for help.

Ironic, isn't it, that women pursue careers because they are too proud to depend on their husbands, who may love them, and so they end up depending for the essentials of life on housekeepers or child-care workers—hired help, who neither give nor expect to give emotional involvement, yet perform the most intimate, emotional-laden activities of life.

Dependent Is Not A Four-Letter Word

We want to be a child-centered society. At least our politicians seem to think that's what we want if we can judge from the way they talk. One basic fact about children is that they are dependent on us. They need us for everything. Being depended upon enables us to feel grand, I suppose, and there's probably not much wrong with getting satisfaction out of doing well the job of taking care of a child so long as we are motivated not by our emotional satisfaction but by meeting the child's real needs.

I am afraid that perhaps our society indulges too much in self-satisfaction with regard to children, however. You know why I think that? Because I don't see much of an attitude of love toward children. The professional child development people, the new industry of chapter 6, have the Rhetoric of concern, all right, but I don't think the yuppie elite have the content right at all. Here's a sample of the attitude a modern woman really has toward children.

> When my husband announced he'd been assigned to Egypt, a place where he hoped I would accompany him, I said, "Fine." Just like that ... I went to Egypt without the smallest notion of what our country calls spouses who heedlessly dash off with their sober, government-employed mates to faraway posts: It calls them "dependent." The word dependent was affixed to the grinning photo on my embassy ID card. It was also affixed to the ID cards of members of quite another category: children.[2]

This author gripes on and on about the insult of being a dependent. She resents having given up her own job to follow her husband to Egypt and blames fate for giving all the fun of both work and love to men only. Being categorized with children is an intolerable insult to her. I wonder, had she been on the *Titanic* when it was sinking, would she have been insulted to be categorized along with children, when it gave her a seat in a lifeboat?

If we claim to value children so much, shouldn't it be a privilege to be in the same category? After all, valuing our children means taking care of them, considering them before ourselves, giving them certain priority, doesn't it? And isn't it an honor to be given certain priority and consideration? Remember the Alamo? Women and children were allowed to leave before the fighting began. Wasn't that a sign of honor, of how much the men of the era valued women and children? No doubt our angry feminist author would have refused to leave, resenting the implication that she deserved any special treatment, or not wanting to be dependent on Santa Anna's mercy.

But perhaps she's just mad because now that her husband earns the money, her feminist dialectic gives him all the power. The oft-repeated cardinal principle of feminism is that all relationships are political. A feminist views every relationship as an activity in relation to power. Every relationship has its more powerful and less powerful member, and the goal of a liberated woman is to be the more powerful member of the relationship. Since who has the money has the power, according to the feminist Marxist dialectic, this angry diplomatic wife feels she is on the powerless end of the stick. Sad for her; if only she realized that relationships are based on love, she might actually be able to enjoy being in Egypt at Uncle Sam's expense.

A woman who is a New York attorney and a CPA who has travelled all over the world doing arbitration has certainly taken advantage of the opportunities for self-fulfillment in the modern world. But when her husband died, Philomene Gates did not want to get out of bed in the morning. It was in that time of shock and grief that she found that relationships meant more than accomplishments: "It was the women I volunteered with at the church and the Girl Scouts and the neighborhood house and the legal aid, it was those wonderful women who had the time to think, 'Phil Gates is alone . . . let's just have her over to supper'. They had the time. Working women don't have that time. If I had had to depend on my professional friends, I would never have gotten out of the house. It is the ladies who aren't climbing up the corporate ladder who have a little more time to think of people."[3]

Destructive Independence

How far do we take our mania for independence? To the extent that we make "quality of life" synonymous with "independence." I have before me a document entitled *Guidelines for Selecting Bias-Free Textbooks and Storybooks,* published by the Council on Interracial Books for Children. This is one of those historic works: it helped set the stage for the de-sexizing of textbooks and more. Consider what this document says about "Handicapism in Basal Readers."

First, it tells us to beware of stereotypes: the ugly hunchback or the hunchbacked old crone. Then it alerts us to occupational stereotypes about disabled people (begging or being a witch, for instance). But here's the clincher: stereotypic story lines. And what is the primary offense? "Are disabled people always shown as . . . in need of help from non-disabled children or adults? Disabled people should be depicted as equals, not as objects of charity—a dehumanizing characterization."[4]

Dehumanizing characterization? To be in need of the kindness of another human being is dehumanizing? What could be more human than needing a fellow human being? What is more human than meeting the need of a fellow human being? Is it not our need for each other that makes us human? Wounded animals do not stop to help each other along the way. I thought we were better than animals and that we, as human beings, would help each other along the way. I thought that whatever we did for the least of the little ones we did unto the Lord. I thought that not even a cup of water offered for His sake would be forgotten! And yet here are the arbiters of school textbook content—the people who set the emotional and moral tone for the moral education of the next generation—inveighing against and insulting and demeaning human kindness! I pity them personally. I lament whatever unhappy experiences have caused them to turn against humanity so viciously. I pity the pride, the independent spirit, that has produced this twisted logic, this pitifully distorted concept of humanity.

You can see how it is the spirit of the age. Where else have we encountered the implicit premise that it is better to be dead than to need help? If helping a fellow human being dehumanizes him, well, then, logically, it is better to kill a deformed baby than to let it live, since the child could only have a dehumanized life.

Where is the logic?

Needing help is dehumanizing;
Handicapped babies need help;
therefore handicapped babies are dehumanized.

A equals B;
B equals C;
therefore A equals C.

The logic is faultless. But the first premise is all wrong.

Needing help is not dehumanizing. Dependent is not a four-letter word. Our Savior Himself came into this world as a dependent. He, who could have come triumphant and blazing with light seven times as bright as the day, with armies of angels at His side, with their flaming swords to cut down everything in His path, with the whole hosts of heaven shouting triumph and glory — did not. He came instead as a helpless, mewling, whimpering infant, who needed His swaddling cloths changed. He stunned all creation by becoming a creature, but He did it. He became dependent on us. His very incarnation was dependent on the consent of a woman. His survival was dependent on the obedience of a man, Joseph, to the warning of an angel — -and then, let's face it, His safe escape into Egypt was facilitated by a cooperative donkey, and depended on unnamed and unsung well owners along the way who were willing to share the water from their wells with travelers. Joseph and Mary and the infant escaping to Egypt were objects of human charity. Did it dehumanize them? On the contrary! It confirmed the humanity of the God-man! And offering charity to them raised to glory those who served them.

This is the Christian view of being dependent. This is the Christian view of helping those who are dependent. The world, which would eliminate dependence, speaks with no authority, but with confused misery masquerading as worldly wisdom.

10

MODERN SOCIETY'S CRUELTY TO WOMEN

(The Parable of Mary and Ellen)

Except the LORD build the house, they labour in vain that build it: except the LORD keep the city, the watchman waketh but in vain.

Psalm 127:1

Fear of being dependent causes our nation to kill its children. Fear of being dependent destroys motherhood and causes women to kill the emotional lives of their children. Whence comes this irrational fear?

It comes, ultimately, of course, from the Old Deceiver himself. He wants us to think that everything depends on ourselves. He wants us to believe that only we can take care of ourselves. It's an easy step from there to concluding that we can't afford to take care of anybody else.

It's worse for women than for men, of course. Women, as the heart of the family, are always more vulnerable to Satan's delusions. He knows that if he can get women thinking about themselves, they won't be thinking about other people, and they won't be seeing the dangers he's busy laying for children and men and society. A woman who gets busy providing for herself will be too busy to evangelize her children, and that saves Satan a lot of work.

In a traditional society the Devil didn't have as many open doors. In a traditional society a woman knew who she was, so she worried about herself a lot less and had more time and energy to work on her relationship with God. (So did a man, for that matter, but here we're talking about women.) She knew who her father was and what his position was in society. Therefore, she knew hers. If her father was a pillar of the community and honored by all, then she was entitled to a reflection of the same honor. If her father was a hardworking, decent yeoman, then she was entitled to the honor given to a hardworking, decent woman. Even if her father was a worthless drunkard, in a traditional Christian society, she was still entitled to respect because she was made in the image of God; if her father couldn't protect her, then the church was there to do it.

When she married, she knew who she was marrying (that's why parental involvement in the choice of spouse was so important) and who she was to become. Now she was John Smith's wife and the mother of his children. She knew her role in the world. If John Smith was a merchant, she had a different role than if John Smith were a farmer or a member of the gentry. She knew how to raise her children; she knew what standards to expect of herself. *She knew whom she could trust.*

Does it seem dull and predictable? Believe me, life was no more dull and predictable than it is today. Children bring their own excitement, and the cavalcade of history continues to pass by, sweeping us up in it from time to time. Events beyond our control come to pass and affect our lives now as they did then.

Was the life of the Proverbs 31 woman dull and predictable? There is a portrait of a traditional woman in a traditional family in a traditional society. Look at her life:

The heart of her husband doth safely trust in her: She has a good two-way relationship, based on adult trust.

She seeketh wool and flax and worketh willingly with her hands: She is in charge of the spinning and weaving and works along with the others at it.

She is like the merchants' ships; she bringeth her food from afar:
She's a bargain hunter, who shops at more than one store.

She riseth also while it is yet night, and giveth meat to her household, and a portion to her maidens: No idler, she gets breakfast ready before anybody is up, even the servants, for whom she is responsible.

She considereth a field, and buyeth it: with the fruit of her hands she planteth a vineyard: Her experience and shrewdness add to the family wealth; maybe the money she made from selling cheese, she saves until she can buy a vineyard. No helpless "I can't balance the checkbook" type, this woman.

She perceiveth that her merchandise is good: She's a shrewd customer and a businesswoman who knows how to turn a profit.

She stretcheth out her hand to the poor; yea, she reacheth forth her hands to the needy: Not only does she manage the family and participate in the family enterprise, but she also initiates charitable acts.

She maketh fine linen, and selleth it: She has another cottage industry on the side.

She openeth her mouth with wisdom, and in her tongue is the law of kindness: She is not ignorant or uninformed about current affairs, but not trying to be "one of the boys" either.

She maketh herself coverings of tapestry; her clothing is silk and purple: No false modesty plagues her. She wants the nicest clothes, and she knows she's entitled to them.

Her children arise up, and call her blessed; her husband also, and he praiseth her: In the course of contributing to the family prosperity, she did not fail to raise her children right. They were not neglected; they love her. And so does her husband.

Give her of the fruit of her hands; and let her own works praise her in the gates: No need to hide her light under a bushel; let her accomplishments speak for themselves; let her enjoy the fruit of her accomplishments.

Not a bad life, when you think about it. The traditional woman was free to use all her talents, all her abilities, to learn anything she could and put it to use. With enterprise centered in the family, she could, indeed, "have it all." And think what the woman in a traditional society was spared! She was spared the frenetic quest that plagues modern woman: Am I good enough? Have I accomplished enough? When can I relax? The traditional woman knew what she had to accomplish, and maybe, for most, it was primarily repetitive domestic chores. But she was able to do it with internal calm because she knew it was what she was supposed to do. And since whatever she did achieve benefited her entire clan, it benefited her as well. Free enterprise in its most original form.

There's another point I want to make: In a traditional society, internal accomplishments or qualities were honored. A woman who was generous to the poor was honored for it. A man who was honest was honored for it. A shrew was publicly criticized; a man who beat his wife was scorned for his uncontrolled temper. Today our internal accomplishments, our qualities of character are ignored. Does anybody care whether corporate executives are kind and honest? Only if they get caught does anybody notice their honesty or lack of it. Maybe they have a different secretary every two weeks because their tempers are so out of control. But that's something joked about around the water cooler; nobody would seriously think it mattered. If somebody beats his wife, he's treated as a criminal, but still nobody talks about self-control in public.

The Limitless Anxieties of Successful Modern Woman

Today we are told that women have limitless choices. And, basically, whether right or wrong, that's correct. Therefore, women's anxiety is also limitless because modern society teaches us that our worth comes from our achievements. Men have the same endless anxiety, too — they've had it for a few centuries longer than women have. Until very recently the innate demands of the survival of the race kept women protected from the same anxieties. Now that reproduction is "under control," however, the emotional pressures on women are out of control.

Think about it. How are smart girls educated? Get good grades, Mary, and you can go to a good college so you can get a good job. Even a generation ago Mary would have perceived that if she went to a good college and got a good husband, her parents would be pleased. But not today. Today chances are the parents want her to get her own good career. They've been made to feel ashamed if "all they want" for their daughter is a good husband. And, too, they know that with no-fault divorce what it is, no marriage can be certain to last, so, since they don't want their daughter to go hungry, launching her on a good career is, they figure, really the best thing they can do for her.

And Mary responds. She learns early that good grades will make her parents very happy with her. They reward her for good grades. When she gets Phi Beta Kappa at college they buy her a car, perhaps. But by now the reinforcement is coming from other sources as well: her teachers praise her and pay lots of attention to her. Clearly, she's the apple of their eyes. When she gets her MBA, she is paraded before all the relatives and praises are lavished upon her. The employers fall all over each other to woo her (federal equal opportunity quota requirements mean they have to hire a certain number of women in management, and Mary's the pick of the litter).

When she gets her first career-track job and then a promotion, the world is really her oyster. Now she can have for herself all the material pleasures the world has to offer: a stunning wardrobe and a condo with a jacuzzi for starters, a sports car to be sure, ski vacations in Europe with the beautiful people . . . all because she worked hard and earned it. Nobody gave her any of this; it's hers by right. She knows who she is: Young Female Executive, on the Fast Track to Success. She has created her own identity. Her paycheck and her titles are her honors. Maybe she sleeps around a little bit, maybe she is ruthless at internal office politics, but who cares? She's carved her niche in the world, hasn't she? And isn't that what was expected of her? Nobody cares anyway what she's like inside.

Her life seems complete. Her parents are pleased that she's successful. Oh, maybe occasionally Mom might hint at grandchildren, but she knows to make a joke out of it . . . there's something about Mary that just—just doesn't seem to go with the idea of domesticity. Mary gets huffy at the idea too. "Mom," she says with exasperation, "I've got an interesting life! Why should I ruin it just for some man?" And Mom doesn't really know how to respond to that. "Well, honey, I've always felt that the greatest satisfactions I got out of life came through your dad and you kids . . ." she says lamely. "But Mom, you didn't have the opportunities I've had," Mary responds. Mary just doesn't have a clue what Mom is talking about.

Mary is not just a quintessential pagan, though certainly women with no religious scruples fill this bill. She could just as easily be your child or mine. Mom and Dad could count themselves Christians; so, for that matter, with a few modifications, could Mary. She is just a typical twentieth-century icon. She is what most college women today want to be when they finish their education.

Is Mary fulfilled? Does she sit back and relax, giving thanks to the Lord at night for all His blessings? Well, it's possible. Being a successful career woman isn't intrinsically incompatible with loving the Lord. But if Mary has a regular prayer time, she's the only fast-track young executive I know of who has.

More likely, Mary is, apart from her fleshly delights, miserable. She probably has to spend close to eighteen hours a day on her job, whether at business breakfasts and dinners or traveling or in the office. She always has to be one step ahead of the other guy: that means she must always be looking for the opportunity somebody else misses, creating opportunities, making the case for her ideas. No going home and relaxing over the sewing machine for Mary: at best, it's reading the professional journals or self-improvement or studying the reports that have accumulated on her desk. Life goes from one project to another; when one is finished, another is waiting. At the end of each one she may receive a little recognition, a pay bonus perhaps, but the next idea has to be forthcoming or she'll get behind. Bright new people who would like to outshine her are coming along. But she has to be the top person — if she became just one of a crowd of managers, she'd be miserable. That's not what she's all about. She has to be the best, and the definition of best is always being rewritten. There is no end to the job.

Since it's the modern world, she has to cope with sex on the job. Her male peers find themselves attracted to her sexually, and expect her to accommodate them. They're not interested in commitment, however, or perhaps they already have wives. If Mary doesn't want these relationships, the burden is on her to avoid them without jeopardizing her working relationship with the men. But she does get lonely, too, so sometimes the relationships may seem attractive . . . even if she doesn't want the sex, she wants the companionship. And, after all, there's no time to find other friends. Maybe occasionally she meets a nice guy, but when he finds out how high-salaried and high-powered she is, he may back off, feeling he couldn't possibly support her at the level to which she has become accustomed.

As she gets older, the unmarried nice guys appear at longer and longer intervals. And she isn't sure she wants to cope with some fellow's children from a previous marriage. Besides, if he blew the last marriage, how's she to know he'd be any different this time around?

What's It All Worth?

Mary gets tired, and she gets depressed. Sometimes, she wonders what she'll be like when she's seventy. Her phone rings constantly, but it's people she's working on projects with. When the project is over, they don't have any reason to call anymore. Hardly anybody calls just to be friendly. They know she doesn't have time for idle chatter. When she gets depressed, she goes to the gym and works out, since physical exercise produces brain chemicals that combat depression. She reminds herself that she knows her worth: she's got that impressive title and that impressive salary and that good pension plan and those blue-chip investments. She knows that's what it's all about, and she's got what she wanted.

To feel better, all she really has to do is look at her friend Ellen. Ellen was a classmate who used to be Mary's best friend. But Ellen quit her job when she had a baby. Now she's home with a couple of kids. To Mary's way of thinking, Ellen is so *boring* now; she can't talk about anything except the kids, never does anything interesting any more. Just no fun. What a dull life that must be, Mary thinks, just to have your world limited to a house and kids. Why, it would be as if you never existed. What a waste of talent, she thinks. Even if she's depressed, thoughts of Ellen reconcile her to her own life. At least, Mary reassures herself, she knows she is *accomplishing* something with her life, not just wasting away as Ellen is.

Mary is a child of her age. She has bought into the world's honor system: paychecks, titles, accomplishments, projects, bonuses. This is how she defines herself. Relationships are a means to an end: you treat people nicely, and they'll cooperate better. When Mary is seventy, she will see the fallacy of it. Indeed, long before then she may understand that something is missing. But will she know what? Will she always need to seek, to strive, to earn her own sense of worth?

Unknown to Mary, Ellen has many internal struggles. She loves her children, and she knows she's doing the right thing by raising them herself. But so often she feels wistful and unappreciated. She wonders whether maybe she's wasting her talents. She used to command a nice salary and knew she was a valuable part of an enterprise. She was an assistant manager when she quit the career track; she had fifteen people working under her and was responsible for a $3.2 million budget. It's hard to go from all those challenges to two toddlers, who can't even get themselves to the bathroom without her help. So what if she gets nice dinners and does the laundry and keeps the house looking spiffy, despite the distractions and fatigue and demands of the kids? What difference does it make? The dinners get eaten and the clothes get dirtied and it all needs to be done again. . . . She hates to keep coming to her husband Chris to be bucked up. She knows he gets tired of telling her over and over again how important she is to him and the kids . . . but she can't help it, she gets so depressed.

She used to enjoy looking sharp. Now she just goes to the local shopping center for cheap haircuts. Since she doesn't bring in any income herself, she doesn't feel right about spending money on herself. She and Chris are planning on private schools, so whatever they can save now is money ahead for that big expense. Maybe when the kids are in school, she can go back to work and come back to life mentally.

Ellen, too, is a child of her age. True, to her credit, she has accepted the responsibilities that come from her decision to be Chris's wife and is doing the best she can by him and the children. But still she is tempted. She can't help it. The life of a suburban wife today is unsatisfying to a woman with an active mind. What use is she anyway? How would the world be different if she didn't exist? What does she have to show for her efforts at the end of the day? She, too, is still seeking a sense of worth from accomplishments.

Mary, Ellen, and the millions of women educated in the postfeminist era, will never be able to relax, to know their true worth, if they rely only on what the world has taught them: that their worth comes from their accomplishments. No tangible accomplishments, no worth. No paychecks, no titles, no value. The world educated them to have functional skills, to be managers, to be executives, to be mathematicians or lawyers or nurses or engineers or teachers or researchers. It is only natural that they want to use those skills. But today there is no place for those skills in the home, no way to harmonize those skills with motherhood. With the rare, rare exception of a home-based or family business, a job-trained woman will feel her talents wasted in motherhood. "Being a mother" is not enough to keep her mind active.

In a more traditional society, Mary or Ellen might have had close friendships with older women, who might have shared with them experience and wisdom and advice on coping. But intergenerational bonds have been broken in modern society: grandmothers bake cookies and invite you to Thanksgiving dinner—they're not your wise confidantes. So Ellen and Mary are isolated from the collective wisdom of their gender.

Mary has devoted herself to rising on the world's ladder of success and has for all practical purposes forsaken any expectation of permanent, meaningful relationships. Ellen wisely chose to give relationships priority but finds that in developing those relationships an important part of her is now useless. She, too, is used to being an activist, to taking on responsibilities. Now she is simply a dependent, in the worst sense of the term. She doesn't mind that Chris supports her; she thinks that's only fair since she's raising the children. But there's an emptiness in her that comes from enforced passivity; she is not a real participant in the economic life of the family, except perhaps as the main spender of her husband's income or as a cottage industrialist, who generates income at home.

To be content with this dependent role, she has to choose: resent the dependence or find grace in it. That's all there is.

Either Resentment or Grace

Either resentment or grace. Modern society is cruel to women. By its very nature it is unkind to and unappreciative of motherhood. If we allow ourselves to be frustrated by the way the world is structured and can't stand the frustration of trying to reconcile motherhood with independence, either one or the other will be thrown overboard. If we abandon motherhood, our children lose, and our future society loses. If we abandon dependency and revert to the way we were trained, to finding our worth in paychecks and achievements, our children lose and our future society loses. It is a no-win situation. Modern society is cruel to women — *if* we accept the modern world's premise about where a woman gets her worth.

Where does the worth of a woman come from? It doesn't come from husbands. It doesn't come from jobs. It doesn't come from children.

Mary and Ellen get their worth from the same place. Their intrinsic worth is a free gift from the same Person. The Son of God died on the Cross for Mary and for Ellen, who never did and never could deserve it. Through the power of that Cross, every emotional need they have can be satisfied. It is not Mary's pay raises or Ellen's children that will matter to them one hundred years from now. But what Christ did for them on the Cross will matter supremely.

God loves Mary and Ellen and all women equally, whether they are chief executive of the world's most important corporation or a nameless housewife or an abandoned prostitute on the streets of Calcutta. In the eyes of God, in the face of His love, they are equal. He knows them alike. All Mary and Ellen need to do is to *allow* God to love them. If they accept God's love, they will know their enormous importance in His eyes. With that will come the peace that passes understanding. Then, having His peace, they can seek His will, and He will give them the strength to do His will each day.

Perhaps Chris will never appreciate Ellen; perhaps Mary will never find a satisfying human relationship. But once they know that they are appreciated — and valued — and cherished by the only Person who matters, His Cross will give them the power to accept gracefully and cheerfully the lot in life He sends them.

If the Lord wants Mary to rise to the top of the corporate world and she conforms her will to His, that's where she will go. If the Lord wants Ellen to be a successful mother and she conforms herself to His will, her family will rise up and call her blessed. But it will not be Mary's efforts that win her promotions, and it will not be Ellen's initiatives that give joy to her family. It will be the Lord building the house of their lives. For "except the Lord build the house, they labour in vain that build it" (Psalm 127:1).

PART 3

THE RESTORATION
OF MOTHERHOOD

ON TALENTS AND WASTE
(How I Came to Be a Myrrh-Bearer)

The wisdom that is from above is first
pure, then peaceable, gentle . . . full of
mercy and good fruits.

James 3:17

A few years ago, I was pretty much like Mary. I had a full-time career on Capitol Hill: I was chairman of the National Pro-Family Coalition, which was a critical ingredient of family politics. An ordinary day began with a breakfast meeting and ended with a dinner meeting. At least once a month, and usually more often, I traveled around the country. I didn't have any great salary, alas, and no blue-chip investments. But I did have a company car that I had been able to choose, and it had a telephone in it. Which, believe me, was used every minute of the time I was in the car.

But in one respect I was different from Mary. I had a husband and two children. Mary, at least, was keeping her life manageable: she had only her own needs to worry about, and with her schedule, that was about all she could manage. My problem was that although my schedule was not too dissimilar from hers, I was trying to meet the needs of a husband and two children. Well, actually, I *wasn't* trying to meet their needs, but I *should* have been.

Today, thanks be to God, I still have the same husband and two children, now teenagers. I am home full time with a two-year-old and a new arrival due in a matter of weeks. (If you're hurrying to read this book, imagine how I'm hurrying to write it!)

When I was a career woman, I believed in the same traditional values I believe in today. How, then, did I come to live the opposite of what I believed?

And, more important, how did I come to where I am today? What changed me? How did I change from total immersion in a demanding career to total (well, almost total) immersion in domesticity?

I was raised pretty much like my hypothetical Mary. From the time I can remember, my mother talked about the careers my sister and I would have and prepared us for them. My mother also urged me, "For heaven's sake, don't get married young. Your life is over when you have children." I couldn't understand how she could say that when she herself had children, but then mothers are inscrutable.

I was sent to Catholic schools for the superior education, not because my parents expected me to take the religion seriously. Nonetheless, when I was in fourth grade I consecrated my life to Jesus and absorbed everything I could understand about pursuing holiness. Alas, my conversion was like the seeds that fell among the weeds. The weeds grew faster than the faith. We changed schools, and the Catholic church changed, too. By the time I went to high school, loving God was an abstract memory.

A friend dragged me to prayer meetings for a while after I graduated from college, and something began to stir in those seeds. But by then I was in love with politics. And shortly thereafter, along came Bill Marshner. From the first time I met him, I knew that I wouldn't be satisfied with any other man, even though it was a year before I saw him for the second time and then another six months before he began courting me. The amazing thing to me now is that I never had the slightest doubt about the rightness of my marrying him: looking back, I count that as a gift of discernment from the Holy Spirit.

Not, mind you, that I was in the least prepared for marriage. I only knew one thing about marriage. But if I had to get married knowing only one thing, it was the right thing to know. Bill and I both knew that it was forever. Period. No ifs, ands, or buts about it. Nonnegotiable permanence. I didn't know how to be a godly wife; I didn't know much about how to be a mother. But I knew that this was going to last. No matter what, we could count on having each other forever.

Nor did I have anybody to teach me. Just as Number One Son was arriving, Bill went to graduate school, and the savings we had accumulated by my working a year were quickly consumed. By the time he finished graduate school, we had two babies and were broke, living in one of the most expensive cities in the country. Guess who ended up back in the work force pretty quickly? Bill completely endorsed my working in politics and believed that as a woman defending traditional values, I had a unique contribution to make to politics. He was my strongest encourager. I loved politics, too, and I loved the chance to make a difference in history. Family issues were just coming into their own; the nation was finally turning its attention to moral concerns. Workers in the vineyard were needed, and I happened to be in the right place at the right time. I felt that God had put me in this position for this reason. And so the priority shifted without either of us realizing what was happening: instead of getting up in the morning wondering what I was going to do that day for the family, I woke up thinking about what I could do to win the political battle of the moment.

By 1980, the year the boys were five and three, I was working full time and traveling on alternate weekends (that year I was on ninety-nine airplanes—I counted them). When my aunt moved from California to Virginia for the express purpose of keeping the kids, there was no holding back. By then, unlimited opportunities presented themselves to my talents. I always figured that as long as I didn't promote myself, whatever happened would be God's will. Of course, I didn't talk to God much—too busy, you know—so I figured that He'd speak to me through events. I was the girl who couldn't say no to a worthy enterprise. My aunt really meant keeping the kids, too. She wasn't interested in any day-care arrangement. They lived with her. So, for that matter, did Bill—since she lived closer to his job than to mine, the family center of gravity shifted. Actually, we had two centers of gravity: Bill had his, and I had mine. On weekends, we met at the place we called "home," which was like a moon to our two suns.

The Seduction of Career

Now why am I telling you all this? Because it's important to understand the *seduction* of a career. I had never intended to have a career. I had always figured that when I had children I would become a full-time mom. But economic necessity, combined with my ability and an opportunity to do more than supplement the family income, just sort of took over our lives. We continued all along to go to the same church and hear the gospel preached, and participate in the sacraments. We just never thought that it would matter to God how *we* lived *our* lives. In principle, I guess at any point we would have told you that God cared about each of us. But in practice, well, we never thought about it.

Why was this possible? I have thought and prayed about it, and I can pinpoint a couple of things that predisposed me to be seduced by career.

1) I had absorbed all that feminist preaching from my mother. I didn't think I was a feminist — in fact, I debated feminists on television. But I lived like one without realizing it. I had learned at my mother's knee that the only things that mattered were the achievements and rewards of the world; that a woman shouldn't have to depend on a man for anything; that life wasn't worth anything if you didn't control your own destiny; and that children were slavery. Does it seem contradictory that I was defending traditional values on the public stage and living such a nontraditional life? It shouldn't. I was defending traditional values out of a deeply held intellectual conviction. But I was living my life out of a deeply held emotional disposition. I still hold the intellectual conviction — it was correct to begin with. But through the grace of God the emotional disposition is being healed.

Maybe you didn't get the feminist preaching from your mother. Maybe you got it at school instead. But it has some attractiveness, doesn't it? It makes you feel important, and you deserve more than a life of mere domesticity. Right? Don't think that just because you're a believing Christian you're immune to the lure of feminism. What your mind believes and what your emotions dictate can be two very different things, and you might not realize the contradiction.

2) I was a lousy housekeeper, and I knew it. I also knew that Bill wasn't too happy with my housekeeping. But I didn't know what to do

about it. I mean, how do you go up to another woman and say, Could you please teach me how to tidy the house before my husband gets home in the evening? At least, when I had a political accomplishment to share with him, he enjoyed it and felt proud of me. Can you blame me for wanting to please my husband? As I saw it, that's what I was doing. The only woman I turned to for advice urged me to hire a maid. Well, we couldn't afford that. But getting the kids out of the way kept the house a whole lot neater.

Most college-educated women today don't know how to keep house. We were never taught—so we can't blame ourselves. But there are books and other resources available.[1] Or better yet, ask some of the Naomis in your church to give the young Ruths like you a few lessons. Would be a great ladies' club talk, wouldn't it? Who knows, popular demand might turn it into a whole series.

3) I was totally unprepared, as was Bill, for little children. The first newborn I ever held was my son Pearse. Apart from the occasional babysitting job in high school, I had never spent any time with toddlers. I had no idea how to handle them. I had no idea what kind of chaos they could create. I had no idea how to cope with it all. And, again, nobody to ask. I felt inferior to women I knew who had raised large families, but I admired them from a distance. The occasional conversational foray about how they did it was always brushed off with a self-deprecating laugh. These women seemed to think there was nothing to their accomplishment, so I felt really dumb and worthless in comparison. Here I was in knots, and they shrugged it off as nothing. What was wrong with me? Much easier to pay attention to the political world, where I could do something and get results that pleased people.

If you are a successful mother and a younger woman asks you how you do it, don't laugh away her question, thinking you're being modest. She's probably crying out for help! Since more and more women are growing up as I did and coming into marriage without any experience of children, a church that wants to be of help to its flock—and here especially, the new Christians, the ones who may not have grown up around Christian families, are needy—might organize a "family internship" as part of the marriage preparation program or maybe before the birth of the first baby. Arrange for—even require—the young couple to spend five days with another family, a family that has young children, just so they can observe them, see them coping, ask them questions, and in general get some idea what to expect for themselves. Later on, the experienced family will be a wonderful close resource for the young family, which in itself will address the biggest problem a new mother has: isolation from other women.

4) We wanted to own our own house someday and knew there was no way we could ever, ever do that on Bill's income. I mean, I *really* wanted my own house. I felt I was *entitled* to it.

5) We had no accountability. Nobody ever suggested we needed to reevaluate the direction of our lives. My parents, needless to say, were tremendously pleased that their little girl was making something of herself—they were pretty unhappy when I married so young and then totally wrote me off when I had a baby less than two years later. So nothing from that quarter but encouragement for my political activity. Bill's parents, if they had reservations, kept them to themselves. And there was nobody else. Our pastor may or may not have been aware of how out of control our lives were, but if he was, I guess he didn't figure it was his business to meddle. We wouldn't have gone to him for advice—after all, we didn't think we needed any. I can see now that anybody who had spoken truth to us would have had a cold reception; we would have defended ourselves to the core.

I don't blame anybody for not talking turkey to us. But if somebody objective and loving and with some degree of authority had spent an evening with us and asked us to evaluate our family life, it just might have provoked some self-examination. I was aware from time to time of gossip about the contradictions in our life—but unless somebody cared enough to say something to my face, I wasn't about to pay attention to it. Hearing such things in the rumor mill only made me resent them. You may know people right now who are living contradictions. How can you help them? Don't comment behind their backs, no matter what! Pray about it, get some facts—it may be that things are not what they seem. But if you still feel concern, don't keep silent. Perhaps a diplomatic conversation with the pastor or deacon might suggest some action that a person in authority could take. If that doesn't work, become friends with the family yourself. Show them some kindnesses—that will give you, in time, authority to speak to them. Even if they reject the advice, continue the kindnesses. You might be surprised at the seeds you have planted in their minds!

Those were some of the predisposing factors. Not excuses. Just explanations of why I was so vulnerable.

I know I'm not unique. I know there are people reading this who are in exactly the same boat, maybe with children still preschool age. Maybe they don't know how they have ended up in the situation they're in and are having a few flickers of doubt.

If that's you, please read on.

What Is Waste? What Are Talents?

If you have doubts about whether you have prioritized your life correctly, if you are feeling torn between your child and something else you do, chances are the Spirit of the Lord is nudging you gently, patiently, to take a look at your life. The Lord nudged me like that a lot over those years of activism, but I didn't look as closely as I should have because I was afraid of what I would see.

I was afraid I would see that God wanted me to be a housewife, that He wanted to sentence me to be the jewel on the bottom of the sea or the flower in the desert — unknown, unsung, and unappreciated — and I wasn't about to let that happen. Not only did He want me to disappear for all practical purposes from the face of the earth, but He wanted to sentence me to the thing I was least able to do!

> Full many a gem of purest ray serene
> The deep, unfathomed caves of ocean bear;
> Full many a flower is born to blush unseen,
> And waste its sweetness on the desert air.

That poem, "Elegy Written in a Country Churchyard," is a classic of English romanticism. I memorized it young and clasped it to my bosom. The point of that stanza is the tragedy of someone's talents being unknown and undeveloped. Now, I had studied the parable of the talents, and I took that to mean that whatever talents God gave you He wanted you to develop. If you had a talent to play the piano, for instance, God sort of expected you to take lessons and practice. I counted myself lucky that my first-grade music teacher had pronounced me singularly without musical talent, so that burdensome task did not fall upon my shoulders. All through life, however, I felt very keenly the obligation to use all my talents.

I could write; later, I found I could speak publicly; still later, I realized that my basic Irish unwillingness to concede a point could make me a "good debater." Well, you can't write with little kids around, and there's no need to speak publicly, and it's not good to argue with your husband—so obviously those talents would be unused if I simply stayed home and wasted my sweetness on the desert air.

There were two things wrong with my thinking. First, definition of "talents." Second, definition of "waste."

In that parable (Matthew 25:14–30) Scripture is not talking about worldly abilities: the Lord is talking about His spiritual gifts to us, His grace! If He gave me the grace to do something and I chose to ignore His grace, He would hold me far more strictly accountable for that than if I left untrained a mere fleshly talent. Yes, God also gives us human talents, and they should be developed, developed to bring glory to Him. And I have tried to develop my children's talents. Far more important than developing the mere human talent, though, is to develop the spiritual disposition to use the talent for the glory of God.

I had grown up with the erroneous idea that God helps those who help themselves. I knew my abilities came from God, so I somehow had the idea that I had to help myself from then on. How many other Christians have the same idea, perhaps not even knowing they do? How many times have you heard the same thing said? But it's nowhere in Scripture. What can be found in Scripture are many instances of God helping those who depend on Him and submit to Him—quite the opposite of relying on themselves.

I haven't met many women my age who share my preoccupation with using my talents. I suspect, however, that women who grew up and were educated ten or fifteen years after me, after feminist attitudes had permeated our culture a bit more, have the same compulsion that I had. And many women my age do share my erroneous idea of waste. Absolutely the best response to that is in a little pamphlet called *Why This Waste?* by Watchman Nee.

Watchman Nee points out that Judas had the same attitude toward waste! That's right. Remember when Mary came and washed Jesus' feet with her tears and dried them with her hair? Then she poured pure nard upon His feet, "and the fragrance filled the house." The host of this house had been remiss in the usual courtesy toward guests: it was the custom to provide a guest with a basin of water to get the dust off his feet. But Mary more than made up for his oversight. Judas, however, resented it. Of all the people to complain that the Master was being shown honor! Of course, Judas disguised his resentment in altruistic rhetoric: the ointment could have been sold and the money given to the poor, he said (John 12:5).

What did the Lord say? "Verily I say unto you, Wheresoever the gospel shall be preached throughout the whole world, that also which this woman hath done, shall be spoken of for a memorial of her" (Mark 14:9). Mary's action has His full endorsement: it is not a waste, He implies, to give all you have to God. Yes, the money could have been used in another way. But use is not what God cares about. "The service of the Lord is not to be measured by tangible results," says Nee. "No, my friends, the Lord's first concern is with our position at His feet and our anointing of His head."[2] Staying at home, fixing meals, vacuuming living rooms — if done out of love for God and for the family — is a modern way of anointing His head.

The Myrrh-Bearers

After the Crucifixion, most of the followers of Christ were frightened and in hiding. But Mary of Magdala wanted to show one last honor to her Lord, so she purchased myrrh and spices to anoint His body. Together with a few other women, she went to the tomb to give the final gift of love and reverence to the Anointed One. That courageous journey, undertaken purely out of love, won for Mary Magdalene the unique privilege of being the first person to whom the risen Lord appeared.

For He appeared to her in the garden while she was still trying to figure out who had taken the body. When she recognized Him who she thought was the gardener, what did He say to her? First, He gently turned aside her spontaneous embrace: "Touch me not; for I am not yet ascended to my father" (John 20:17). Then He told her "Go to my brethren, and say unto them, I ascend unto my Father and your Father, and to my God and your God" (John 20:17).

Mary, a woman, became the first messenger sent by the Lord Himself to announce the good news of the Resurrection. She was the apostle to the apostles.[3] Not because she was especially brilliant, not because she had led other people. Simply because she was *faithful to His needs*. She served Him. That's all: she just followed where service led.

The importance of this began to dawn on me after I heard a sermon by David Hester. In the life of the church, women, he noted, are analogous to the Holy Spirit. The essence of femininity is response. The church is feminine, since it is a response to a call from God. So, for that matter, is creation. The Holy Spirit also responds to our needs, coming with His light and His comfort. "The Spirit of truth . . . shall not speak of himself. . . " (John 16:13). The Spirit does not exalt Himself, but He does what needs to be done; He "shows you things to come." Holy women do not exalt themselves, do not speak of themselves, but respond to the needs of those they love.

Who is the preeminent myrrh-bearer of our day? Mother Teresa of Calcutta, without doubt. There's a woman who influences the lives of millions. But feminists don't admire her. Why? Because her influence is unsought, because it comes through service. From love and service, Mother Teresa establishes true authority. Not power, not the kind of power feminists see lurking under every bush. But real authority.

A mother is the ultimate myrrh-bearer. The essence of motherhood is response: our bodies respond to the first hint of pregnancy; our emotions and minds continue to respond. The baby is born, and everything in us wants to care for him: cuddle him, swaddle him, nurse him, keep him close. Some of this is spontaneous and natural; some of it is learned. But long after the first rush of those maternal hormones at the time of delivery, mothers are still serving. It is a decision of the will that enables a mother to submit herself to the reality of other people's needs.

That's what it is: submission to the needs of others. Certainly not to their wills (mothers who fail to maintain authority rear whining spoiled brats), but a willing suspension of one's own desires for the welfare of the children. Sure, Mom would love to save herself some work and buy gourmet stuffed pork chops, already stuffed by the butcher. But they cost $7.00 a pound, and because she doesn't want the kids to go without milk, she settles for some regular pork chops instead, which she can get for less than $4.00 a pound. More likely, she waits until chicken thighs go on sale for $.48 a pound and then stocks up on them and rice. Mom would like a new outfit, but the kids have outgrown theirs, so guess who gets the new clothes?

Dad, too, would love to buy tickets to the playoffs and go see his favorite team compete for the championship. But he knows the school tuition payments are due, so he denies himself. The Christian ideal is for husband to submit to his wife and children. Far from being the petty tyrant that feminist caricatures make of him, the godly husband is motivated by the needs of his wife and children and in love serves their needs before his own desires and needs. Whatever his personal, intimate response to his family, his primary responsibility is to go out and earn money amidst strangers so that the mother of his children can minister personally to them.

It's not that Mom is a martyr. To be sure, sometimes she may feel like one, and so, for that matter, may Dad. But that is a dangerous, destructive temptation of self-pity. Giving in to such a temptation will not only undermine the good the actual sacrifice may accomplish; it will destroy the parents' relationship with the children and with each other, and it will feed a progressively greater depression. Satan loves self-pity; it gives him such a field day.

Rebellion or Submission

Mothers make sacrifices willingly, out of love. Christian mothers make them gladly because they are myrrh-bearers. Like the Holy Spirit, a mother responds to the needs of her children (and husband!). Because often those needs control her life in turn, serving them is indeed submission of her will to God's will. But if you're doing what God wants you to be doing, how can you be wasting yourself? If God thought of you from all eternity and created you so that this moment you could respond to the cry of that child, whom He also thought of from all eternity and gave to you and nobody else to mother—how can you be wasting yourself? This is what you were born for! So what if the baby will cry again and the meals will need to be fixed again? You were created by God, from all eternity, to comfort that baby and feed that family.

There are only two responses: one, decorate it how you will with high-sounding rhetoric, comes down to this: "I don't want to." The other comes down to this: "Yes, Lord." Rebellion or submission. No other choice.

Submission is an unpopular word today. Self-determination is all the style. But self-determination puts Self in the driver's seat. Don't we want God to be in charge? He always is in charge, of course, but do we want to continually fight Him? The only way around it is to submit our will to Him, not just to *do* what He wants us to, but to *want* what He wants. That's the spirit of obedience, of submission.

This kind of submission requires more strength than leadership because the challenge is not to compete with other people but to compete with the flesh and the Devil. Boring? No way. It's the greatest struggle in the world, the same struggle that occupied every hero or heroine of the faith you have ever admired. There's glory in submission, not shame. That's the secret a Christian knows that the world does not.

After all, even God Himself did what He is asking mothers to do. He came down and took flesh and walked among us—to serve us: "Who, being in the form of God . . . made himself of no reputation, and took upon him the form of a servant . . . and became obedient unto death" (Philippians 2:6–8).

Reevaluating my idea of waste showed me that nothing done out of love for God is wasted. Learning about myrrh-bearers helped me to understand service as the essence of femininity. Realizing that my Savior had stripped Himself of fame and power in order to be an obedient servant gave me access to humility I did not know I could have. This new understanding was the beginning of the spiritual struggle to hang on to the grace and the energy to live according to it.

It was a new idea, and once I was used to it, I rather liked the idea of being a myrrh-bearer. At least it gave me something to be, now that I could no longer say I was "editor," "chairman," or member of the executive committee of this or that. "Myrrh-bearer." Sounds nice as a job title, doesn't it? Next time I have to fill out a form that asks for my occupation, should I write in "myrrh-bearer"?

OPTIONS FOR A WORKING MOTHER

(From Tag Teams to Home Businesses)

O LORD, give me understanding according to thy word.

Psalm 119:169

B y now, some readers are mad at me. "Okay, Connie," they say, "this is all fine. I knew it already. I never had your hangups about waste and talents and that sort of stuff. But I'm a mother of young children, and I work outside the home. What does that make me in your view, some kind of pagan?"

No. Not at all. It's your own internal disposition, your own attitude, that decides how God feels about your working. I would not presume to judge you, and neither should anybody else. Only God knows whether you are working out of an attitude of service and love or out of less pure motives. Only you know your circumstances. Only you, and your husband if you have one, can make decisions for your family.

I do want to tell you one thing, though. If you're working and your children are small, *be careful*. When I was in politics, I thought I had the best possible substitute-care arrangement for my boys. It was so good, I never worried about it. My aunt was more patient and more fun loving than I. And she loved the boys enormously. I thought that was all that was necessary. She lived in the country, in a big house on a mountain, where they could have dogs and cats and open air. I sincerely believed the kids were better off there than they would have been at home with me. Now that the two boys are teenagers and the doting aunt is out of the picture, they're suffering a lot because they weren't disciplined adequately and because Bill and I weren't the ones to meet their needs as small children. I mention that by way of warning anybody who may be where I was ten years ago: the piper will have to be paid sooner or later, and when your innocent children are the ones who end up paying, it hurts you triply. You suffer for them, you suffer because of them, and you suffer with them.

Tag-Team Parents

How can you minimize the harm to your children of your working? Well, the first way is by attention to your schedule. If your job and his permit it, arrange with your husband to be Tag-Team Parents.

Can you arrange to work when your husband is home? If so, the kids may notice that Mom has gone, but since Dad is here and attentive to them, it makes scarcely any practical difference. If Dad can do what you do when you're home—namely, pay attention to the children, talk to them, listen to them, follow the schedule and practices they are familiar with—consider yourself very lucky. More likely, Dad reads his paper or works on his projects while the children play around him. When it comes to feeding them or putting them to bed, he'll do it in his own way—maybe not on your schedule and maybe not with the food you had planned to serve. But it'll get done, and they'll all be with each other at home, so don't sweat the small stuff. If Dad keeps forgetting to give a certain medicine or ignores a certain diet, deal with it as soon as you notice it because fathers are creatures of habit, and habits get set early with fathers and kids.

One word of caution: try to keep a brake on Dad's amusing the kids to death. When I traveled before my aunt came, Bill handled the home front on weekends. Twenty-four hours a day! I usually had meals prepared ahead and didn't expect any domestic chores to get done, but even so, as you can see, Bill is an unusual husband! Things seemed to go smoothly enough. He was happy; the boys were happy. Later on, I discovered that one of the ways he passed the time was to take the kids to the movies, complete with popcorn and candy, or otherwise out for entertainments. When I was on duty, of course, I did just routine things, and they yearned for more sparkling entertainment. Naturally, the boys got to think their Dad was infinitely more fun than Mom . . . an attitude that has persisted to this very day. At the time I was just glad the kids were being taken here or there, but in retrospect I can see that I should at least have been along with them so that they could think of their mom as capable of having fun. As it is, one of the charges I'm always hearing from my teenaged know-it-alls is that I don't know how to have any fun. Even though all teenagers say something like that at some time, this oversight on our part may have given ours a basis for it. They hardly ever saw their mother having fun.

The other big downside to tag-team parenting is that the adults have hardly any adult time with each other. They may see each other across a breakfast or dinner table but find themselves primarily exchanging scheduling information and child-status reports: "I have to be in early every day next week; we've got big shots from out of town coming." "Katy had a runny nose." "Lemuel next door has chicken pox. We'd better be watching fourteen days from now to see if ours get tired or feverish." "My boss is thinking of shifting me over to afternoons. If he did that, would you be able to go in at six and get home by four?" And so on. Too much of this can put a damper on even the fondest relationship.

The answer? If you can afford it, hire a babysitter and go out on a date with your husband, maybe even an overnighter together. But you probably wouldn't be working if you could afford luxuries like that. So just resolve that one night a week, whatever night suits your schedule, will be sacred time. Both of you will be home that night (nobody can routinely work seven nights a week—it isn't humanly sustainable), and make a genuine effort to get the routine stuff out of the way before the kids get to bed. In other words, don't tell yourself you'll pay the bills then or do the bathrooms, no matter how strong the temptation may be. Promise each other and stick to it. When the kids go to bed, take the phone off the hook, and pay attention to each other. Bake up a foolishly fancy dessert together; then turn out all the lights and eat the dessert by candlelight in front of a window (or outdoors if it's summer). Watch a romantic movie together. Work on the family photo album together, and reminisce while you do it. Take a bath together. Anything you can enjoy. Just do it faithfully, and try not to talk about the kids or money while you're doing it. After all, you have this tough schedule because you loved each other so much that you had these children to whom you are now devoting your energies. Don't get so preoccupied with the needs of the children that you forget how you came to have them in the first place![1]

"Doubletime" Mothering

The next most popular way to have a job and take care of your children yourself is "doubletime" mothering.

What is "doubletime" mothering? It is having your children present at the same time you are earning money. You know, what those tremendously well-paid television anchorwomen do when they demand a nursery next door to their office after they have a baby. Not too many office jobs allow you to take your child or children with you, of course. But other types of work may: being a school bus driver comes to mind as one example. With infant seats in the school bus, the driver can care for her own small ones while she earns some supplemental income.

Most young women who earn money at home practice some kind of "doubletime" mothering. The range of home-based business is as unlimited as your imagination. In many ways, it is an idea whose time has come. Home employment has grown by about 7.5 percent every year since 1985. The Bureau of Labor Statistics of the U.S. Department of Labor indicates that about 2.5 million Americans were employed full time at home as of 1987. If the figures include part-time or occasional work, the total expands to 23.8 million home workers. This was up from the expanded total of 18.1 million in 1985! This growing trend obviously benefits women, but 52 percent of those working at home are men![2] Many of them working for other employers.

Men and women who have advanced to a certain level in certain careers are able, thanks to the miracles of microtechnology, to turn their homes into offices through computers, facsimile machines, copiers, and other high-tech machinery. In the kind of career where results matter more than time logged in at the office, telecommuting is a growing trend. In the era of highway gridlock, when commuting from home to work can occupy three or more hours a day, many high-level producers are simply not willing to put up with the hassle. Their employers don't want to lose them to another firm, so arrangements are worked out. "If you do the job and do it well, then it doesn't matter where you work," says one woman who runs a firm out of her kitchen.[3]

But it's not just self-starters who are able to take advantage of the trend. The Travelers insurance company, for instance, finds that allowing employees to telecommute can increase worker productivity by as much as 25 percent. Routine computer work doesn't always need to be done in an office, and smart companies who don't want to lose trusted employees are willing to experiment.

Many businesses are run from the home, and about 70 percent of such businesses are managed by women. Home-based business is a wide-open arena for energetic, creative women who have a skill to sell. A woman in Minneapolis makes liturgical garments in her home. A woman in New Jersey consults with architects and builders on energy efficiency. Women run travel agencies and camp consulting businesses in their homes. Flavia Moskaitis, one of my neighbors, runs a baking business from her home. Her partner, Kathy Hinkle, lives nearby. The county (which considers it a catering business) requires that cooking be done in inspected facilities, so when there's an order to fill, they rent a restaurant kitchen during mornings or late nights to get the job done. Having a partnership means they can trade child care during the summer, and their pre-schoolers are learning a lot about baking at a young age!

Lots of women have typing and secretarial businesses at home. Psychologists can continue their careers from their homes. Calligraphy and other design work are popular among women who formerly did it for one employer. Accounting is popular; translators frequently work from home. Plant counseling and care are enterprises that wouldn't survive everywhere, but Sherrill Boggs in Columbia City, Indiana, has made a go of it. Moving consultant is a fairly new job description, but with close to 20 percent of the American population moving every year, why not? One of the newest ideas is lactation consulting: women who have been deeply involved in La Leche League are finding a way to turn a few dollars out of their expertise, selling their advice instead of dispensing it for free.

Arlene Enos in San Bruno, California, was a dental prosthetic technologist who not only made dental devices but had a sideline in jewelry. Another neighbor of mine, Dee Dahm, is a former teacher who supplements her income with tutoring. Her home-schooled children have a bread-baking business as well. Well, I think you get the picture: aspiring home-based business led by women is a movement that is here to stay.[4]

Be aware that any home-based business that deals with the public or gets fairly large is likely to come to the attention of local bureaucrats one way or another. Jealous and officious neighbors might make sure the local government knows what you're doing. Many counties, particularly in urban areas, have beastly regulations. Some counties even have special "residence employment" taxes that they'll slap on to home-based workers. You might want to check into such things before you begin; I have a friend in Fairfax County, Virginia, who didn't and got some surprise bills for back taxes from the county.

Home Business Pitfalls

There are other pitfalls to generating income at home. If you are working on deadlines and must gather information from the outside world during regular business hours, you will need to have somebody else supervising your young children in the home during working hours.

Let me tell you a story. It's hilarious to me now, but at the time it was awful. I was writing a series of articles for a newspaper chain on Planned Parenthood. Now, this was way back in 1979, back when I was only working part time and Planned Parenthood was still something of a sacred cow. I had to interview Jeanne Rosoff, then the head of the Washington office. I called her early in the day, hoping she might return my call while the boys were napping. But no such luck, of course. I was fixing dinner when the call came back. Since I had a deadline, I had to take the call right then. Nowadays, I'd be cool and tell her secretary that we needed to schedule a telephone appointment, but I was young and anxious, and that never occurred to me. Besides, this was Planned Parenthood! I wanted to seem professional—and of all the people to be interviewing with children's noises in the background! I was embarrassed at the thought. It was summer, and the kids were playing on the back patio. So I quietly locked the patio door while I ran upstairs to take the call. It went on longer than I expected, and the boys became unhappy in the back yard. Finding they couldn't get in the door, they left the yard and went to the neighbors' house. I conducted most of my interview to the sounds of the boys crying outside, telling the neighbor that "Mommy went somewhere and left us alone," and hearing the neighbors (another mother got in the act) tsk-tsking and conferring under my window about what to do. I was glad that Jeanne Rosoff couldn't hear all this, but regarding my neighbors it was one of the most embarrassing moments in my life. Somehow, the interview was conducted, and I raced downstairs to greet my distressed children, and reassure my neighbors that indeed I had not abandoned my children.

My problem with the Planned Parenthood interview was unusual, but my sister-in-law Susan faced the same situation every day for years. Susan and her husband ran their computer services company out of their home. They rented a house that had a large basement, which they filled up with computer equipment and printers. Employees came and went throughout the day and evening.

When the babies first came, Susan tried to stay upstairs. But employees came upstairs and seated themselves at the kitchen table for lunch, expecting her to chat. They didn't seem to realize she was busy as well. Eventually, to save the expense of hiring somebody, she took over keeping the books for the business. She kept her desk upstairs so that she could have some measure of quiet to order supplies, call customers who hadn't paid their bills, and so forth. Before her children started school, though, it was a constant struggle. At one point she hired women to come in and watch the boys during her office hours. But since she couldn't hire somebody full time, nobody lasted very long, and just as the boys became comfortable with one woman, she'd be off to a full-time job.

During the summer it was easier: outdoors beckoned, and junior-high girls in the neighborhood could be found to take care of the kids for a couple hours. But there was no clear distinction in the children's mind between Mommy at the Desk and Mommy otherwise. So still there were interruptions. The boys came to her with complaints about the babysitter: "Mommy, make her give me a popsicle." Occasionally, my son babysat. If he tried to enforce a command the boys didn't like, they went right away and interrupted their mom with their complaints.

I, too, did a long stint of working at home. When I finally came to the conclusion that full-time political employment wasn't right for me, I began to phase out of activism by degrees. One of the stages was to edit *Family Protection Report* at home while I was still chairing the Pro-Family Coalition. Producing this monthly newsletter required me to be in the office supervising the actual production only about two days a month. Several other days, on average, were required to attend events about which I was writing, and maybe twenty hours a month of interviews and information gathering by telephone. This work load was compatible with being a full-time mommy. But running the coalition was never-ending because it not only involved keeping current on all the developments on Capitol Hill affecting family politics issues; it also required continual networking with the forty or so members of the coalition. Still, thanks to a telephone answering machine, I was able to home school my children in the mornings and work at the desk in the afternoons.

My kids were older than Susan's—third and sixth grade—when we began this system. After morning home school, we ate lunch. Then I went to the desk and they did homework and special school projects. While I might leave the desk briefly to help with homework or remind about chores, afternoons were primarily Mommy's office hours, and the boys knew it. The system worked, but in my commitment to my desk I forfeited part of the fun of home school.

After homework, Pearse and Mike did their chores, usually until their friends came home from school. My boys understood that if they came to Mommy when she was on the phone, they'd better stand in silence until she hung up. When they couldn't wait for the conversation to end, they learned how to pass me notes: "kan i pley with josh?" is one I came across in a file just the other day.

Eventually, I realized that having office hours all afternoon, which was necessary to do the job and keep my political self current, was depriving the boys of a mommy who was just a mommy: they saw me as teacher and businesswoman, but rarely was I just a mommy. I was constantly preoccupied from what the Lord was increasingly showing me was His will for me, namely, mothering those boys. So, eventually, I was moved to write my letter of resignation from *Family Protection Report* and the National Pro-Family Coalition. As if to ratify my decision, shortly thereafter I discovered I was pregnant, something we had wanted for a long time. It was as if the Lord said: All right, Connie. Now that I know you're serious about doing right by the children I have given you, I will send you another.

Guidelines for Home Work

If my job had been more limited, say just writing the newsletter, I think I probably could have kept it going for years. But the unpredictable and unending telephone work was a killer. First advice to aspiring home-based businesswomen: *put limits on your work.* Decide what your job will be, and then say no to add-on projects. Whether you're working for yourself or for somebody else, set your limits and stick to them.

Second advice: *decide what your image will be.* If you want to appear professional, you will have to build higher walls between your maternal self and your business self. You have to decide what your market will bear and what you're comfortable with. People who are ordering five thousand brownies probably don't care if they hear children playing in the background; clients who are calling for investment advice might not like it; people who haven't paid their bills might not take you seriously if they think you're just a mom-and-pop business. After you've thought this through, decide how you're going to handle your child-care duties.

Third advice: *plan your hours so your work time doesn't conflict with your mothering duties.* If you work alone at something creative, like designing jewelry, and the work isn't deadline driven, then plan on napping when the kids do and working into the night. If you're trying to do your work during the same hours that your children need you, you'll go crazy: one or the other will have to take priority, and if it's the children, your work will suffer.

If your work is for somebody else and is deadline driven and your children are small, plan on making arrangements for the children outside the home. Or get in-home care, but squirrel yourself away in a closed room and *be unavailable* and mean it. This will cost, but it will be a business expense. Then you can have certain mornings and certain hours when you belong to the company. For your peace of mind, as well as for getting the job done, you need this. As the children get older, perhaps you can have your company hours when they are present, but you must teach them from the beginning that you do not belong to them during those hours. This is tough. It is not ideal. You may feel guilty (After all, it's my kids' home. Why can't they be in it? . . . I'm their mother. Why can't they have access to me? . . .). If you do, home-based business might not be what you need right now. If you're constantly feeling guilty, your kids will sense your vulnerability and instinctively play on it. You won't be an effective disciplinarian to them. Remember that if you're doing this work to buy them food, you don't need to feel guilty; plenty of kids throughout the history of mankind have had to endure worse afflictions.

Some kinds of work, like certain crafts or plant-care or pet-care or cleaning businesses, can be done with well-behaved children around. And children can even be meaningfully involved in some home-based businesses.

Still, it's evident by now why the most common way of "double-time" mothering is to take care of other children for money while you're taking care of your own for love. This is the burgeoning industry known as family day care. More about that shortly.

Relative Care

Meanwhile, back to your child-care options as a working mother. Having a relative take care of a baby under a year old is the most popular child care for working mothers of infants. That's understandable since the relative is likely to be the baby's grandmother and can be counted on to pay lots of attention. Nationally, about 11 percent of all child-care arrangements for preschool children involve relatives. Many of the arrangements are free, an added attraction.

The solution is not problem proof, however. Relatives who are older than you may do things their way if they have a mental attitude toward you as a perpetual kid yourself. With an infant that probably won't matter so much. But by toddlerhood, the handling of discipline and eating habits can be very important. Lifelong problems with food can begin before age two, you know. And by preschool age, training both in behavior and attitudes is probably the paramount issue in a child's life. If you and your relative cannot be on the same wavelength on this point, you have to make some changes. Painful as they may be to the relative ("I was good enough when you needed me, but now you think somebody else can do better"), to you ("I do love you, and I do appreciate you, but I know what's best for my children"), and to the children ("You're mean, Mommy, to make us leave Nana's house"), if you can't get all the significant adults in your child's life to sing off the same sheet of music on basic authority issues, you're doing a long-range kindness to your children to remove them from the situation.

How drastic you must be depends on how serious is the undermining of your authority. If Grandma is telling your children that you and your husband are fanatics because you go to a weird church and it is unfair that you force the children to go too, that should not be tolerated. If she merely gives them more cookies than you want them to have, you might want to change your standards a little bit. Of course, even unlimited cookies can be serious if one of your children is diabetic. You must use good judgment to protect your children and preserve basic parental authority.

Perhaps the relative who is taking care of your children has deep racial prejudices, and your children are beginning to pick up attitudes and terminology that signal their absorption of those attitudes. No, daycare workers may not be perfect either, but at least they won't be likely to express their personal opinions on the job. They know they might get fired for it. Maybe your children make fun of each other, and you want them taught to repent to each other and forgive each other, and your relative says: "Don't be silly. They don't know what repentance means, they're only three and four. Besides, they might as well get thick skins now, the world isn't going to be sensitive to their feelings." Now, a worker in a day-care center isn't going to teach repentance and forgiveness either, but at least she will not be a *significant* adult to the children. Children can understand "This is the way we do things in our family. Strangers may do it differently, but this is our way." But they can't understand "This is the way Mommy and Daddy do it, but Grandma will want you to do it differently." That confusion is harmful. And if Grandma happens to be doting and indulgent, Mom and Dad will suffer by comparison in the child's mind. That lays the groundwork for confusion and conflict later on.

Family Day Care

The most popular day care for preschool children is family day care. Probably about 40 percent of the nation's day-care children are in licensed family day care; those in unlicensed family care would undoubtedly raise that percentage. You can find any number of family day-care providers advertising on the bulletin boards of the local grocery store, neighborhood women who are staying home with their own children but trying to supplement their income. The closeness to home, the similarity of environment, the presence of a limited number of other children usually of similar ages, and the fact that they will be dealing with another mom all make this a comfortable choice for many mothers.

Family day care is as good as the individual who does it. How do you know the individual? Ask questions. Observe. Talk to other mothers whose children stay with her. A woman in a three-bedroom townhouse who keeps eighteen children for pay is probably not someone you would choose to keep your toddler. But how can you be sure she doesn't keep eighteen children? Drop by without warning.

Yes, of course, there are regulations, some state but mostly county or city, governing family day care. But only licensed providers are bothered by regulations. And don't count on government to do your homework for you. It's not their job to protect your children; it's yours. If they help at all, it's fine; they can, for instance, reassure you that the nice neighbor down the street doesn't have a police record for child abuse in another state.

Regulations cut both ways, however: not too far from my home last year a group of neighbors wanted to put out of business a woman who provided care to handicapped children. Perhaps it made them uncomfortable to see the "defective" children in the neighborhood. And so they tried to force her out of business through zoning regulation, arguing that her work diminished the property values of their homes. Also, plenty of perfectly good providers are not licensed because of the bureaucratic hassle. The inspectors may require a house be repainted if they find lead-based paint, even outside. While putting in a few extra smoke alarms is no problem, putting in new bathrooms might be prohibitive. Some counties even stipulate how high the ceiling has to be, and if a basement misses by an inch, a license won't be issued, no matter how well-qualified a woman may be to take care of kids. Regulations have their limits.

Here are a few things you can look for before you entrust your children to a stranger: Is the woman like you? Do you think your children will be comfortable with her? What are her reasons for doing day care? Does she go to church? Is she a believer? Is she enthusiastic about keeping children? What does she say she will feed them? What will they do with their time? Where will they take naps? What are her rules about behavior? How will she enforce them? By going to different homes with your children you can get a wide variety of answers to these questions. How experienced the woman is might influence how businesslike she seems: one day-care mom writes contracts for her customers, but most are less formal.

Once the children start going to Mrs. Jones, assuming they're old enough to talk, you can learn how to ask leading questions. What did you have for lunch today? Did you watch cartoons today? Did you make anything to show Mommy? Did Susie take her nap today? Did Billy misbehave again today? What happened to him when he did that? Questions like "Did you have fun?" or "What did you do today?" will get you no information. Notice whether your children look forward to going or dread it.

Family Day Care as Ministry

Being a family day-care provider is a great way to doubletime.

One mother, Cheryl Ewings, in Wheaton, Illinois, has three boys, ages seven, five, and infant. She has been home with them all the time. "One way we've been able to afford to have me home for our boys is I run a state-licensed day care from my home," she wrote to me. She takes her job seriously and serves on countywide boards governing day care. She has been a family day-care mom for six years now. "I usually have eight children in my home. This provides me with a salary of far more than I could ever make by placing my children in day care and finding a job." It's not always easy, she cautions. "I do lots more than 'babysitting' — I teach preschool, do crafts and teaching projects, and go on field trips with my kids. I have cared for some children for two or more years. This is their second home. . . ." And along with earning the money, she has the satisfaction of being able to put family first: "I always put my own boys above the day-care kids — first and foremost. They are my God-given responsibility." Not many jobs will spare a mother the hassle of finding child care, pay her a good salary, and also enable her always to be able to put her children first.

Being a family day-care provider is a great way to brighten the corner where you are. Think about the opportunities to set an example for younger mothers. One woman who worked outside the home from the time she was married wrote this to me:

> We were fortunate to find a woman (Christian) mother of five nearly grown children who opened her home which was a superior setting to an institution. This woman cared for both my children during the day for the next eight years. I knew that this woman was better able to provide a solid foundation for my children than I was at the time. (Had only some older woman been there for me to show me the way.)

Can't you just feel the gratitude this working mom had for the wise Christian woman who helped her raise her children? Many a church that has a Christian school finds that within a few years many of the new members of the church itself are parents of children in the school. What does that say? It tells me that people will be grateful to somebody who helps their children and is willing to listen to them on other subjects. Not right away, of course, but after credibility is established. A mother who loves a child who comes to her house day after day and establishes a mother-to-mother relationship with that child's mother may also be laying the groundwork for bringing both to the Lord.

And even if things never get to the point of explicit evangelism, time spent in a Christian family day-care home may be the only exposure a child has to obedience, order, kindness, or just saying a grace before eating. And one can never know what yearning for these forgotten comforts may appear later in the heart of a tormented young adult.

Tips on Being a Family Day-Care Mom

If you don't mind mess, have a family that's pretty tolerant, enjoy kids, and have an extra dose of patience, being a family day-care mom may be just the thing for you. As long as you're not expecting to get rich, but can be satisfied with a little extra income; as long as you expect it to be as demanding as any other job; and as long as you realize that it is probably other adults, not the kids, who will give you your biggest headaches — you won't be likely to be disappointed because your expectations will be realistic.

What adults will give you headaches? You will probably want to be certified. The first headache will come from the county day-care office, which will want you to take a course or two. They'll send a social worker to check you out. They'll inspect your house and yard. The fire department may do its own inspection. Someone may interview your neighbors about you. You'll have paper work to fill out. You'll need to contact your zoning board to find out if your home is zoned to allow it. You'll need to contact your homeowner's insurance company to find out what keeping children in day care will do to your insurance costs. In fact, licensing may take months. But thirty-four states at last count have state regulation, and more are getting it. Twenty-seven states require some form of training. If you do get licensed, you'll be one of nearly two hundred thousand licensed family day-care homes in the country.[5]

The next set of adults who will give you headaches will be your clients. Parents will take you for granted; they won't be there when they say they will to pick up the kids; they'll assume it's okay with you if they "pay you next week"; a child will get sick and you'll discover that the parents changed jobs and neglected to give you their new phone numbers; parents will fail to bring a spare set of clothes and you'll find yourself sending your charges home in your own children's clothes. . . . But there will also be wonderful ones: mothers and fathers who will cooperate with you splendidly, who will always be prompt and won't waste your time with idle chatter, who won't send their children to you

if they're sick, who will give you Christmas presents, who will appreciate the difference you make in their children's lives, who will bring you
tools of your trade and resources like learning toys and scrap paper. You
will have, in short, the human race to deal with. Misunderstandings can
be avoided best by having agreements up front, at the beginning of your
relationship. A typed sheet listing the rules of your house will help: put
it in the parents' hands at the first interview, and keep a copy posted by
the front door as a gentle reminder.

Tag-team parenting; business at home; relative care; family day
care—these are the best options available to you if you are a mother
who needs to earn money. Happily, most of the children of working
mothers are in fact cared for in one of these time-honored arrangements.
Only 11 percent of the children in the nation spend their time at day-
care centers. But, as the next chapter shows, that is quite enough.

VIRUSES, IQ's, AND EMOTIONS
(The Harm of Institutional Child Care)

> *Can a woman forget her sucking child,*
> *that she should not have compassion on*
> *the son of her womb? Yea, they may*
> *forget.*
>
> *Isaiah 49:15*

Yes, she can. Institutional day care is designed to encourage her to forget. And institutional day care of one kind or another is integral to the vision of social parenting.

Social parenting advocates are strangely silent about the possibilities of women working at home. They don't mention family day care much. The very possibility of relative child care they dismiss as a throwback to the days of Ozzie and Harriet—nowadays, they point out, grandmothers have their own careers to think of (which may be true enough, actually).

Fundamental Principles of Social Parenting

Whether or not anybody says it, the real reason that institutional day care is the child care of "professional" choice is this: only institutional day care is compatible with the fundamental principles of social parenting. The other forms of substitute care retain too much closeness with the mother and too much responsiveness to the mother's authority to achieve the purposes of social engineering. Don't forget the ideological premise that "society" has to parent children because they get wrong ideas from their parents (or grandparents, or other mothers, etc.) Now, I am not accusing every professor of child development of a hidden agenda. And most owners and operators of child-care institutions truly believe they are providing a necessary and useful service and truly want to help the children in their care.

That does not alter the ideological winds blowing behind the trends, however. "The care of children . . . is infinitely better left to the best trained practitioners of both sexes who have chosen it as a vocation, rather than to harried and all too frequently unhappy persons with little time nor taste for the work of educating young minds."[1] There speaks a leading feminist who makes little effort to disguise her distaste for motherhood. Her premise — that mothers are not very good people to be raising children — is stated explicitly; it is implicit in much other literature of social parenting. Feminist ideology has always maintained that the destruction of the family will occur hand in hand with the liberation of women: "The collective professionalization (and consequent improvement) of the care of the young . . . would further undermine family structure while contributing to the freedom of women."[2]

Where have we heard this kind of talk before?

> Under the socialist system, when there will no longer be a domestic household and children will be brought up by society from the day of their birth, other forms of the union of the sexes rather than the family will undoubtedly come into being.[3]

This ambitious pledge, made in a work published in Leningrad in 1925, reflects the Communist Manifesto, which proclaimed that the "bourgeois family" (that means nuclear family, with parents raising their own children) would "vanish as a matter of course" when capitalism vanished.

The original Communist thinking on the family is evident in another work, *The Origin of the Family, Private Property, and the State* by Karl Marx and Friedrich Engels.

With the transfer of the means of production into common ownership, the individual family ceases to be an economic unit of society. Private housekeeping is transformed into a social industry. The care and education of children become a public affair; society looks after all children equally, whether they are born in or out of wedlock.[4]

That was written in the nineteenth century. It anticipated the Communist revolution. But we are in the twentieth century (what's left of it), in a non-Communist country. Around the world, Communism is being explicitly rejected, root and branch. And yet, here, in our "free world," we're following the very trends they're rejecting. Hasn't the family ceased to be an economic unit of society, with the rare exception of the family-owned industry or the home-based business? Are not the education and care of children increasingly becoming public affairs? Does not society, through the welfare state, look after all children equally, if they come to it fatherless and in need of help? Is not the family withering away, to judge by the statistical trends of unmarried motherhood, divorce, and living together without marriage?

How do we come to be fulfilling the dreams of Karl Marx in the destruction of our families?

The answer is alarmingly simple. Historically there is a close connection between feminism and socialism. Ideas about women and the family which are fashionable today among liberal opinion makers can be traced to Karl Marx. Feminist ideological leaders are not ashamed of their left-wing origins and sympathies. Their demands for a restructured economy may be couched in terms of "benefiting women," but those demands are for a government-controlled, centralized economy nonetheless. This is what is called socialism in economic textbooks. Unfortunately, in political reality, fear of feminist reprisals has caused the business community in our historically free-enterprise nation to ally with this particular crocodile, in the hopes that the crocodile will eat it last. Such are the compromises that occur when practicality, not principle, is the guiding motive for decisions.

Now, in light of the warm fuzzy feelings generated by Gorbachev and glasnost, it is unfashionable to talk of such things as "Marxism" or even "socialism." Many people have the idea that both are dead. They're not, for ideas always have consequences, but obviously it isn't effective today to argue against social parenting by invoking the specter of Karl Marx. It just won't persuade many people.

And there doesn't need to be a political reason to oppose social parenting anyhow. It's a feminist (read: Marxist) principle that all relationships are political.

All politics aside, there is one overarching reason to oppose social parenting: it harms kids.

Day Care Harms Kids

The mental health profession takes as a given that the infant-mother relationship is the most crucial one we experience. It is the basis for our personality, our intellect, our conscience, and our ability to receive and give love. These foundations are laid in the first three to five years of life. Whether or not a person will be able to learn, to have self-control, to care for others, to cooperate in society — all these qualities are sown in those crucial early years. If the seeds are not sown at this critical time, they may never be able to be sown. The mind is able to receive certain input only at certain times in development.

I'm not saying that a person who did not experience a mother's love and concern is ruined for life. Let me make that clear from the beginning. The existence and efficacy of divine intervention in our lives are real. God can heal our memories and our minds. God can provide for every emotional need we have, no matter how great. But before God can heal what needs healing, the need has to be felt. And the only way our emotional needs are felt is through suffering. And I've never known of one person suffering who did not involve others in his (or her) suffering, causing them to suffer as well.

So yes, the deficits of the early years can be laboriously almost made up. But only at the cost of great suffering, only through the grace of conversion, and even after the divine intervention, sometimes only through much time-consuming and costly human intervention. Do we want to subject our children to the risks of great suffering? to the risk of hoping the right human help comes along? to the chance that conversion will not occur before they have done permanent damage to themselves or others? Those are the risks to children of social parenting.

You will not hear of those risks in the propaganda you're handed when you leave the hospital with a new baby. You won't hear about those risks in the women's magazines that cater to working women. Your pediatrician most likely doesn't read the behavioral science journals and isn't aware of the emotional impact of day care from a young age. And, too, thanks to feminist infiltration of the field of child development, data that reach unfashionable conclusions are not always published or, when they are, are disguised.

Pediatric Jackpot

For pediatricians, group child care is a jackpot. Most pediatricians are overworked, their offices overcrowded, their practices filled to the limit. Without day care life would be much slower for baby doctors. Day-care environments, particularly large institutional ones, are germ factories. I remember my mother lamenting that we were pretty healthy until we started school and then we were sick all the time. Well, the same phenomenon is true today; only instead of the illnesses starting at age five or six, they are starting at five or six months and continuing. It's obvious why: germs like warm, moist environments. How often do babies and toddlers put their hands in their mouths? Think about children and their hands, mouths, toys, sneezes, and diapers — and then try preventing them from touching each other.

That's an obvious explanation. Here's a subtle one. A pioneer field of medical research today is called psychoneuroimmunology. That's the study of how the mind influences the immune system. Research shows that stress can, in effect, turn off certain genes that are crucial to the body's immune system. In other words, the immune system doesn't work as well when individuals are under severe stress.[5] We know — if we are willing to admit it — that children in day care are under stress. Not only are there studies finding high adrenalin levels in day-care children, but just think of how so many day-care babies and children cry when they're dropped off. Think how stressed you would have to feel in order to cry like that. And then realize that the main difference between that baby and you is that you have learned to explain things to yourself and to channel your stress. This will give you some measure of the child's stress. No wonder day-care centers are such centers of disease propagation: children may not able to resist infection as well as they would at home. Christopher Coe, chairman of the monkey lab at the University of Wisconsin, has studied long-term immunity changes in monkeys that grew up wholly or partially out of contact with their mothers. He surmises that the illnesses children get in day care are related to impaired immune function as well as to the increased number of germs they are exposed to.[6]

- Children in day-care centers had fewer than half as many normal ears as children reared at home or in family day care.

- Day-care kids are at two or three times the risk for persistent ear infections as home-reared children.

- Just in case you think an ear infection is a ho-hum sort of thing, realize that $2 *billion* a year is spent on otitis media (ear infection). Since it causes hearing loss, ear infection is responsible for some of the impaired intellectual and academic achievement, speech difficulty, and consequent emotional difficulties of American children.

- The average American family was found to experience two gastrointestinal illnesses a year; the rate among day-care children was more than double that.

- Day-care centers whose personnel diapered children and also prepared or served food had three times as much diarrhea as centers that kept those functions separate.

- Hepatitis A is generally a mild infection for children, although serious for adults. A whopping 88 percent of households with at least one case of Hepatitis A had children under the age of three in day care.

- According to the Centers for Disease Control, the normal rate of Hepatitis A is 11 per 100,000 people. But one study found that among children in day care, the rate is 2,200 per 100,000 children. Among other members of the family with the child in day care, the rate is 4,000 per 100,000 adults. And among day-care staff, the rate is 12,100 out of 100,000!

- Meningitis is a killer disease. As many as 30 percent of infants and children who survive meningitis have permanent consequences:

blindness, brain damage, and so on. H influenza, type B (HiB virus), causes more meningitis in preschool children than any other organism. One two-year study found an occurrence rate of HiB among home-reared children at 40 per 100,000. In the same county, among children attending day care, the rate was 75 per 100,000. Among children under six years of age, the risk of meningitis as a secondary infection from HiB is 585 times as great as the risk to the general population.

- Cytomegalovirus (CMV) is the leading cause of congenital viral infection in humans, leading to CID, or cytomegalic inclusion disease. Eighty-seven percent of children born with this disease experienced at least one of the following symptoms: some degree of mental retardation, serious hearing loss, premature death. One very recent study found that fewer than 20 percent of children reared at home had CMV—but 57 percent of day-care children were infected. The disease is not so serious for children as for women who might catch it from them and unknowingly affect unborn children.[7]

Handicapping the IQ

We live in an information age. The professions today are, in essence, built on handling information: whether it be facts about the law or facts about medicine, information is the basis of the jobs of today. What does a person need to be successful in the information age? The ability to communicate and a good IQ. It is often charged that this society overemphasizes IQ. I agree—virtue is more important than intelligence, and our society, alas, ignores virtue altogether. However, the emphasis is a fact of our era.

That's why it is so ironic that the campaign for social parenting is coming from the successful, intelligent, articulate yuppie elite—the very people whose path to success is built on modern information-age skills. They push for social parenting, day care, new social forms, without realizing that they are handicapping their own children by consigning them to such a life.

Ed Zigler at Yale; the Women's Center at Wellesley; Dr. T. Berry Brazelton at Harvard—all key thinkers, activists, or propagandists for social parenting. More yuppie, more establishment, more information-age-oriented than Yale, Harvard, and Wellesley it is hardly possible to be. And yet, when you think of young professional mothers packing their infants off to day care, don't you think of Harvard types first? I do, and perhaps that is an unfair stereotype. But let's at least acknowledge the reality that the trends toward social parenting are being pioneered by the graduates of Ivy League and similar institutions, where feminism and socialism have always been hospitably received.

Understanding that, savor this further irony.

The conclusion of years of research and thousands of studies of human growth and development is that 50 percent or more of mature intelligence develops between birth and age four. Dr. Burton L. White, who is perhaps the nation's foremost authority on the subject, goes even further. In his view, the origins of human competence can be found between birth and eighteen months of age, with a particularly critical period coming between months eight and eighteen. The child's experiences during these brief months do more, White says, to influence future intellectual competence than any time before or after. White is former director of the Harvard University Preschool Project.

What is it that builds this intelligence during these crucial months and years? It's the things that mothers do as a matter of course and substitutes do not. And interestingly, the intellectual development of little boys is more affected by their mother's behavior than is the intellectual development of little girls.[8] It is physical handling, holding, eye contact, looking at, talking to, reacting to a baby. It is interrelating with this tiny human being so acutely that you know what he's going to do next before he opens his mouth. Mothers can have that kind of interrelation; paid caretakers can't — simply because they have too much else to do. A mother who picks up a crying baby teaches the baby the first thing he ever learns: that someone will respond to his needs. That first step is essential for all future emotional development, including development of conscience.

Yet in some day-care centers, helpers are not allowed to pick up a crying baby! After all, pick up one, you have to pick up all — and who has time for that?

A child development specialist named Alison Clarke-Stewart did a study of how middle-class mothers interact with their children, compared to how low-income mothers do.[9] The middle-class mothers were more verbal, spontaneously as well as in response to the child; they talked face to face with the child more; there was less distracting background noise; there were more questions and references to things, fewer commands, more complicated and varied talk. They imitated the children more frequently, rewarded them more often, including verbally. They put fewer restrictions on exploration, offered more toys and less TV, and were more sensitive to what a fretful state might indicate.

All of that is a description of good mother-child interaction. Think about it: babies rarely come in litters, so mother generally has lots of one-to-one interaction with her infant during that first crucial year or two; the children around in the next several years will be likely to be of different ages. Watching a helpless new baby makes the toddler feel accomplished and grown up: being around someone who is totally helpless is a wonderful way for compassion to develop. In the experience of the household children can see the meaning and reward of hard work; the need for rules; how trust works; the importance of sacrifice for others. The ebb and flow of household life provides times of organized activities, times of quiet reflection, and times of personalized attention.

Now think about what a day-care center, even a good one, is like. First, it is an artificial environment: numerous children of the same age are grouped together for the entire day; a "herd" mentality develops; rather than compassion, they may develop scorn for the child who is smaller or slower; they are denied the experience of the consequences of their actions (few centers expected a child to clean up the mess she made: after all, there's a schedule to keep). No boredom is allowed, no time for thought. Group situations must be kept structured and organized. The adults have little face-to-face talk with each child; lots of background racket provides a constant distraction. Adults give lots of commands and repetition and can pay but little attention to children's questions, let alone give thoughtful answers to them. In short, the whole atmosphere is more like the low-income mothers than the middle-class ones.

By the way, don't be put off by the socioeconomic descriptions: income level has nothing to do with mothering skills. You know the saying: behind every successful man stands a very attentive woman. That is true, especially if the woman is his mother. That "middle-class mothers" happen to have the maternal skills that produce intellectual development is behavioral science's way of noticing that kids with attentive mothers tend to achieve more in life. The academic jargon is used to avoid other descriptions of the mothers in question.

The Family in America is one of the finest family policy publications in the country. The research behind that newsletter is first-rate, and the worldview thoroughly harmonious. Here is how Allan Carlson stated the naked, unpopular fact: "While the issue remains in dispute, there is a growing body of research showing that full-time mothers have children with higher cognitive abilities and academic achievement, as compared to working mothers with children."[10]

What an irony is here! If mothers are going to work to keep their families in the economic middle class, is it not a bitter irony that their children are being raised like members of the lower class? What is the mother's sacrifice worth in the long run if the child's intellectual potential is compromised by her making the sacrifice?

Oh yes, one last word about Alison Clarke-Stewart. Knowing what she does about how children's intelligence is developed, does she urge mothers to raise their children themselves, to give them full advantage of love and attention? No, that would be insufficiently feminist for her. Instead, she urges more sophisticated government social parenting: "policies on child care should show variety that respects and accommodates differences in age, need, and cultural values."

Ideology first, children second. The rhetoric may be about how much we care about children and want them to reach their full potential. But the reality is that if we cared about children and wanted them to reach their full potential, we would do everything we could to encourage their mothers to raise them.

Making Emotional Cripples

Institutional day care is a medical disaster zone. It is a handicapping parlor for the intellect. But none of these effects can compare in sheer evil with a third area. Maternal abandonment—that key ingredient of social parenting—reaches its full effect in institutional day care. There, it wreaks devastation and destruction in the emotional lives of children.

The emotional havoc caused by day care is enormous. It is incalculable. It is producing a generation (really a second generation now) of children who are not only handicapped emotionally, but incapable, for reasons they may never understand, of becoming happy, stable, productive members of society.

Carol Gifford appears to be a Mrs. Typical America. That's how *USA Today* treated her, anyway, in a cover story on day care. She has two-year-old twins and a five-year-old. She searched for months for the right day-care arrangement and finally found one. But she's not happy. "I can't see any visible psychological signs that my children are being harmed by day care," she told the newspaper, "but I keep thinking maybe there are signs that I'm not seeing." But since Carol feels her family couldn't survive on just her husband's income, she has to suppress those fears. "I keep telling myself that everything will be OK," she says.[11]

Carol is deliberately deceiving herself. So are hundreds of thousands of other mothers who also keep telling themselves everything will be okay. Their instinct tells them otherwise. Their knowledge tells them otherwise. But they don't see any visible signs of damage, so they are able to reassure themselves and make themselves ignore their better judgment.

The day of reckoning will come. Few children show ill effects from institutional day care right away. It takes a few years for problems to start manifesting themselves, a few more for the full dimensions to become clear.

The basic psychological job of a mother and a baby is to form what psychologists call an attachment. Attachment is defined by John Bowlby, the premier researcher in the area, as a warm, intimate, continuous relationship between mother and infant in which both find satisfaction. If the attachment is weak enough, the situation is considered deprivation. Deprivation is a specific syndrome apparent in adults, which results from a lack of nurturing, affirming love by a significant adult during the vulnerable years of growth and development. Essentially, it is emotional retardation, showing up as extreme self-centeredness, anxiety about one's own worth, an inability to experience a wide range of emotions, and an inordinate need to please others at all costs.

It is the nature of attachment that the two individuals who are attached tend to remain in proximity with one another. If separated, they will get back together. They will resist any effort to separate them.

Think about how honeymooners behave: that is attachment at its most visible. The maternal-child attachment is essentially the same.

Not that a child is to be dependent always on the mother. Once infancy passes, various levels of self-reliance are achieved and should be. But the mother should be an always available emotional refueling base for the child. A toddler may explore the house and the yard, but he likes to come back and check that Mommy is still around. Reassured, he continues to explore. Without the reassurance, he will no longer be able to explore because an intense emotional stress will have taken the place of security.

How does behavioral science measure attachment? The measuring devices are admittedly crude. Something called the "strange situation" is used. Its basic pattern is this: A mother and child are subjected to two three-minute abandonments. First, the child is left in a strange, empty room. Then mother returns. The child's reactions are observed. Then mother leaves again. A stranger enters. The child's reactions are observed. Then mother returns. The child's reactions are observed. Here is how the child's reactions are interpreted:

- Securely attached children immediately seek closeness and/or physical contact with mother; resist when mother attempts to leave

- Insecurely attached children avoid physical and/or visual contact, or may approach, but turn away before reaching the returning parent. Insecurely attached children are divided into two sub-categories: insecure/resistant and insecure/avoidant. Insecure/resistant children will push away the mother, or push away a toy she offers, or may seek contact with the mother but then cry angrily and push her away. Insecure/avoidant children will avoid any psychological contact with their mother: move away from her, avoid eye contact, not approach her and so forth. The latter category is the most serious.

Now, of course, no test procedure is foolproof. But this strange situation test is pretty generally accepted as a barometer of the emotional development of children. Dr. Craig Peery, a child development specialist at Brigham Young University, described it to me as a "radar screen." If a problem in the relationship shows up in a strange situation test, it's already a pretty big problem. By the time there's an attachment disorder, as it's called, the child has already suffered extensive emotional harm.

Using what you know about the strange situation methodology, see what you make of these study results:

- Children who began day care at 25 months of age sought little proximity to or contact with the mother upon reunion but showed heightened proxmity- and interaction-avoiding tendencies.[12]

- More full-time day-care children (but not part-time children) were found to display avoidance of the mother during the final reunion episode of the strange-situation procedure than did non-day-care children. The length of the daily separation appears to be an important determinant of day-care effects on infant-mother attachment.[13]

These studies are just two, ten years apart, of a multitude that found the same or similar results. The first study, by Mary Curtis Blehar at Johns Hopkins University in 1974, found clear disruptive effects of frequent daily separations. The second study, by Pamela Schwarz at the University of Michigan in 1983, found the same thing in younger children. The same kind of thing is still being studied abundantly, and the same results are coming in. In the Schwarz study the infants being compared were eighteen-month-old infants in full-time, part-time, or non-day-care situations, from intact middle-class homes. All the day-care infants had been in day-care homes before nine months of age. Nine months with their mothers, and yet after another nine months without her, they are already showing signs of serious problems!

Nor are these findings in any way exceptional. As Jay Belsky, perhaps the nation's leading specialist on the effects of day care on children, put it,

There is, then, an *emerging* pattern here in which we see supplementary child-care in which nonmaternal child care, *especially* that initiated in the first year, whether in homes or in centers, sometimes is associated with the tendency of the infant to avoid or maintain a distance from the mother following a series of brief separations.[14]

What an answer this is to the people who advocate six-week "parental leave" policies on the grounds that if a mother can have six weeks with her baby they'll "bond" and be all set for life. What an answer to Harvard's T. Berry Brazelton, this generation's Dr. Benjamin Spock, who urges a mother to spend the first four months taking care of her child and then confidently place him in day care.

Proof in the Pudding

The problems started by early institutional day care only get worse as children get older.

- Based on eight months of observation in the same setting, nineteen 3- and 4-year-olds who had been in day care from infancy were compared on nine behavior traits with matched subjects who had had no day-care experience prior to the study. The infant day-care group was found to be significantly more aggressive, motorically active, and less cooperative with adults.[15]

- Kindergarteners and first-graders who had been reared on a full-time basis at a university day-care center throughout their first four years of life were rated by school teachers as "more likely to use the aggressive acts, to hit, kick, and push than children in the control group." Second, they were more likely to threaten, swear, and argue. Third, they demonstrated those propensities in several school settings — the playground, the hallway, the lunchroom, and the classroom. Fourth, teachers were more likely to rate these children's aggressiveness as a serious deficit in social behavior. Fifth, teachers viewed these children as less likely to use such strategies as walking away.[16]

- A study in Bermuda found that two-year-olds "who experienced predominantly center group care in the first two years of life," at two years of age were found to have poorer communication skills than children cared for at home. . . . Center group infants were rated by teachers as more apathetic, less attentive, and less socially responsive.[17]

- A group of 156 three- to five-year-olds "who began group care in infancy were rated as more maladjusted than those who were cared for by sitters or in family day-care homes for the early years and who began center care at later ages" and were judged to be more anxious, aggressive, and hyperactive.[18]

- Eight-year-olds in Dallas "who had extensive child care beginning in infancy" were rated by teachers and parents as being less compliant and having poorer peer relationships compared with children who began full-time child care after infancy. Full-time child care from an early age also correlated with poorer study skills, lower grades, and reduced self-esteem.[19]

Shall I continue, or have I made my point?

What conclusions do you, a Christian parent, draw from these reports? Be glad you are not a behavioral scientist, because if you were, you would have to conclude, as Belsky does from his comprehensive review of forty-odd pages chronicling the ill effects of day care, that "it would be misguided to attribute any 'effects' of nonmaternal care to the care per se." Too many variables: Are the mothers working? Are they happy? Perhaps the family situations are unhappy as well. Other family practices may affect the children, too. . . . The rationalizations can go on forever. And maybe they're valid. For the sake of argument, I'll concede for the moment that maybe the children in day care in all these studies have had behavioral problems for other reasons than the day care itself. As a mother, I still ask you: so what? No matter what the excuses, do you want your children associating with children who have these problems when, if you kept yours home, they might avoid them?

Can a woman forget the babe of her womb? Can a mother harden her heart and risk endangering her child's future health, happiness, and ability to succeed in life?

Yes, unnatural though it be, she can. And thousands upon thousands do.

But the Lord, our God, is more faithful to us than even our mothers.

ATTACK AND COUNTERATTACK

(The Answer to Creeping Materialism)

But my God shall supply all your needs according to his riches in glory by Christ Jesus.

Philippians 4:19

All right now. What do we have so far? The attack on motherhood is premeditated. It is intellectually grounded in the most profoundly anti-Christian ideologies of modern times. The goal is the restructuring of human nature to conform to ideologies of "equality" or "liberation." The means is the mistreatment of children. The consequence of the campaign is social disorder: disorder between parents and children, which yields in time disorder between adults, which yields in time the destruction of the human community.

Why are there such dire consequences to what is said to be only a simple redistribution of the tedious routines of child rearing?

Because of the Way God Made Us Human Beings

Human beings are created in God's image and likeness. But the image was distorted by the fall of man. Through grace, the likeness can be restored partially in this life, completely in the next, if we respond to God's call to perfection, sometimes called God's gift of grace. Grace works through the human mind, body, and soul, however; and following God is a constant struggle between the flesh and the spirit. Human beings learn to imitate God's perfection in their relationships with each other. The mother prepares the infant's heart to receive God's grace. Without love at the foundation of the mother-child relationship, sin finds fertile soil. When the most fundamental human relationship, that of mother to child, is compromised, mind and flesh are disordered, reflecting the disorder introduced with the Fall.

How can we possibly imitate the Creator in our relationships if we don't learn from our mothers to give of ourselves, to offer ourselves in love to another, and to control our fleshly impulses for the sake of another? Not knowing it, how can we practice it? And if we do not know it in human experience, how can we understand it of God's love? How can we believe in the self-giving love of a heavenly Father when we have not known such love from a human mother? And if we do not believe in it, we will not live according to it.

In our parents' generation, this spiritual wisdom was already fading, but the social structures established to support it were yet present. Community standards were high, and most people conformed to them. Because society was living off the spiritual capital of its ancestors, self-control and deferred gratification were the norm, even though the spiritual reason for them may not have been comprehended. Social conventions prevented much harm. In our generation, the spiritual capital has been almost consumed. Some of us grew up with spiritual convictions; more grew up seeing hypocrisy where our parents saw order. And so our generation threw away the superstructures, thinking them meaningless because they were hollow. And the restraints against harming each other became fewer and less compelling.

Human beings cannot make human society on their own; God is the Author of society, of human nature. But our generation does not want to know that; we are afraid that knowledge might entail obligations, which might interfere with our pleasure or our "freedom." Our generation's idol is the Self. Pleasing the Self guides our actions. But self-gratification is no basis for human society. If everyone operates for self-gratification, nobody can depend on anybody else for consolation. And so we are lonely, whether we know it or not. Achieving our own goals, disregarding the effect we may have on others, and finding oblivion in drugs and alcohol become substitutes for the demands and rewards of human relationships. How far we have come from imitating the perfection of God!

Do I sound dire? I hope so.

What are we to do? What are God's people to do? What is the church to do?

The Church and Social Parenting

Is the church aware of the trend? Can church leaders see the forest for the trees? Is the institutional church today more of a hindrance or a help? Has the church stood athwart the tide of the times with prophetic power to speak the truth, or has it climbed onto the bandwagon and abetted the cause of social parenting?

What can the church do—what should the church do—to prevent the further deterioration of the quality of life for America's children?

If I were a pastor, I would not know the right thing to do. On the one hand, I could preach about the family (though I've never even heard of a sermon exhorting women to pursue motherhood), but on the other hand, the women of the congregation are working and something must be done for their children.

Church Day Care: Major Industry

The immediate problem has occupied the minds of many churches. Some estimates say that 80 percent of the institutional day care in the country is church-related. If that figure seems very high, compare it with this: a National Council of Churches study of fifteen of the NCC's member denominations found that those fifteen denominations alone enrolled between 375,000 and 1,309,000 infants, toddlers, and preschoolers in denomination-related day care. That is between 5 and 20 percent of all three- and four-year-olds in the country!

That does not mean that between 5 and 20 percent of all three- and four-year-olds in the country are hearing the gospel. It does not even mean that churches are running that many day-care centers as ministry. It mostly means that some enterprising businessperson rents the church's unused Sunday school classrooms and playground to operate a day-care center Monday through Friday.

Among those few churches that do see day care as a ministry, only 10 percent of the toddler programs, only 16 percent of the preschool programs, and only 14 percent of the after-school programs list "Spiritual development" as one of their three most important goals. "Provision of love and warmth" leads the list, "providing child care for working parents" is next, and "creating a positive self-image" is third. Hardly the attitude of a ministry, eh?

These are, however, more liberal than conservative denominations; many of these same denominations may have been on the list of the Alliance for Better Child Care, which launched the ABC bill. The small, independent evangelical and fundamentalist churches that operate an uncounted number of day-care centers do have more a sense of ministry. Their goal is not only to provide help for working parents and love and warmth for children, but also to teach the children about morality and the Author of morality. This segment of church day care is the target of vicious antichurch day-care provisions in the various versions of the Act for Better Child Care and other proposed bills. Time and again, in version after version, the discrimination against religious child care is blatant, ranging from requirements that any "religious artifacts or symbols" be removed to requirements that the federal government supervise the employee pay scale. The implicit assumption is always that the federal government will have the authority to write church day-care regulations. Anyone who believes that federal aid to child care will in any way be allowed to benefit church child care must also believe in the Tooth Fairy. The attack on motherhood could hardly be waged by subsidizing motherhood's last remaining bastion!

In general, the church has been strenuously nonjudgmental toward the growing trend of social parenting, in effect giving implicit approval. One widely respected moderate Christian monthly emphatically stated that "Christian leaders should speak out for more and better day-care facilities."[1] Another otherwise excellent Christian magazine concluded an informational article about child care with this piece of classic gobbledygook: "Whatever child care option they choose, concerned Christian parents who are committed to making the right choice for their family can have the confidence that they are investing in a Biblical priority."[2] As if all choices were created equal!

On the national scene, Dr. James Dobson has always been a clear voice in the defense of motherhood, and the entire Focus on the Family ministry is built around supporting and advancing motherhood by helping mothers with their real problems. Dr. Tony Campolo has written a few pieces urging women to rethink the career choice. Neither of those men is even a spokesman for "the church"! But apart from those two voices in the wilderness and an occasional other, the Christian press has been discouraging on this issue.

I can understand the pastoral imperative to avoid laying more guilt on women who are already carrying too much (as most working mothers are). I can understand the arguments about "if we help them with their daily needs now, they'll be willing to listen to us preach later." I can understand the argument that since "somebody's going to be raising the kids, it might as well be Christians." I could be more sympathetic to these arguments if the children were really being evangelized in church day care. But as it is, I can imagine that the same rationalizations for indecision were used twenty years ago with respect to abortion. The danger is in becoming so open-minded that our brains fall out, as a teacher of mine once said. At some point, the understanding and the sympathy and helpfulness have to be set aside so that the truth may be preached. And I simply don't see that happening. If you do, please let me know.

Perhaps the church can take up its prophetic call by addressing the issues that underlie the lemminglike rush for day care. The ideological campaigns of social parenting, after all, would have remained ivory tower ideas unless conditions had made society ripe for it. Child care is really a symptom of a very serious disease. I wish I saw the church addressing more of the real causes of the disease.

What Causes the Disease?

Let's face it: the campaign for social parenting is succeeding because society sees social parenting as an answer to some needs. Society has created a need for social parenting. As long as those needs continue to grow, the attack on motherhood will continue apace.

What causes the need for day care?

First of all, divorce. Divorce and the fear of divorce probably compel more mothers to stay in the work force than any other single factor. Where 33 percent of mothers with children under six work, 50 percent of divorced mothers of children under six work, and at that, most of them have a bare-bones existence. Churches are falling over themselves to "win" as members the divorced person and to assure the single mother that she is welcome — as indeed she should be since the church's primary mission is to win souls. But somewhere along the line the compassion has become so great that the truth of God's law concerning divorce is kept mighty quiet. Where do we hear the church speaking out against no-fault divorce laws?

Another reason day care continues to be a growth industry is that mothers prefer working outside the home to staying home with children. "I'd go bananas if I stayed home" is an expression we have all heard from working mothers. Why would she go bananas? Probably because her children are undisciplined. This woman doesn't need a job; she needs some practical teaching about raising obedient children.

Then there's the social expectation: mothers get more approval from society (to say nothing of a paycheck) for having interesting jobs than they do for working in the home to develop their children's spirits. What is the church doing to counteract this acute self-image crisis? Some small churches can do a great deal, but the large denominations seem oblivious to the problem.

But probably the most common reason is that people want more money. Materialism is the bane of our existence. *Working Mother* magazine asked women why they worked: 94 percent said they worked for money; 69 percent also said they felt freer to spend money on themselves after they started working.[3] These statistics suggest that only about 31 percent of working mothers are working out of real need. Yet most women believe they are working out of financial necessity.

I don't dispute the financial necessity for one second in the case of most divorced or single mothers. I know that in the year after a divorce, the man's standard of living goes up 42 percent while the standard of living of the wife with children goes *down* 73 percent. I know the child-support payment statistics. I know that alimony went out of style as feminism came in. I know that in divorce the wife and children lose their home. I know that most divorce judges expect the woman to be able to support herself and her children within a year or two. I know how totally egalitarian divorce policy has become, which is to say how totally unfair to mothers with children.

But I want to probe the case of working mothers with employed husbands. Back when I was working, I would have said I was working out of economic necessity. To begin with, when I was working part time, that was true. When I was working full time, though, it wasn't true any more. My husband's college salary would have been close to the margin, but probably adequate, if we had lived in the small country town where the college was. But we didn't want to live there. We preferred to live in the suburbs of Washington, D.C., one of the most expensive cities in the country. Can we honestly say I was working out of necessity? Necessity to support our choices, yes. But the choices weren't defensible. They were emotion-based, not reason-based.

I remember a woman who was desperately seeking employment. "We absolutely have to have the income," she said. It turned out they absolutely had to have the income to pay for their swimming pool. Her statement was true—the family did indeed need extra income. But why did they need it? For an unnecessary expense they had chosen to incur.

Wants Versus Needs

We, as individuals and as a society, want far, far more than we need. We want so much. Do we ever stop to examine the source of these wants? They come from our memories and our imaginations. We see what other people have and want it. Then we get angry if we can't have it. We see our friends cruising around a lake on their very own boat, and we get resentful that we don't have one. We can just see ourselves, in our mind's eye, doing the same thing, and somehow, we feel entitled to it. Or we go to a fine restaurant once on a special occasion and keep remembering it and thinking about it and wanting it again. We see total strangers on television wearing chic clothes and having a hilariously wonderful time snow skiing, and we realize it's been three years since

we had a family vacation anywhere, and we begin to feel sorry for ourselves and resent our ill fortune.

But we're only reacting to an artificially stimulated appetite.

Here's an example as close as your mailbox: the catalog-created desire. I refuse to go into the department stores between mid-October and
January as my personal protest against excessive "holiday" hype. Hence,
I do the family Christmas shopping out of catalogs. Back when I was
working, I didn't have the time to go shopping, so I shopped by mail.
Okay, I admit, I brought this flood of colorful, irresistible catalogs upon
myself. I'm safe if I stand by the trash can when I bring in the mail and
pitch them right in, toss, toss, toss. They don't touch my life if I do that.
But when I am weak — or, worse, if I take the mail with me as I leave the
house to drive car pool and allow myself to look at them while I wait for
the kids to come out of school — immediately I'm in trouble. I can't help
looking and ever so slightly *wishing I had this, that, or the other*. If I
hadn't known it existed, I'd have been perfectly happy without it for the
rest of my natural life. But once I've seen it, my appetite is stimulated;
time is wasted; images enter my mind to clutter and distract it. Sometimes I can brush it off by reminding myself that it's only junk anyhow.
But sometimes an item takes hold in my memory and imagination.

Fortunately, I rarely buy the stuff because I keep the checkbook and
know what the balance is. But I keep the catalog around and look at it
occasionally and feel wistful. We have a family word for this: *concupiscing*. We made the word up from the noun *concupiscence*, meaning
an inordinate or strong desire.

I'm no different from any other American: we all grow up with the
habit of wanting more than we have, more than we need. My mother
could never ride through a nice residential neighborhood without noticing the houses in great detail: "Look at that porch. I wish we had a
screened porch." "Too close to the neighbor." "Lovely landscaping."
"Now that's a good-sized house." Now, since my mom and dad bought
and sold something like forty houses in their life together (no, I'm not
kidding — Daddy was in the Navy), I can understand how she picked up
this habit. But I picked up the habit too. No matter where I lived, I
always compared it to someplace else, someplace I imagined to be better. And by the time the boys were ten and eleven, they were doing it

too. Because our church happens to be in a very posh residential neighborhood, every Sunday we all made ourselves discontented with our home. Finally, I realized that in complaining about the home we had I was in essence telling God He had made a mistake in not giving us a bigger one. The word for this bad habit isn't nice: sin. So I stopped concupiscing over houses.

The temptation still comes around, however. And it isn't unique. In fact, a very considerable national industry is built around this habit. Real estate is a growth industry in our country. People rarely stay in the same house more than five years. Even if they stay in the same job or same city, the expectation is that they will "move up." Same thing with cars. Who keeps cars until they fall apart these days? Nobody who is status conscious, that's for sure. The thing to do is to "move up."

It's the American way, all right; I suppose libertarian economists would argue that constantly wanting more is the engine that drives our economy. And I won't dispute that our economy is doing better than almost any other in the world, providing more benefits for more people than any other system, so I certainly am not proposing any system change. But I am asking for a spiritual perspective on our economic behavior.

Isn't it a fundamental spiritual mistake never to be content with what we have? When we're always wanting more, aren't we really being dissatisfied with what God, in His wisdom, has given us? We act as if we believed that enjoying ourselves and satisfying our every whim were what this life is all about. But it isn't, and if we stop to think about it, we know it isn't. We know we are here to know, love, and serve God, and to find our joy and satisfaction and happiness in knowing, loving, and serving Him. But being creatures of habit and members of our consumerist culture, we forget to think about it. Of course, we are free to enjoy the amenities of life. Jesus told us we were entitled to our daily bread. He even taught us to pray for it! But did He mean for us to pray for French napoleons with real whipped cream and genuine chocolate on top? Somehow, I don't think we're *entitled* to such things. They're nice if they come, but we have no right to them. And certainly no right to orphan our children so that we can have them.

Children as Pampered Pets

We've all seen the estimates, originating with the U.S. Department of Agriculture, that the cost of raising a child from birth to age eighteen in an urban midwestern area is about $92,228. Of that, housing accounted for 34 percent and food for 23 percent. No wonder parents shiver at the prospect and mothers plan to go back to work. I hate those figures. I am glad that for several thousand years of human history nobody published figures like that. The globe would be pretty sparsely populated if all our parents had considered how they were going to afford us.

I talked about concupiscing for adults. Guess what? Concupiscing on behalf of children is even more addictive and expensive.

> They splurged on Laura Ashley bumper pads, crib linens and a wallpaper border of red-coated toy soldiers. And Cyndi Tabb, 25, had her heart set on an oak rocker with a bowed back. "The rocker cost a little over $300, but I really fell in love with it." . . . There are $500 "Dynasty Cradles" just like the one used on the television drama. One hot new item . . . is a $30 "Electric Wipes Warmer" that heats containers of disposable baby wipes to 110 degrees Fahrenheit and also acts as a night light. . . .[4]

Do babies need this sort of lavishness? Of course not. Many a perfectly happy baby came into the world to sleep in a drawer lined with towels and be washed with a washcloth with whatever water was handy. One farmer's wife in Colorado has the perfect answer: "We're the third generation of Barry's family to live in this farm house. We have half as many children and are the first to have a bathroom at all. They all grew up to be wonderful people. We can live here and raise a happy family too."

The yuppies who buy Laura Ashley bedding for the baby will probably also hesitate to have a second baby until they have another bedroom ready. Do these young urban professional parents have the idea that if they don't give their baby decorator crib linens and a gorgeous private nursery, they are somehow failing to be good parents? Or is it the competitive urge? Do they want their friends to know that they have really arrived, that they can afford such things? More likely, they are acting on the emotional presumption that having beautiful surroundings will make them — or the baby — happy.

The same thing continues as the child grows up. First, it's toys: the ones that are advertised most heavily, of course, because the more you think about them, the more you realize they must be the "best." And lots of them because we are accustomed to finding our happiness in *things*. Without thinking, we train our children from the tenderest ages to find happiness in the same place, and they soon demand this or that new item from us. They are vulnerable to the television advertising beamed at them, and a mother's love can be shortsighted enough to indulge whims.

Here is another fallacy we all fall into: "I was depressed, so I bought something." Material things do not buy happiness; they do not turn disobedient children into quiet little angels, they do not make selfish girls into good mothers, they do not bring joy to an unhappy relationship. But as long as we think things will work such magic for us, we will keep on acquiring things we don't really need, and our need for more income will go up and up and up.

We tie ourselves up in knots because of our material possessions. We organize our lives around acquiring them or the money that will enable us to acquire them, and then we have to organize our lives around housing the junk. Why do so many people want larger and larger houses? Because they are saddled with a growing mound of material possessions. And not only do they have to house the stuff; they have to care for it: the VCR goes on the fritz, and they have to drive across town to get it fixed, then drive back again, killing a few gallons of gas and two afternoons of irreplaceable time. Every new material possession entails hidden costs.

We did not get a color television set until the boys were seven and eight years old (and then it was a gift). Could we live without it? Sure. We have locked it in the attic for eighteen months at a time. We have a stereo too. Could we live without it? You bet. The turntable has been broken for six months now, and we haven't really missed it. When we get the money to get it fixed, it will cost our time to take it apart, put it in the car, take it to the shop, then go pick it up and repeat the process. When I got my microwave oven, I felt behind the times because most of my friends had already had one for years. Could I live without it now? Of course I could. But when I got it, I didn't think so.

Nor is it just material possessions that we think we can't live without. The same thing can be said about vacations. What do they do except cost us money, wear us out, and create appetites for ways to spend more money? Can the same thing be said about private schools? Many mothers go to work to pay the tuition at the Christian schools they think are absolutely essential for their children's well-being. And perhaps they are. But the expense is considerable. When I began phasing out of paid employment, the first thing to go was private school. I worked part time so that I could home school. Not everybody can do that, of course. But it is an option. Later, the boys went back to private schools, different ones, and we were not too proud to apply for financial aid.

Kids Don't Need to Cost a Fortune

The cost of having children — or the fear of the cost — is scaring women away from motherhood or driving mothers out of the home. This is not necessary. Fifty years ago people didn't feel they had to have air conditioned houses before they could have children. They felt no obligation even to have separate beds for the children, let alone separate bedrooms! Sharing beds didn't prevent the children from growing up happy and wise in the eyes of God and of man. What wisdom did our grandparents have that our technological society has forgotten?

Parents didn't feel they had an obligation or a right to own their own homes, either. But our generation feels both. We expect to own our own homes, whatever we have to do to acquire them. We forget that before the post-World War II era of affluence and low interest, it wasn't typical for young families to be homeowners. Many of our parents grew up in apartments or had landlords. Yet we consider buying our own home almost a prerequisite to having children. I didn't go quite that far, but until we had our own home, I was perpetually discontent and afraid that the landlord would toss us out (it happened once, and it scarred me forever).

When I was preparing to write this book, I mentioned it on one of my *Focus on the Family Weekend* commentaries and asked people to write to me with their experiences of surviving without sending Mom out to work. The flood of letters that came to me was enormously touch-

ing and humbling. Most of the letters were from the American heartland
(as opposed to the East or West Coast, yuppiedom's strongest foothold).
Many of these letters contained advice that had survived the test of time.
Here are a few samples:

From Florence, South Carolina:

We drive a 1984 used station wagon and a 1971 used truck, I arrive at
the grocery store at 8:00 A.M. when the out-dated meat has just been
reduced to half-price, we eat meat only once a day. . . . When one of
us is sick, we consult God first, not the doctor first. . . .

From Petoskey, Michigan:

I planted a large garden and preserved a lot of our harvest. My husband did much of the home repairs and cut firewood for home heat-
ing. I also bought used clothing and gladly accepted used, good clothing for our growing children. . . . We feel that TV commercials tend
to stimulate a sense of materialism and our whole family can better
avoid that temptation without a TV in the home. Many of our best
times have been walks in the woods, swims at the beach, visiting
friends and other basically low- or no-cost activities.

From McClue, Pennsylvania:

Over the past couple of years I have been making crafts at home.
Most of the crafts our children, 13, 11, and 6, are able to help
with. . . . We also had the opportunity to buy a chicken house last
year which is totally a family project. . . . I have taken in some mend-
ing from time to time. . . .

From Twin Lake, Michigan:

We try to buy very little, if anything, that we don't have cash for. We
have no credit cards: never have; never will. Our monthly bills cover
utilities, rent, food, and one student loan. Our future goals aim toward
gardening and putting food up (canning, freezing, and drying) such
that our bills will be minimized to utilities and rent alone.

From West Palm Beach, Florida:

We leave the water heater to "off" until about 10 minutes before we'll
want to use hot water. . . . we wash with only cold water and also line-
dry the clothes. [Note: This would not work in the winter if you live
in Minnesota!]. . . . I breast-fed exclusively for the first eleven

months. . . . We recycle toys. We give our daughter hand-me-down toys. We don't give her all her toys at once, but we rotate them, so when she's tired of the ones that are out, we put them away. . . .

From Coolidge, Arizona:

The sacrifices that we have made in order for me to stay home have included living in a small home (800 square feet) with a leaky roof, no heat, and plenty of cockroaches. This was very hard on my ego. We recently moved into a nicer home and I am thankful to the Lord for the way He has provided for us. I am "stranded" at home as my husband uses our one vehicle to go to work. We are unable to visit our families as often as we would like.

From Ocheyedan, Iowa:

I raise a year's supply of corn, green beans, and tomatoes in my garden. They are the crops that yield the most for the amount of space and work required. . . . It helps to learn to do simple household repairs myself. The public library has a wealth of how-to books available. . . . I have learned to paint walls, and finish and refinish furniture and woodwork and floors. The more you can do yourself the less you have to hire done. . . . It is important to take the time to plan all of my menus for a month at a time. By planning I know exactly what I need when I go to the grocery store and don't spend on what I won't use.

Do these tips sound old-fashioned? You bet they do. But kids shouldn't have to cost a fortune. And with care and good habits, they still don't. Thrift is one of those old-fashioned good habits. "Use it up, wear it out; make it do, or do without" is an old American slogan — but not a slogan of the consumer society. Thinking about how to make ends meet, how to save a penny here or there, sounds tedious and boring only because we have conditioned ourselves to think of thrift as tedious. It shouldn't be. It gives wonderful play to creativity: a woman who is aggressively thrifty never need feel her talents are being wasted. Several women who wrote mentioned the fun they have making hand-crafted presents, using materials free in nature; many mentioned sewing, everything from recycling men's pants into babies' rompers to making quilts from scraps.

There are other rewards for the thriftiness it takes to keep a mother home with her children:

From Manhattan, Kansas:

We get a lot of compliments on our children and I honestly feel that the financial sacrifice that we have made has been well worth it. . . . The more I learn and understand about child development, the more I believe that daycare is a cruel and inhumane place for children. . . .

From Las Vegas, Nevada:

I have seen many women take on jobs, full time and part time, and I have yet to see it benefit them financially. There is this great hope to get ahead or out of debt, but in actuality they have gotten further into debt. As I see it, because of the added pressure of both parents working you end up justifying indulgences to counter it. . . . In the beginning of my marriage my husband used to bring up the matter of me getting a job, thinking that I had it too easy at home. There was that temptation to get a job just to prove to him how much worse off we would be. But instead I humbled myself as the Lord says to do. . . . Years later my husband began to appreciate the fact that I stood to my convictions and the effect it has had on the children. He saw a security in them that he believed was a direct result of me staying home with them as well as other godly principles. . . .

From Aloha, Oregon:

As a personnel professional for nine years . . . I saw many women, particularly first-time mothers, struggle with the issue of return to work vs. stay home. Those who chose to stay home quietly faded from the scene. . . . Those who chose to return to work were inevitably teary-eyed about the separation from their babies. Their anxiety led them to be preoccupied and not concentrating on their work. They were obviously in an emotional battle and not sure which side was right. . . .

From Tyler, Texas:

Sure we give up things with just my small salary. . . . However, we feel we gain much more by Jan staying home with the boys. Such as: less sickness, better disciplined, respect for adults, strong family ties, less hurried lifestyle, quality and quantity time, and, finally, we instill our values, not others.

From Aberdeen, South Dakota:

Yes, we have sacrificed brand new cars, the latest in clothing styles, diamonds, and steaks. But we are content to drive an '82 Chevy Impala, we're thankful for casseroles, and our clothes are not that bad. At least when I am 60 or 70 years old I won't look back on my life and have to say I sacrificed my children for worldly goods that don't truly mean much anyway.

Woman after woman wrote to tell me how she enjoyed her work but knew that God had called her to work at home instead. One military wife found herself stationed in Panama and saw real poverty there: "I was so humbled. Here I was, thinking of how poor I was compared to other Americans, and I was rich compared to these people! My life was changed."

The Counterattack on Divorce, Disobedience, and Discontent

Her life was changed. Therein lies the answer. To escape slavery to materialism, our lives must be changed. But what can change lives?

The people of God must fight against the attack on motherhood; the church must resist the drive for social parenting. The church's weapon must be the only weapon the church has: the Word of God, sharp as a two-edged sword. That alone can pierce through our self-delusions and self-deceptions. That alone can change our lives.

The situations that predispose us to conform to social parenting must not be tolerated. And the Word of God speaks to all of them: divorce, disobedient children, discontented women, fear of poverty, materialism.

Divorce must be made harder to obtain, made less respectable, perhaps, just as marriage must be made more difficult to obtain. Better not to contract a marriage that's doomed to fail. With serious preparation and instruction, marriages can be more successful. The church has its part to do to change its policies—a considerable task since 90 percent of Americans are still married in some sort of church ceremony. And we, the citizens, also have to do our part to change our laws.

The church needs to come into the breach left by the breakdown of Western civilization and systematically and thoroughly teach the flock how to raise children. People may be out of practice with the customs of yesteryear, but the knowledge has not disappeared. It can be found in books, and some parents have acquired it and practice it. The highest levels of church authority must support and encourage their efforts. Pastors cannot assume that all is well if a marriage simply holds together: they must be concerned about the quality of love and discipline the children receive. Teaching from the pulpit for the entire congregation (it makes an impact for a child to hear on Sunday morning from the pastor himself that God expects him to obey his parents) must be followed up in regular training and evangelizing. Parish retreats for married people should include units on love and discipline. The older women should organize their instruction of the younger women; young people past elementary school age continue to need instruction on living a godly life.

In our technological society, the father of lies feeds deceptions to women to foster misery and discontent. Why do we and why does the church allow him unlimited access? Why don't we protect women with the sword of truth? True teaching about women — not feminist rhetoric about thier being identical to men, but true teaching about women as myrrh-bearers, like unto the Holy Spirit — must be sought out and revived.

And men need to be taught how to value women. Women's common fear of dependency comes in no small part because many men do in fact scorn their wives' dependency — they don't appreciate the value of what their wives do for them and the family at home. Men need to learn more respect for women from Scripture, just as women need to learn it so that they can have more self-respect. This teaching is not new; lay leaders in various family life movements have been doing it for years. The time is long overripe for the church to avail itself of the experience of years of family ministry and to exercise its authority in spreading sound teaching to defend motherhood and womanhood.

The Word of God answers the pervasive, creeping materialism that enslaves us all. What could be clearer than "Lay not up for yourselves treasures upon earth, where moth and rust doth corrupt, and where thieves break through and steal"? (Matthew 6:19).

"For we brought nothing into this world and it is certain we can carry nothing out. And having food and raiment let us be therewith content" (1 Timothy 6:7–8) is advice needed today as never before. That is the answer to the incessant pressure to "move up" and "have better": be content with the food and clothing you have. If your material means happen to be abundant, be sure your heart does not take inordinate delight in your material possessions.

Be content. It sounds so easy. But what about the fear of catastrophe? What if my husband loses his job? What if he has to take a pay cut? What if we don't have insurance and one of us becomes seriously ill? How can we survive *if. . . ?*

One of two things will happen. Either God will bless you for your trust in Him, and all the "what ifs" will pass you by. Or the "what ifs" will come to pass, and you will be poor.

What If You Are Poor?

What if you are poor? Is being poor the end of the world? We have the word of our Lord and Savior that being poor is not the end of the world. It is in fact the opposite:

- Blessed be ye poor: for yours is the kingdom of God.

- Blessed are ye that hunger now: for ye shall be filled.

- Blessed are ye that weep now: for ye shall laugh.

(Luke 6:20–21)

Most of us are probably more familiar with the version of this passage in the Gospel of Matthew, which talks about "hunger and thirst after righteousness." But here, the Lord simply says "ye that hunger." It is a noble thing to hunger and thirst after righteousness; it is something we are all called to do, actually. But Jesus is talking about something else as well: He is pronouncing blessed those who care not for wealth, who are free of the love of money and the things it brings, who do not choose the display of earthly riches. He is not talking only about extraordinary mystics, living in caves in the desert. He is not talking only about the Mother Teresas of the world. He is talking about everyone who follows Him and practices the life of an apostle. He is talking about you and me and our fears of being poor in an affluent society.

In the corruption of these declining days of Western civilization, simply to follow Christ may mean embracing some form of poverty. If one way to make money is to be a doctor but medical training requires you to participate in the performance of abortions, then to be faithful to Christ, you may not be able to be a doctor. You will perhaps be an X-ray technician and make less money. Certain career choices simply may not be available to followers of Christ.

Following Christ means raising our children to be His sons and daughters. That can hardly be done without mothering the children. This may mean that your family will limp along on a single income for as long as there are children home. This may indeed mean having neither silver nor gold nor two coats. It may mean having to endure hardships. It may mean never owning your own home. It may mean no vacations, no second car, no dinners out. It may mean wearing secondhand clothes, raising your own simple food, playing charades instead of going to the movies. It may mean turning on the hot water only a couple of times a day. It may mean not having indoor plumbing. It may even mean being scarcely able to obtain food. These are real sufferings. And they may happen to those who follow God.

Talk is cheap. It's easy to say that to follow Christ is to be at enmity with the world. It's easy to say that God will take care of us. It's even easy to intellectually comprehend it. What's hard is to know it in your bones and to practice it, especially if you were raised in middle-class comfort and didn't expect yourself to be poor. Only the grace of God enables you to do it. *But you have to ask for the grace.* When I had the challenge, I didn't ask for the grace, and I regret it.

When our first baby was born, Bill quit work and returned to graduate school. For two years we lived without any steady income, and another baby came along during those years. Tension and worry were my primary occupations during that time. In retrospsect, I see how absurd, how foolish, how counterproductive, how harmful it was to be so entirely concerned with exactly the things that Jesus says in Luke 12 we should not be concerned with. The worry did make a difference — it made me an unhappy, fretful, ill-tempered woman. But it didn't do a bit of good.

It took years to overcome the effects of it. When Bill finally did get a job, we were determined that we were not going to go through that again. For a year we were okay because we had a low-rent apartment. But when we lost the apartment and had to move, I was quick to go to work — and you know the rest of the story. Nearly ten years were spent reacting to two years of student poverty, to the detriment of every member of the family.

The irony was that, even then, I knew *intellectually* that God would take care of me, but I didn't believe it. For me, prayer was a formality and an irregular one at that. If I did pray, it was only to ask for something. I was too absorbed in myself, in my own concerns, to praise God. In order to praise, you have to set yourself aside, and I wasn't mature enough to do that. I was accustomed to having security in this world — I thought I was entitled to it, somehow. And I thought that God helps those who help themselves, so I focused my attention on myself, not on Him.

Just recently Bill went through a brief period of unemployment and finally ended with a job that pays two-thirds of his previous salary. It was almost like a flashback to fifteen years earlier — two babies and poverty (with two teenagers now as well). I was surprised to find that, even though I have given my life to the Lord in the meantime, I experienced the same feelings as I had then: the same tension, the same fear, and same anxiety. *How can this be?* I wondered. *I know better!* But such is the power of our fallen flesh that we can be so easily seduced by its desire for security and comfort, guaranteed by our own efforts, that the temptation to self-pity is almost imperceptible. Which, of course, makes it all the more dangerous.

God does not permit us to wallow in self-pity. If we make these sacrifices for His sake, we can cling to the promise of the gospel: those who hunger now, and otherwise suffer in the flesh, because of their following Him, *shall be filled.*[5]

"Many are the afflictions of the righteous: but the LORD delivereth him out of them all" (Psalm 34:19). The Word does not promise that the deliverance will come in this life. There are spiritual blessings in store; there are delights that eye has not seen nor ear heard in the place He has prepared for us. Why should we let our hearts be troubled if we are only at a station along the way to our real destination? Worrying ourselves only weakens us; it only makes us vulnerable to attacks from the evil one. Of course, we do what we can, even the best we can, to provide for our material needs. But then we are content with what we have, whether it be abundant or meager. Our Father in heaven knows our needs; He decides whether to fill them now or later. If we are His followers, we trust Him.

My God shall supply all your need according to his riches in glory by Christ Jesus (Philippians 4:19).

PUBLIC SOLUTIONS
(What Government Could Do)

LORD, how long shall the wicked, how
long shall the wicked triumph?

Psalm 94:3

The fundamental flaw in the nation's politics regarding mothers and children can be distilled from two simple quotations. These are entirely typical observations, the sort of thing you've probably read many times and not even noticed.

The first is a passing comment in a news roundup story of all the different proposals before Congress affecting families and children: "Underlying the political discussion about children's issues is the emerging bipartisan consensus that children are a valuable resource and must be protected."[1]

There may be a bipartisan consensus that children are a valuable resource and must be protected, but I don't share it. Children are not a natural resource, like coal or timber. Yes, they should be protected. But we should protect them the same way we protect the bald eagle or the snail darter: leave them in their natural habitat. And the natural habitat of children is the family, with a mother and a father. If politicians want to protect children, let them protect motherhood.

215

The second is a paragraph by William Raspberry, a liberal columnist, urging increased funding of one of the oldest and best-established programs of social parenting:

> Americans love Head Start, because they know that it works. Not only does it get youngsters ready for academic success, but it also socializes them and develops their values. . . . But it does even more than that. By building self-esteem and school success, it reduces the likelihood that poor youngsters will grow up to become jobless, hopeless wards of the welfare system.[2]

After reading this, one wonders what, if anything, the program fails to do. Buy the children Christmas presents? Replace the phrase "Head Start" in this paragraph with the word "mother" and you would have a far more effective, less expensive solution to the same problems. The author of this column is a liberal, whose concern for the well-being of the underclass is sincere. The tragedy is that he believes a government program can do for children what in reality only committed people, usually known as mothers, can do.

Actually, there is some question about whether Head Start does all the things it is claimed to do. Some 1960s Ypsilanti, Michigan studies of early childhood education for "at-risk" children suggested some slightly lower level of juvenile delinquency for children who had the early intervention, some slightly higher levels of school performance, and the like. People advocating social parenting as a solution to the problems of poverty still cite those studies. Why? Because many subsequent studies of other children in other places with other staff have not replicated those results.

But you get a taste of the miracles social parenting is expected to perform.

It is no wonder that we expect miracles out of social parenting programs: the programs are costly, they are radical (at least, when they began they were), and for Congress to continue to expand them, the hype has to be tremendous. Raspberry's column is an example of precisely that kind of hype. Many organizations in Washington suck money from well-intentioned people around the country for the express purpose of persuading Congress to expand social parenthood. Their public statements allude to "promoting welfare of all children," of course, but in translation they mean expanding the welfare state and social parenthood.

Let's be honest. Government policies have led the attack on motherhood. Yes, it is a spiritual battle too, ultimately with a spiritual answer (see chapter 14). The spiritual battle must primarily be waged by those most directly affected: mothers and fathers of young children. The political battle must be waged by all Christians and all citizens. It is not necessary to be a Christian to understand that babies need mothers and to see the harm in destroying motherhood as an institution.

The church is influential in America. I know this is hard to believe when you take a look at some of the plagues that run rampant through the land. But we have the highest percentage of churchgoers of any large, modern, Western nation. And that means that pastors and priests and preachers have access to the minds of more people in this country than in any other similar country. What is said from a pulpit has a larger audience and receives more attention than practically anywhere else on earth. True, the Christian message must compete with more television and movies and other sources of ideas—but it still is there. The enormity of the opportunity magnifies the tragedy when the church merely repeats the message of the world instead of challenging it.

Christians are uniquely capable of defending the family because they are uniquely committed to it. Yet most American Christians would not be able to answer the question, *What does government do to encourage the destruction of motherhood?* So how can they begin to know what to want their elected representatives to change? And unless our understanding has some depth, we are in danger of being snookered by shrewd politicians with the right-sounding rhetoric.

The Power to Tax Is the Power to Destroy

That old slogan was never more true. Government's attack on motherhood has been relentlessly conducted over the past decades with that irresistible weapon, the tax code. Not with much publicity, but with great effectiveness.

The Personal Exemption

Forty years ago, when inflation was low and tax policy was profamily, most working-class families with children did not pay income tax. That was by conscious decision to exempt fathers from taxes because it was understood that the benefit to society of having mothers home to raise children far exceeded the monetary value of the taxes. During the same era four out of five jobs paid well enough to support a family. Interest rates were low, and home ownership was a growing phenomenon.

In 1948 the median-income family of four paid no income taxes and about 1 percent of its income in Social Security taxes. In 1989 the median-income family of four paid 7.51 percent of its income in Social Security taxes alone and slightly more in income taxes.

There's something fishy here: taxes are proportionally considerably heavier on families with children; and the more children, the more the proportion has changed. Singles and married couples with no children, however, have escaped this dramatic tax increase. Why?

In 1948 a single person paid 9.7 percent of income as taxes; in 1989 a single paid about 12.7 percent of income as taxes. In 1948 a childless two-income couple paid about 6.5 percent of income in taxes; in 1989, about 9.8 percent. Not a tremendous difference in percentage, really (though the dollar amount looks like a lot more). In 1948 a two-income couple with two children paid about .3 percent of income as taxes; in 1989, about 8 percent. In 1948 a one-income family with two children paid 3.4 percent of income as taxes; in 1989 the same family paid 8.9 percent of income as taxes — more than twice as much as in their parents' generation![3]

These figures, by the way, are very conservative. Phyllis Schlafly, a staunch defender of motherhood, uses different figures. She has this to say:

> When I had my children 30 years ago, the average couple with two children paid only 2 percent of its income in federal taxes. Today, the average couple with 2 children pays a whopping 24 percent in federal taxes. That explains why families feel the crunch about child care.[4]

Whatever figures you rely on, the point is clear: one way or another, to a greater or lesser degree, government punishes us financially for having children.

How does it do this? Through the personal exemption. The personal exemption was $600 in 1948 and did not go up again until 1972 when it became $750. In 1979 it became $1,000.[5] It became $2,000 only in 1989 — and that only with the support of President Ronald Reagan and after a tireless year-long effort by every Christian and profamily organization in the country, to write into the 1986 Tax Code revision a phased-in increase. Despite the occasional adjustments from time to time, the exemption has not kept up with inflation or with cost-of-living increases. The personal exemption of 1948 protected about 75 percent of a median-income family's income from taxes. The exemptions for the same median-income family today would shield less than 25 percent of household income.

To mean the same thing that it meant in 1948, the personal exemption today would have to be about $6,300 per person.

Think about that. Imagine, when you sat down last April to compute your family tax bill, if instead of taking the number of children and multiplying by $2,000, you could take the number of children and multiply it by $6,300. Think of how much lower your final tax bill would be! Think and weep.

That would be a measure of social justice. It would be the most important thing government could do to reverse the large-scale abandonment of our children to strangers. But unless every parent in the country demands it, countervailing interest groups will prevail.

If families could spend all the money they earned, most of them could take care of their own needs. Families would be strong. And then how could liberals argue that families "need" this or that government program? Families wouldn't need social parenting; they could afford to do their job themselves. But if present trends continue and families are rendered less and less able to provide for themselves economically, they will of necessity look to government for help in rearing their children. The people who believe in social parenthood are writing this scenario.

Public Policy Recommendation Number One: Raise the personal exemption to $6,300. Politics is the only reason the personal exemption could not be raised to $6,300 per person.

The nation is beginning to suffer the effects of a declining population: not enough children are being born to sustain a growing economy and social benefits for the future. The working poor are hardest hit by heavy taxes on their children. A significant increase in the personal exemption would not only help these families to make it into the middle class; it would create a tremendously strong incentive to stay off welfare. Raising children should be regarded as an "investment" for tax purposes, not as a "consumption" item.

After all, if children are a "valuable resource," they deserve tax protection like other valuable resources. Let the economists squabble over how much tax protection children are worth. If the pressure is strong enough, they'll come around to seeing things our way. When I was leading the fight on Capitol Hill to double the exemption from $1,000 to $2,000, even our conservative allies were against us at times. Different economists said government couldn't afford it. But through the grace of God we managed to generate enough pressure on both left and right that eventually all the theories yielded to political reality. The exemption finally was doubled.

The Child-Care Tax Credit

In 1954 Congress allowed working mothers to deduct expenses up to $600 a year for day care.[6] Under the presidency of Jimmy Carter, when feminists were riding high, the deduction became a tax credit. By 1985 this credit became a $3-billion pass-through subsidy to the day-care industry. And no wonder! Working parents who paid someone to care for a child aged fifteen or under could take a tax credit equal to 20 or 30 percent of the total cost of child care, up to a maximum of $4,800 for two or more children. The tax reform of 1986 limited the maximum effect of the credit to those with the lowest adjusted gross incomes, but the general drift is obvious.

Does something strike you as wrong about the whole idea? Here's government telling mothers that if they pay somebody else to raise their children, they'll get a tax break. But where does this leave mothers who stay home? Maybe they could work, maybe at wonderfully high salaries, but they decide to do what is best for their children. Do they get the same tax break? On the contrary! They subsidize the tax credit to the women who work. Is this fair?

I wouldn't see it quite the same way if the child-care tax credit helped mothers who were poor and struggling. But in fact, most people taking advantage of it have above-average incomes. It's the tax loophole for the two-income family.

If your retired mother lives with you and you want to help her keep some of her dignity by paying her to look after your children while you work—guess what? You can't claim the child care tax credit. Dependent relatives are not eligible. If you stash Mom in a nursing home and hire a stranger to mind the kids, well, that's fine in the eyes of Uncle Sam. One more strike against the extended family and in favor of social parenting.

Since the credit only covers care for two children, it's one more antichild instrument in government's arsenal. We've had a below-replacement birthrate for a decade now, and through the credit government communicates the message that when it comes to children, "fewer is preferred." Not only is this the wrong message, it is the immoral one.

I think I've said enough for you to get the message: the child-care tax credit rewards abandoning children and subsidizes the retreat from motherhood. It subsidizes the burgeoning day-care industry at the expense of struggling, one-income families trying to live on average or below average incomes.

Can we get rid of it? Not likely. Several million taxpayers take advantage of it, and not just left wing feminists either. Most of the working parents you know probably benefit from it, the conservatives as well as the liberals.

Public Policy Recommendation Number Two: Universalize the child-care tax credit.

That's right. Let mothers at home be eligible for the same credit. After all, they're taking care of children, aren't they? Why should both parents have to be working out of the home for government to value raising children? Why should the double-above-average-income families get the most tax breaks? Let the single-average-or-below-income families get one too.

And eliminate the two-child cap for the credit. If you're home raising five children, you should be entitled to five times the tax break of somebody who is raising one child. After all, you're raising five contributors to the Social Security Trust Fund for the next generation; your friend is raising only one. You're benefiting society five times as much in the long run.

Other Attacks on Motherhood

Being a mother is a worthy occupation. For too long government tax policy has treated motherhood as if it were completely dispensable. Every father in the country ought to be up in arms to defend his wife's motherhood. (So should every mother be defending her own motherhood, but let's be realistic and recognize that the mothers with little ones are too busy to do much in politics. Let the older mothers fight for the younger ones' rights.)

Direct Federal Aid to Day Care

In the 86th Congress in 1958, it was Jacob Javits' Day Care Assistance Act. In the 100th Congress in 1988, it was the Act for Better Child Care. Ten years from now in another Congress it will be another Act.

The drift will always be the same: the creation of a federal bureaucracy to supervise local child care; the promulgating of federal regulations with the force of law to govern local child care; the expenditure of your money and mine to pay the bureaucrats and enforce the regulations — all for the purpose of making motherhood a poor second choice to social parenting. In the name of facilitating the flight from motherhood of those who wish to flee it or of economic necessity, such legislation forces more mothers out of the home. That's the bottom line, disguise it how the lobbyists and advocates will.

If my church wants to help working mothers by offering a little nursery school, what right does the federal government have to regulate it? None at all, according to my reading of the Constitution. But every federal day-care bill tries to bring under its control not only the fifty thousand or so group care centers in the country, but also all the one or two million informal, unlicensed, neighborhood mothers who keep other kids during the day. The control of religious day care would be tantamount to persecution. Federal legislation would require federal "training" of all day-care personnel. States would have to bring their laws into conformity with federal standards. A federal bureaucracy would be created to develop the standards.

Would any of this help the mother who needs help in finding day care? Not on your life. Currently national day-care spending, private and public, is about $15 billion per year. If the increased regulations and "quality controls" envisioned in federal legislation go into effect, that could easily be 20 to 25 percent more. *Child Care Review,* the leading day-care industry journal, estimated that the ABC bill would increase parents' costs by nearly $1.2 billion. It would also force the closure of 12,600 existing day-care centers, pushing almost eight hundred thousand children out of care. That's not all. The proposed ABC legislation, supposedly intended to make day care more available and affordable, would actually raise day-care costs by as much as $16.21 per week.[7] So much for warmhearted rhetoric about "helping" working mothers.

Public Policy Recommendation Number Three: Enact no legislation, adopt no policy, promulgate no regulation that will create any federal agency or any federal government authority over nonfederal day care. This recommendation includes any federal standards, licensing requirements, plans, advisory committees, or other measures to extend federal authority over child rearing.

There are enough attacks on motherhood in government policies. Our culture is stridently antimotherhood. The social and political forces bent on destroying the traditional family are strong enough. Creation of any federal authority over child care would serve only to institutionalize the social parenthood clique in a position of legal supremacy, give them an unchecked influence over state government policies, and finance their schemes to advance their own agenda. Any legitimate problems with child care can — and should — be solved at the level of government closest to the problem, not by Washington bureaucrats.

Whatever Happened to a Family Wage?

In 1960, the traditional married couple with a wife at home had only 1.8 percent less income than the median income for all families. By 1985, there was an 11.5 percent difference in income. By 1989, families in which the wife did not work had 32.6 percent less income.[8]

In 1989, the census bureau reported that only about 29 percent — or 26 million — of the nation's 89.5 million households had enough left over for luxuries after payment of all basic costs to provide a "comfortable style of life." Of these 26 million households, nearly two-thirds were families with at least two people bringing home a paycheck.[9]

One-third less income if the wife does not work. Two-thirds of the households in the nation with not enough left over after basic costs for luxuries. It's obvious that even with the practice of serious thrift—even with a spiritual detachment from worldly things—many families cannot make ends meet on one paycheck.

Inflation is harder on middle- and low-income people than it is on the rich. And inflation was out of control for the decade of the seventies. Social Security taxes increased 58 percent between 1970 and 1981, and the wage base on which the tax was calculated increased more than 70 percent. Social Security taxes rose another 13 percent between 1981 and 1988. All of this took more money away from families.[10]

Meanwhile, federal spending on social programs has not diminished. All the policies that promote family dissolution are still in place.

Interesting, isn't it, how society's ideas have changed over the century? In 1910, liberals discouraged the employment of women so that they could be free to fulfill their higher function as mothers; in 1990, liberals encourage the employment of women and the destruction of motherhood in the name of liberating women.

The idea of a "family wage" used to be a major demand of organized labor: that a man's salary should be adequate to support a family in decency so that wives would not have to work and children would not be motherless. That noble old idea disappeared with feminism. Suddenly, it became necessary to give "equal pay for equal work"—no matter whether the woman collecting the man's salary was the wife of a wealthy man and chose to work for fun or whether she was the single mother who needed every penny. Justice in wage scales had to be sacrificed to a rigid ideological "equality." The consequence? A woman who relied on the single income of her husband was forced to find a job because her husband's income was no longer adequate.

Public Policy Recommendation Number Four: Amidst all the federal regulation of wages and the workplace, explicit permission and encouragement should be given to the concept of "head of household wage," i.e., that an individual who is the sole support of other dependents should be eligible, should the employer wish thus to reward him or her, for a "head of household wage differential," thus making possible a family wage. I would never make such a wage scale mandatory lest it become an excuse for hiring young or single or childless employees and discriminating against family men and women.

This cosmetic reform would benefit few people. Of greater benefit to large numbers of people would be some down and dirty economic reforms to help control inflation: cutting government spending, lowering taxes, meaningful welfare reform. Some maintain that amending the Constitution to require that the government's budget be balanced would also address the problem, as would the line-item veto which would allow the president to veto unnecessary special-interest spending. Both these measures are intended to secure the future and control the damage that politicians can do with a mindset of "let the next generation pay for it." Limiting the terms of members of Congress might also have the same effect. I'm not an economist, and this is not a book about economics, so I'm not going into more detail. If you want to pursue this further, check the endnotes for this chapter and read the publications of the Rockford Institute Center on the Family in America.

Divorce

If I could wave a magic wand and change one thing about the country in the last twenty years, just one thing, to protect motherhood and families, that one thing would be this: repeal no-fault divorce laws. When one in twenty people got divorced, it didn't matter so much. But when half of all marriages are predicted to break up, it is a national epidemic of destruction.

Not only has no-fault divorce produced a generation of walking wounded, of people who lived through a divorce in their childhood and have been carrying the scars for twenty years already. Not only has no-fault divorce created a whole new class of the poor: formerly-middle-class divorced women with children. Not only has the accessibility of divorce instilled in young women such a (realistic) fear of being abandoned that they dare not choose their children over their jobs. Not only has the large-scale separation of children from their fathers been the greatest social catastrophe of the century for blacks. Not only has large-scale father absence produced higher levels of teen suicide, mental illness, increased violence among adolescents, and increased drug use.[11]

But the longer it all continues, the more it becomes a vicious cycle. The more single mothers there are, the stronger the case for social parenthood: obviously, goes the argument, people cannot manage their own lives, so they need institutional parents. That kind of thinking has been applied to the poor for generations already and has resulted in permanent welfare dependence; now the same kind of remedy is being applied to the middle classes ravaged by divorce.

The more institutional support there is for single parenting, the more attractive that option becomes. And the more dependence there is on the institutional support, the higher taxes must be. And the higher everybody's taxes become, the more women will have to go to work to pay the taxes. And the more they will come to rely on the institutional substitutes for motherhood.

Private acts have public consequences. Your divorce affects my family's ability to make ends meet on my husband's income.

Public Policy Recommendation Number Five: Repeal no-fault divorce laws. This is a matter for fifty states, operating on impetus within the state. It is not a matter of federal intervention.

Right now, the mood of the public is shifting. Until recently, divorce was a sacred cow. But it has become such an epidemic, and so much pain is so obviously connected with it that the climate is shifting. Today, one criticism of no-fault divorce comes from all sides. Politicians are not yet ready to lead on the issue, however: they are still cautious followers. They need to be made aware of public willingness to experiment with major changes. I predict that a politician who bites the bullet and takes some leadership to repeal no-fault with empathy and compassion will have a bright future. Herewith, I offer some suggestions for such a politician:

Mandate waiting periods. Mandate reconciliation attempts. Return divorce to traditional fault standards; let there be a reason for the divorce. Let one party defend the marriage. Until the twentieth century, fathers often got custody of children in divorce. That was a pretty good system: it gave both women and men an incentive to stay married, which should be exactly the goal of laws pertaining to the family. The common situation is that women want to keep their children and men want their freedom — and the current practice of giving women custody enables both to get what they want with easy divorce. If men were automatically given custody, they might think twice about encouraging the breakup. And that would be good for the children and for the family.

Many, perhaps most, of the divorces in the nation could be prevented if doomed, hopeless marriages never occurred in the first place. Make marriage harder to obtain: enforce a long waiting period; mandate serious preparation. These requirements ought to be a minimum of church practice and reinforced in secular laws as well.

Don't be swayed by the argument that if they can't marry, they'll just live together anyway. Let them if that's their inclination. At least then, neither one of them will be deceived into thinking the situation is permanent. At least then, the fickleness will be seen for the philandering it is and won't corrupt the good name of marriage. And if at the same time certain tax or other benefits are *reserved for* married couples, the unwillingness to marry will not be a matter of indifference.

One friend of mine, a marriage counselor, had a suggestion so novel and outrageous it just might have some potential. Let there be two different types of marriage contract, he said: Type A and Type B. When the dewy-eyed lovers stroll up to the marriage bureau to apply for a license, the clerk will ask them whether they want Type A or Type B. They'll ask for an explanation. Here's what the clerk will say: Type A is the simple, temporary kind: we agree to live together as long as it pleases us, we plan no children, and we can dissolve this contract by mutual consent at any time, with a 50–50 distribution of property acquired during the span of the contract. We make no pretense of preserving even a ghost of Christian matrimony with a Type A contract; we just formalize a civil arrangement. Type B is the other kind: here each partner pledges permanent fidelity, agrees to the permanent support of children, and all the rest. Type B contracts can be dissolved only with great difficulty. Upgrades are allowed from Type A to Type B and are mandated in the event of a birth to the union, but Type B cannot be downgraded to Type A. Here's a brochure to read with further information. Now, which type of contract did you want?

It was my friend's position that just confronting the issue that starkly would bring to the fore hidden incompatibilities within the couple. My hunch is that most women assume that they are entering a Type B (permanent) marriage while many men operate on the assumption that they are entering a Type A (temporary) marriage. If the Type B contract had enough teeth in its enforcement, which it would have to have, the folks who are not really seeking a permanent union would avoid it. Right then and there, standing before the clerk's window, a sweet young thing might decide to reconsider her wedding plans. One more divorce and all its accompanying misery just might be avoided.

Radical idea? Yes, for a lot of reasons. But it intrigues me. I hope that someday some legislator looking for creative solutions to the no-fault epidemic may read about it and modify it until it becomes practical.

Conclusion

I think we have covered the waterfront.

- Economic attack on the family through the tax code;

- Subsidizing of the institutions of social parenthood;

- Destroying the family as a viable economic unit by the diminution of men's wages; and

- Attacking motherhood by no-fault divorce, which robs motherhood of its last protection, marriage.

All of these put together add up to a clear government bias, bias against God's plan for women and children, and, yes, for men as well.

What are we going to do about it? Our first responsibility is our own spiritual one. Each and every person who calls himself or herself a Christian must first know and follow God's will for himself, herself, and their family. There is no substitute for that tall order.

But Christians are citizens as well. And nowhere are we told to accept passively whatever government dishes out to us. Government policies on family and children have been shaped for the last thirty years by professionals who are following ideological visions, not by people whose priority is the family.

Every Christmas we celebrate how Jesus Christ Himself honored the family by taking flesh in a human family, how He depended on a mother and lived under the protection and authority of a human father. If that example does not remind us of our obligation to protect the family, what will? Many political issues deserve the attention of Christians.

I don't wish to diminish the importance of any one of them. But I do say this: unless the family is strengthened, none of the other social ills *can* be solved.

> There is no longer doubt that emotional illness, in almost every case, is a continuance of patterns of response to some sort of mistreatment or mistraining or both over long periods during early childhood; it is a disorder in the feelings toward others.[12]

Unless motherhood is restored and honored—unless children are reared once again in security and attachment in a whole family and given the opportunity to develop a conscience and emotional competence—unless children experience love and discipline from parents—*they will not be able to discipline themselves. They will not be able to take responsible care of another person.*

Unless motherhood is restored, an orderly society will not be possible. The hemorrhage of people into homelessness will not be stanched; the increase of homosexuality will not be reversed; the plague of promiscuity and illegitimacy will not be solved. Band-Aids may be applied, I'll grant. But solutions there will not be. Because the symptoms of social decay ultimately stem from people's inability to cope with reality. And we develop an ability to cope with ourselves and our lives at our mother's knee. Economic conditions and other things may be factors, to be sure, just as tax policy is a factor in the destruction of the family. But when all is said and done, social decay is not the fault of institutions or policies or programs; it is the fault of people. A loving, competent mother, provided for and protected by a faithful father, is the foundation of the human personality and therefore of human society.

Christian political energy must focus clearly, consistently, and relentlessly on protecting motherhood. Restoring motherhood to a position of honor and value must be the priority underlying all other political alliances and judgments. Averting the attack on the heart of the family must not be an incidental add-on to a list of political concerns; it must be fundamental to Christian political involvement.

16

A FEW BOTTOM LINES AND AN EXIT MANUAL

(How to Change Your Life Radically Without Rocking the Boat)

To everything there is a season, and a
time to every purpose under the heaven.
Ecclesiastes 3:1

Now you know about the attack on motherhood in contemporary society: the subtle psychological warfare feminists wage against mothers; the federal tax system's explicit economic attack on motherhood; the intellectual fashions of the "working family" and social parenthood. I hope you are also more aware of the hidden physical and emotional dangers to children of group day care.

I pray you are a bit more alert to some of the wiles of the old deceiver Satan and to your own vulnerability to creeping materialism. I hope that, being now aware of modern society's vicious cruelty to women, you are better able to protect yourself from delusions that your life is just wasted if you devote yourself to other people.

If your life has been spared the all-too-common conflicts of motherhood and career, count yourself lucky. But don't be quick to judge others. Remember 1 Samuel 16:7: "For the LORD seeth not as man seeth; for man looketh on the outward appearance, but the LORD looketh on the heart."

Take comfort in that same verse as well if you are a mother who, of necessity, with absolutely no choice, must work. If your heart is in harmony with God's will, that's what matters. "Refrain thy voice from weeping, and thine eyes from tears; for thy work shall be rewarded, saith the LORD" (Jeremiah 31:16). The Lord knows your circumstances; He has allowed them to happen to you; He will support you and protect your children if your heart is completely His. "We know that all things work together for good to them that love God, to them who are the called according to His purpose" (Romans 8:28).

Can You Have It All?

But maybe you are of two minds. Perhaps you are a professional and enjoy your work and make a valuable contribution to the world. Perhaps you are a prolife nurse in a secular hospital — and you have opportunities to witness at work that few other people could possibly have. But you also want to be a good mother. You wonder whether perhaps you can have it all. Reading this book has made you uneasy. It has stirred some sleeping doubts in you, concerns you thought you had dealt with long ago. Now you are not sure whether you are "called according to his purpose" or are simply hearing your own desires and wishes.

Let me assure you, you can have it all. But not all at the same time. Like a tree, your life goes through seasons. Right now, if you have young children and have freely chosen to work, this season of your life may be meant for nurturing motherhood. The season will soon end, and nursing will be there for you when it does. But your children will never again look to you as they now do, never again be in need of so much of you. You will have other chances to advance your career; you will never have another chance to form your children.

But you're not sure. . . . On one hand, the kids are doing fine, and God really has put you in an extraordinary position to serve Him. And your husband is free of worry because of your income. All these facts point to keeping things as they are. But on the other hand, you're agitated by what you have read in this book. All of a sudden, you're not so sure; it occurs to you that you may be deceiving yourself. What are you to do?

Remember Psalm 34:22: "The Lord redeemeth the soul of his servants: and none of them that trust in him shall be desolate." If you do God's will, you won't be desolate. One way or another, He will take care of you. "Taste and see that the Lord is good; blessed is the man that trusteth in him" (v. 8). The Lord will deliver you from your fears (v. 4); the Lord will save you out of all your troubles (v.6).

"Trust in the Lord with all thine heart; and lean not unto thine own understanding. In all thy ways acknowledge him, and he shall direct thy paths" (Proverbs 3:5–6). Trust Him, and then pray for guidance. Examine your own heart, and then set aside your desires, your habitual ways of thinking, your preferences, your wants. Open yourself totally to Him. Seek to know *His* heart and *His* mind for your life. Ask Him to speak to your heart through His Scriptures, through His ministers, through your husband. Tell God you are willing to do what He wants, but that you need to hear something so clear you can't possibly misunderstand it. Pray steadily. Tell the Lord you are willing for Him to fulfill His promise in Ezekiel 36:26–27: "A new heart also I will give you, and a new spirit will I put within you; and I will take away the stony heart out of your flesh, and I will give you an heart of flesh. And I will put my spirit within you, and cause you to walk in my statutes, and ye shall keep my judgments, and do them." An answer may not come for a long time, but when it does, you will know it.

Exit Manual

Changing your life does not have to be sudden and abrupt. In fact, phasing out of the world and into the home is best accomplished by degrees.

Budget

Money is the first thing to go if you quit, so think about it well ahead of time. Even if you intended to stash your income in a savings account, there's been leakage. And the whole family has grown accustomed to some things that are "brought to you by Mommy."

Examine the family budget. Do not ask the question, What can we live without? That's starting at the wrong end. Instead ask, What do we need to live? Start with rent and food, and enhance it the least you can. Don't forget that with less, income taxes will be less. Anticipate major expenses for the next two years. Are there debts that have to be paid? School tuitions coming up? A new baby in the offing? Which of you carries the health insurance for the family? Consider all these things, and factor them into the planning.

Your husband should have a frank talk with his employer about what his career path looks like for the next two to five years. If the boss has been thinking about abolishing your husband's department, prudence might suggest that your husband get a more stable job before you rock your boat. But if his boss assures him a cost of living raise every year, then you know where you stand. If you can live with that, with reasonable sacrifices, keep reading. If you honestly can't live with that, go back to chapter 11 and think about home-based business options for yourself. A part-time, home-work schedule might be better for you than the desperation of fighting the wolf from the door every month.

But suppose you decide to make a go of it on your husband's income . . . at some point in the future. What's the first thing to do? The very, very first? Immediately, begin stashing your entire paycheck in the savings account. Well, tithe out of it, but *no other exceptions.* Wean yourself from depending on it. Let it keep coming, and know that you are building a buffer for a rainy day, but *do not depend on it.* For anything. The sooner you all adjust to the reality of one income, the easier everything will be.

Plan Your Retreat

As you plan your departure, you want it to be amicable. You want the goodwill of your boss and coworkers when you go. After all, it's a form of witness. Sooner or later, you're bound to tell someone that the Lord had something to do with your career change. And you don't want people to mutter, "Remember Sally? And how she left so abruptly, and we had all that crisis because she just up and quit without warning? Did you realize she was one of those religious crackpots?" Much better if you handle your departure very professionally, with minimum disruption of everyone else's work routine. Then they'll respect you and your convictions.

This means nothing sudden. Stay until you are replaced; help find and train your replacement if you have the opportunity. Perhaps you can quit in stages. Be willing to work part time for a while and then to consult or come in on an "as needed" basis for a time. You might even do occasional projects in the future, on a per-job pay basis. If your children are already in full-time day care, it won't hurt them at all to phase into part time. A period of part-time work will help to tighten the family belt in stages, as well.

If you're pregnant or planning to be, it's easy to explain that you've had a change of heart about your career: reorganizing priorities with pregnancy is common. If you're not pregnant, be prepared to explain and defend your change of heart about working, especially to feminist coworkers and younger women workers who may regard you as their trailblazer.

Prepare Yourself Emotionally

Be prepared, once you announce your departure, to be a nonperson instantly. While before you were involved in decisions, now you won't be. Although formerly people came to you for advice, now they won't. Your successor will get all the attention.

Don't be surprised if you hear your boss saying things like, "Well, she did a fine job, really, but I guess the job has just become too much for her." That happened to me, and let me tell you it hurt. It implied that I was losing my competence. I wasn't! I was just as smart and able to do the job as I had been a year before, but I was reprioritizing my life. Later, I realized that while I had used that phrase to myself, I had not described my actions to other people in those terms. So, to spare your own feelings, ask yourself what you would like people to say about you, and then say it about yourself first.

Prepare Your Family Emotionally

The younger your children are, the easier it will be. Promises of more trips to the park with Mom will probably be all it takes to win them over. (Remember to keep the promises.) Plus the freedom to sleep later in the morning. But if they're into the preteen stage, they've already become materialists, and they may have bragged about your job to other kids. On both counts they're likely to resent what the change means to them. No more impulse stops at fast-food restaurants. No more feeling superior to the other kids in the "my parents earn more than yours" game. No more lording it over the other kids: "Well, we went to Canada on our vacation, you just went to visit your grandma, ha ha."

Your parents may not be pleased either, especially if they sacrificed to put you through college and now see their investment eroding. Or maybe they truly don't like your husband and didn't mind your working long hours for an employer, but the thought of your working long hours for "that man" just burns them. When I reprioritized my life, one relative told my children that I didn't count any more, that I had become a mousy little Christian with no mind of my own. You can imagine what this kind of comment did to enhance the contempt my children already felt for me. You might anticipate such problems and discuss with your husband how you're going to handle certain relatives. Perhaps together you can devise a strategy to inoculate your children against vicious comments.

Prepare your husband as well. He may have unrealistic expectations that with all your newfound "free time" the house will look like one of those mansions on TV and dinners will be his favorites every night and you'll be bursting with energy at bedtime too. You may expect all that of yourself, too. You may have visions of yourself sitting around the kitchen table, following instructions in art-and-craft books with the kids. Or maybe you have visions of yourself in the garden, surrounded with gorgeous vegetable crops as the children contentedly putter nearby.

Forget it, and tell your husband to forget it. You will be busier at home than you ever were before. You will feel further behind than ever before. And you'll wonder how it happened. Here's one clue: when you both were working, and the kids out of the house for eight or ten hours a day, there wasn't anybody making work in the house eighteen hours a day. Now you and the children will be living in the house all day, actively affecting your environment: using scissors and leaving schnibbles on the floor and forgetting to put the scissors back; making dinner from scratch and dirtying six pans and the oven every day. Even your grocery budget will go *up*, not *down*, when you quit working and geometrically increase the amount of food prepared and consumed at home.

Prepare Yourself Spiritually

You will be frustrated. You'll look at a day, then a week, and ask yourself, What did I accomplish today? Three meals a day, big deal. No, not three. Three times the number of people: nine, twelve, or eighteen meals a day. That is a big deal.

Decide what your sources of self-esteem will be in the new order. Will you feel satisfied if you make a new recipe one night a week and give yourself a sense of accomplishment from achieving that goal? Or will you not allow yourself to relax until you have repainted the girls' room? Decide for yourself what you want to do, and then tell yourself what your reward will be for achieving your goal. Give yourself the reward too. Don't expect other people to be grateful for what you do for them. Kids will take it all for granted, and once the novelty wears off, husbands aren't likely to spend much time in appreciation either. They'll be glad they don't have to pick the kids up at day care anymore or fix dinner two nights a week themselves, but the time that they once spent doing those chores will disappear without a trace. Don't expect it to be devoted to companionship with you.

Your need for adult companionship will increase enormously, not at first, but after a few months when the novelty wears off. Alas, simultaneously your contact with the adult world will have diminished from dozens or scores of adult conversations a day with many different adults to . . . one. Husband. Warn husband ahead of time that he will be your only contact with the adult world, and tell him what that means in practical terms. Your being around more won't automatically drop time into both your laps. You will want to schedule time together, structure it, plan it. You'll need it more than ever, and don't feel shy about getting it.

This changing of life is a response to a call from God. You must renew the calling each morning. There is no substitute for dedicating each day to the Lord. The pace of the work world is hectic, but it enables us to excuse ourselves: "I didn't pray today, but gosh, I had to save the world instead." Now you have no more excuses like that. And the consequences are sure: no prayer = bad moods, problems; prayer = peace. It's that simple, and I have seen it a million times. Being human, I still fail to pray some days. And always regret it. But such is the nature of the stubborn sin inside us.

Now there will be no excuse for not confronting the sin in yourself. Or for failing to see how much you need the Cross. To avoid depression, you have to confront the least desirable things in yourself: laziness you never thought you had, impatience you thought you had overcome, self-centeredness you thought was somebody else's problem, resentments you didn't realize you still had, self-pity you thought you had outgrown.

While you were active in the world, the pace was fast enough that you didn't need to come to grips with these weaknesses. You were dealing with enough other people that you could avoid seeing yourself. But at home, where the job of spiritually forming children is on your shoulders, you will soon realize that before you can lead anybody else to holiness, you have to pursue it yourself. If you are forming somebody else's character and trying to develop gentleness in your children, you must be aware of your anger so that you can get rid of it. If you are teaching your children to forgive, you must see the resentments you cherish so that you can get rid of them. In other words, as we mothers at home are trying to change our children and our families, we must be changing our own hearts with steady discipline and prayer. We're going into the spiritual hothouse, so let us not go in unprepared for the spiritual battles ahead. The last thing Satan wants is mothers training children to be holy. So holiness is the first thing we must pursue.

We cannot pursue it alone, however. As you plan your new budget and your phase-out from work, be also planning your spiritual life. It is imperative that you have a support group of other mature women with whom you stand on no ceremony and don't have to pretend to be anything other than yourself. It is imperative that you pray and read Scripture regularly. But without the friendly nosiness of someone else to remind you, that good intention will be buried in an agenda of busyness. You know it will. So don't kid yourself. And don't delay in finding a spiritual comrade with whose help you can arm yourself for the coming struggle.

> *Put on the whole armour of God, that ye may be able to stand against the wiles of the devil. For we wrestle not against flesh and blood, but against the principalities, against powers, against the rulers of the darkness of this world, against spiritual wickedness in high places. Wherefore take unto you the whole armour of God, that ye may be*

able to withstand in the evil day, and having done all, to stand. Stand therefore, having your loins girt about with truth, and having on the breastplate of righteousness; and your feet shod with the preparation of the gospel of peace; Above all, taking the shield of faith, wherewith ye shall be able to quench all the fiery darts of the wicked. And take the helmet of salvation, and the sword of the Spirit, which is the word of God, praying always with all prayer and supplication in the Spirit, and watching thereunto with all perseverance. (Ephesians 6:11–18)

Go forth now, in peace, to love and serve the Lord and your family.

NOTES

Chapter One: Whatever Happened to Motherhood?

1. Vera Chatz, "A Day in a Daycare Center" *The Doctor's People*, 2, no. 1. This medical newsletter is available from 1589 Sherman Avenue, Suite 318, Evanston, IL 60201.
2. U.S. Department of Commerce News Release, no. CB89–119, 27 July 1989.
3. "Child Care," *American Family*, December 1988.
4. Renee Schafer, "Some Parents Deny Kids What's Needed Most," *Plano Star Courier*, 12 Oct. 1988, reprinted in *Couple-to-Couple League Family Foundations*, May-June 1989.
5. ArLynn Leiber Presser, "Mom a Sound Concept," *Chicago Tribune*, 20 November 1989.
6. Theresa Wetzel, quoted in "The Working Mom's Handbook," *Ladies Home Journal*, August 1989, 58.
7. Story reported by Katarine Runske, long-time chairman of the Family Campaign of Sweden, at the 1989 Annual Conference of Family Solidarity in Ireland. Reported in an article "Sweden — a Nightmare for Christian Parents," *Family Solidarity News* 3, no. 10, Winter 1989, 5. (Family Solidarity, 17 Montague Lane, Dublin 2, Ireland)
8. Pierre Thomas, "On the Commuter Treadmill: Virginia Family's Life Driven by Rush Hours," *Washington Post*, 3 December 1989, A1 ff.
9. All the quotations are from actual children, ages six through eleven, cited in "Ask the Kids," *Ladies Home Journal*, August 1989, 76.

Chapter Two: Who Are the Lonely?

1. David A. Mrazek, et al., "Insecure Attachment in Severely Asthmatic Preschool Children: Is It a Risk Factor?" *Journal of the Academy of Child and Adolescent*

·*Psychiatry,* 26 (1987), 516–520, cited in "The Breath of Life," *The Family in America,* November 1987, 3.

2. Claudia Pap Mangel, "Licensing Parents: How Feasible?" *Family Law Quarterly,* 22, Spring 1988, 17–39.

Chapter Three: Olive Shoots or Weeds Underfoot?

1. Ken Wilson, *The Obedient Child* (Ann Arbor: Servant Books, 1988), 52.
2. Susan D. Holloway, Kathleen S. Gorman, and Bruce Fuller, "Child-Rearing Beliefs Within·Diverse Social Structures: Mothers and Day-Care Providers in Mexico," *International Journal of Psychology,* 23 (1988): 303–317.
3. Ibid., cited in "Between Two Worlds," *The Family in America,* April 1989, 4.
4. Cited in Marian Tompson, "A discussion of daycare," *The Doctor's People: A Medical Newsletter for Consumers,* 2, no. 2. The newsletter address is 1578 Sherman Avenue, Suite 318, Evanston, IL 60201.

Chapter Four: Time, Guilt, and Strong Families

1. Vicki Whitney, Jennifer Trynin, and Nicola Knipe, "Work and Families," an account of a seminar in Boston by Penelope Leach, T. Berry Brazelton, and Benjamin Spock, *Washington Parent,* November 1988, 1–5.
2. Cited in "Briefly," *Focus on the Family,* July 1989, 11.
3. Bradley Googins and Dianne Burden, "Vulnerability of Working Parents: Balancing Work and Home Roles," *Social Work,* 32, no. 4 (July-Aug. 1987), 295–299, cited in "Job-Family Strain," *The Family in America,* November 1987.
4. Cited in Nancy Kerns, "The Part-time Payoff," in "Parenting Extra," *Parenting,* June/July 1989, 20.
5. Nancy Gilmore Hill, "How to Send Your Child to School Healthy," *Today's Christian Woman,* September/October, 1985, 63–64.
6. "Unhappy on the job," item in "Babynews Questions and Answers," *Pampers Baby Care 9–12 Months,* 1988. The item is condensed from *Parents* magazine, 21.
7. Research by Ann C. Crouter, associate professor of human development at Pennsylvania State University, published in *Developmental Psychology* 23, 431–440, and cited in "Married with Child," *Psychology Today,* February 1988, 14.
8. Mollie Klapper Bersin, M.D., "How Working Mothers Solve Problems at Home," *Today's Health,* 38, no. 1, January 1960, 40–75.
9. Ibid.
10. T. Berry Brazelton, "Nurturing the Nurturers," *World Monitor,* March 1989, 14–17.
11. Ibid.
12. Bersin, 40–75.

13. Ibid.
14. Karl Zinsmeister, "Child-Raising and Today's Social Environment," paper delivered at Eagle Forum seminar on child care, 10 January 1989.
15. Charlotte Montgomery, "Can Working Wives Make It Pay?" *Better Homes and Gardens,* November 1957, 68–138.
16. Mary Rowland, "Can You Afford Not to Work?" *Woman's Day,* 28 March 1989, 54–58.

Chapter Five: What Is Day Care, Anyway?

1. Gathorne-Hardy, Jonathan. *The Unnatural History of the Nanny* (New York: Dial, 1973), 180.
2. Ibid., 148.
3. Ibid., 258.
4. Ibid., 136.
5. Ibid., 136.
6. Ibid., 122.
7. Quoted in Marguerite Hoxie Sullivan, "Looking for Mary Poppins," *The Washington Woman,* October 1986, 49.
8. Quoted in Diane Granat, "Are You My Mommy?" *The Washingtonian,* October 1988, 199.
9. Mike Folks and Enrique Gonzales, *Washington Times,* 26 January 1989, 1.
10. Sandra Evans, *Washington Post,* 2 February 1989, 1.
11. Leah Y. Latimer, "When Day Care Goes On Into the Night," *Washington Post,* 23 January 1989, A1.

Chapter Six: Ideas and Consequences

1. "Conversation" with Steve Kemper, *Hartford Courant,* 20 March 1988.
2. Quoted in Dennis Meredith, "The Nine-to-Five Dilemma," *Psychology Today,* February 1986, 42.
3. Quoted in Robert J. Trotter, "Project Day Care," *Psychology Today,* December 1987, 38.
4. Figure cited in Joan Walsh, "The 21st-Century School," *Parenting,* December/January 1990, 127–130.
5. Testimony of Jule M. Sugarman before the Subcommittee on Education and Health, Joint Economic Committee, U.S. Congress, 14 December 1988.
6. Ibid.
7. Cited in Elizabeth Ruppert, Ph.D., "The Absent Parent: Targeting the Issue," testimony delivered to the Intergovernmental Advisory Council on Education, 12 May 1988, published by Family Research Council of America, 1988.

Chapter Seven: On Sweden and the United States

1. Fred M. Hechinger, "About Education," *New York Times,* 17 August 1988, B9.
2. Ibid.
3. "Child Care in Sweden," part of the series *Fact Sheets on Sweden,* published by the Swedish Institute; Stockholm, Sweden, April 1987.
4. Quoted in Allan C. Carlson, "Work and Family: On a Collision Course in America?" *Persuasion at Work,* May 1986, 5.
5. Ibid.
6. Neil Gilbert, "Sweden's Disturbing Family Trends," *Wall Street Journal,* 24 June 1987, 27.
7. Ibid.
8. Ibid.
9. David Popenoe, "What Is Happening to the Family in Sweden?", *Social Change in Sweden,* no. 36, Swedish Information Service, Swedish Consulate General, New York, December 1986.
10. Gilbert, "Sweden's Disturbing Family Trends," 27.
11. Ibid.
12. Paul Lindblom, "The Swedish Family: Problems, Programs and Prospects," *Current Sweden* (Stockholm, Sweden: Svenska Institutet), August 1986.
13. Richard Kollodge, "Sweden's Gays move out of the back streets," *Washington Blade,* 27 May 1988, 1.
14. This quotation and much of the analysis that follows is from Allan C. Carlson, "The Decline and Fall of Mom and Apple Pie," *Persuasion at Work,* 7, no. 1, January 1985. (Rockford, Ill.: The Rockford Institute)
15. Testimony of Douglas J. Besharov, resident scholar at the American Enterprise Institute for Public Policy Research, before the Subcommittee on Human Resources, Committee on Education and Labor, U.S. House of Representatives, 21 April 1988.
16. Marcella D. Hadeed, "A National Daycare System: Foundations Well Set," *Family Protection Report,* October 1985, 3–6.

Chapter Eight: The Most Dangerous Enemy of Motherhood

1. Boye de Mente, *The Whole Japan Book* (Phoenix, Arizona: Phoenix Books), 324–5.
2. These regulations are quoted in Taketoshi Kodama, "Preschool Education in Japan," National Institute for Educational Research Occasional Paper, April 1983; Tokyo, Japan: National Institute for Educational Research. Document within the ERIC System, no. ED 235 876.
3. Irene S. Shigaki, "Child Care Practices in Japan and the United States: How Do They Reflect Cultural Values in Young Children?", *Young Children,* 38, no. 4, May 1983, 13–24.

4. Ibid.
5. Carol Simons, "They Get by with a lot of Help from Their *Kyoiku Mamas,*" *Smithsonian Magazine,* n.d., 44–52.
6. Emiko Hannah Ishigaki, "A Comparative Study of Educational Environments of Preschool Children in Japan and Israel," ERIC, no. Ed 279 414 (1986), 9.

Chapter Nine: Dependent Is Not a Four-Letter Word

1. Bureau of the Census press release CB88–157, 30 September 1988.
2. Judy Bachrach, "Follow the Leader," *Savvy,* February 1989, 108.
3. Philomene Gates quoted by Don Oldenburg, "Life After Death: Overcoming the Loneliness of Widowhood," *The Washington Post,* Style Plus, May 17, 1990.
4. *Guidelines for Selecting Bias-Free Textbooks and Storybooks,* Council on Interracial Books for Children, 1841 Broadway, New York, NY 10023, 60.

Chapter Eleven: On Talents and Waste

1. *Begin with Clean Report: A Cleaning Center Help Bulletin and Catalog,* a collection of resources to teach you how to organize and clean, and offering you the equipment to do it all. The Cleaning Center, P. O. Box 39, 311 S. 5th Ave, Pocatello, Idaho, 83204. Telephone: (208)232-6212.
2. Watchman Nee, "Why This Waste?" a chapter from *The Normal Christian Life,* reprinted in pamphlet form by Christian Literature Crusade, Fort Washington, PA., 1984.
3. I am indebted for the analysis of Mary Magdalene to *The Life of the Holy Myrrh-Bearer and Equal to the Apostles Mary Magdalene,* trans. Isaac E. Lambertson (Liberty, TN: St. John of Kronstadt Press, Liberty). It seems to be a translation from a 1910 publication in Moscow.

Chapter Twelve: Options for a Working Mother

1. One source of good suggestions for inexpensive dates is Debra Evans, "Romancing for Life," *Christian Parenting,* January/February 1990, 44–50.
2. All figures from "Home-Based Employment Increases," *Family Net,* 13 March 1988, published by the Family Research Council, Washington, D.C.
3. "Escape from the Office," *Newsweek,* 24 April 1989, 58–60.
4. Marion Behr, president, and Wendy Lazar, vice-president, are national spokeswomen for this growing movement. Their directory, Women Working Home, is a valuable resource. Contact WWH at 24 Fishel Road, Edison, New Jersey 08817, (201) 548-7524.

5. Statistics from the 1988 Family Day Care Licensing Study, reported in the *Family Day Care Bulletin,* December 1988, published by The Children's Foundation, 815 Fifteenth St. NW, Suite 928, Washington, D.C. 20005. This organization favors licensing and regulation of family day care, but it also provides some potentially helpful materials if you are a family day-care provider.

Chapter Thirteen: Viruses, IQ's, and Emotions

1. Kate Millet, *Sexual Politics* (1970; report, New York: Ballantine, 1978), 506.
2. Ibid., 86.
3. Cited in Igor Shafarevich, *The Socialist Phenomenon,* trans. William Tjalsma (New York: Harper and Row, 1980), 12.
4. Ibid.
5. "First Evidence That Stress May Turn Genes On and Off," in "The Cutting Edge," *Washington Post Health,* 24 January 1989.
6. Michael Segell, "Of Human Bonding," *Parenting,* May 1989, 58–62.
7. All data on medical aspects of day care come from a special supplement to *Pediatrics,* "Day Care and Illness," June 1986. These data have been regularly updated; if anything, some of these figures are more conservative than later research has shown.
8. Alison Clarke-Stewart, *Child Care in the Family: A Review of Research and Some Propositions for Policy* (New York: Academic Press — A Carnegie Council on Children Publication, 1977), 26.
9. Ibid.
10. Allan C. Carlson and Bryce J. Christensen, "Of Two Minds: The Educational and Cultural Effects of Family Dissolution," *The Family in America,* 2, no. 8, August 1988, 3. The Family in America is published monthly for $21 per year by The Rockford Institute, 934 North Main Street, Rockford, IL 61103–7061.
11. Nanci Hellmich, "Babies Need Stability, Experts Say," *USA Today,* 29 November 1988, 1.
12. Mary Curtis Blehar, "Anxious Attachment and Defensive Reactions Associated with Day Care," *Child Development,* 45 (1974): 683–692.
13. Pamela Schwarz, "Length of Day-Care Attendance and Attachment Behavior in Eighteen-Month-Old Infants," *Child Development,* 54 (1983): 1073–1078.
14. Jay Belsky, "Infant Day Care a Cause for Concern?," Septmeber, 1986, *Zero To Three,* published by National Center for Clinical Infant Programs.
15. J. Conrad Schwarz, Robert G. Strickland, and George Krolick, "Infant Day Care: Behavioral Effects at Preschool Age," *Developmental Psychology,* 10 (1974): 502–506.
16. R. Haskins, "Public School Aggression Among Children with Varying Day-Care Experience," *Child Development,* 56 (1985): 689–703.
17. J. C. Schwarz, "Effects of Group Day Care in the First Two Years," paper presented at the biennial meeting of the Society for Research in Child Development, Detroit, MI, April 1983.

18. This refers to research by Schwarz, et al. (1974), Haskins (1985), and Rubenstein and Howes (1983), cited in Jay Belsky "The 'Effects' of Infant Day Care on Social and Emotional Development" in *Advances in Developmental and Behavioral Pediatrics*, 9, Greenwich, CT: JAI Press.
19. Deborah Lowe Vandell and Mary Anne Corasaniti, "Variations in Early Child Care: Do They Predict Subsequent Social, Emotional, and Cognitive Differences?", unpublished paper delivered at the International Conference on Infant Studies, Washington, D.C., 22 April 1988.

Chapter Fourteen: Attack and Counterattack

1. "Working Mothers," *Christianity Today*, 15 July 1988, 21.
2. "New Concerns about Child Care," *Christian Parenting*, 10 September 1988, 53.
3. Pamela Redmond Satran, "Who Are the Happiest Working Mothers?" *Working Mother*, May 1989, 163–167.
4. Jura Koncius, "Designing Schemes for Babies' Dreams," *Washington Post*, Washington Home supplement, 9 March 1989, 20–32.
5. I am indebted for this insight to St. Cyril of Alexandria, who delivered a sermon on this point sometime during his life in the fourth or fifth century.

Chapter Fifteen: Public Solutions

1. Kim A. Lawton, "Politicians Discover Children," *Christianity Today*, 17 March 1989.
2. William Raspberry, "Head Start: A Program That Works," *Washington Post*, 19 January 1990.
3. Thomas M. Humbert, "Ending the Tax Code's Anti-Family Bias by Increasing the Personal Exemption to $6,300," *Backgrounder*, no. 687, published 30 January 1989 by the Heritage Foundation, 214 Massachusetts Ave NE, Washington, D.C. 20002.
4. Phyllis Schlafly, "The Big Child Care Divide," *Washington Times*, 28 October 1988, F2.
5. Warren Brookes, "Taxing the Family into Federal Child Care?", *Washington Times*, 4 August 1988.
6. Jacob K. Javits, U.S. senator from New York, "Day Care for Children When Mothers Must Work: A Call for Federal Aid to Help Solve a National Problem," *Parents Magazine*, May 1959. This article is an interesting footnote to the long history of federal social parenting. Javits was even then arguing that "the Federal Government has an obligation to work cooperatively with the states and municipalities to provide day care for the overwhelming majority of children for whom such care is not available. The time to discharge this obligation is now."

7. *Child Care Review,* April/May 1988, cited in Phyllis Schlafly, "The Challenge of Child Care Costs," *The Phyllis Schlafly Report* 22, no. 7, Section 1, February 1989.

8. Richard K. Vedder, "Shrinking Paychecks: The New Economics of Family Life," *The Family in America,* 3 no. 1 (January 1989).

9. Spencer Rich, "Prescription for Good Life: 1 Household, 2 Paychecks," *Washington Post,* 25 May 1989, A9.

10. Warren Brookes, "Income Gap Didn't Begin with Reagan," *Washington Times,* 24 August 1988.

11. For a comprehensive, readable article on the effects of fatherlessness, read Nicholas Davidson, "Life Without Father: America's Greatest Social Catastrophe," *Policy Review,* Winter 1990. *Policy Review* is published by the Heritage Foundation, 214 Massachusetts Ave NE, Washington, D.C. 20003.

12. Leon J. Saul, M.D., *The Childhood Emotional Pattern and Maturity* (New York: Van Nostrand Reinhold, 1979), xii.

ABOUT THE AUTHOR

C onnie Marshner is recognized as one of the founders of the pro-
family movement in contemporary politics. She was co-founder
and chairman of the National Pro-Family Coalition, which organized
pro-family participation in the White House Conference on Families in
1980, and went on to spearhead the successful drive during the 1984-85
tax reform debate to double the personal exemption. She was founder
and first editor of *Family Protection Report*, a monthly newsletter which
monitored what Washington was doing to the traditional family. She
founded, and for seven years chaired, the Library Court Meeting, the
key pro-family strategy meeting in the nation's capitol.

During these years, Connie was writing political works, such as
Blackboard Tyranny, Blueprint for Education Reform, and *Future 21*.
As Connie describes in *Can Motherhood Survive?*, the Lord began to
move her heart to phase out her political activity by degrees. Today,
with four children ranging in age from fifteen to six months, she is a
home-based writer and speaker. She does regular commentaries on Dr.
James Dobson's Focus on the Family *Weekend* program, and writes fre-
quently for Christian publications. She is a member of the Council on
Biblical Manhood and Womanhood. Her husband, Bill, is Professor of
Theology at Christendom College, Front Royal, Virginia.

The typeface for the text of this book is *Times Roman*. In 1930, typographer Stanley Morison joined the staff of *The Times* (London) to supervise design of a typeface for the reformatting of this renowned English daily. Morison had overseen type-library reforms at Cambridge University Press in 1925, but this new task would prove a formidable challenge despite a decade of experience in paleography, calligraphy, and typography. *Times New Roman* was credited as coming from Morison's original pencil renderings in the first years of the 1930s, but the typeface went through numerous changes under the scrutiny of a critical committee of dissatisfied *Times* staffers and editors. The resulting typeface, *Times Roman*, has been called the most used, most successful typeface of this century. The design is of enduring value to English and American printers and publishers, who choose the typeface for its readability and economy when run on today's high-speed presses.

Substantive Editing:
Michael S. Hyatt

Copy Editing:
Donna Sherwood

Cover Design:
Steve Diggs & Friends
Nashville, Tennessee

Page Composition:
Xerox Ventura Publisher
Printware 720 IQ Laser Printer

Printing and Binding:
Maple-Vail Book Manufacturing Group
York, Pennsylvania

Cover Printing:
Weber Graphics
Chicago, Illinois